Inventing a Non-Homeless Future

American University Studies

Series XI
Anthropology and Sociology
Vol. 29

PETER LANG
New York • Bern • Frankfurt am Main • Paris

Madeleine R. Stoner

Inventing a Non-Homeless Future

A Public Policy Agenda
for Preventing Homelessness

PETER LANG
New York • Bern • Frankfurt am Main • Paris

Library of Congress Cataloging-in-Publication Data

Stoner, Madeleine R.
   Inventing a non-homeless future : a public policy
agenda for preventing homelessness / Madeleine R.
Stoner.
        p. cm — (American university studies. Series XI,
Anthropology & sociology ; vol. 29)
      Bibliography: p.
      Includes index.
      1. Homelessness—Government policy—United
States.   2. United States—Social policy—1980-
3. Mentally ill—Housing—United States.   I. Title.
II. Series: American university studies. Series XI,
Anthropology and sociology : vol. 29.
HV4505.S78   1989   362.5'8'0973—dc19   88-36781
ISBN 0-8204-1048-9   CIP
ISSN 0740-0489

CIP-Titelaufnahme der Deutschen Bibliothek

Stoner, Madeleine R.:
Inventing a non-homeless future : a public policy
agenda for preventing homelessness / Madeleine
R. Stoner. — New York; Bern; Frankfurt am
Main; Paris: Lang, 1989.
   (American University Studies: Ser. 11,
   Anthropology and Sociology; Vol. 29)
   ISBN 0-8204-1048-9

NE: American University Studies / 11

© Peter Lang Publishing, Inc., New York 1989

Printed by Weihert-Druck GmbH, Darmstadt, West Germany

For homeless people everywhere.
You deserve better.

Contents

Acknowledgments

With appreciation to the many people who encouraged me to synthesize my earlier work and experiences with homeless people since 1969 and to include all of this material in a book. Among these are Robert W. Roberts, former Dean of the School of Social Work at the University of Southern California, Wilbur Finch, Samuel Taylor and Bruce Jansson. Special gratitude and admiration go to Frances Lomas Feldman, who has been my mentor and sometimes editor. Lawrence Long, who shared his NIMH research on self-help groups among homeless mentally ill people, merits gratitude for his excellent research and exemplary collegiality. Stephen Goldston's presence in Los Angeles has been an important reminder that a conceptual framework of primary prevention remains useful and imperative. Finally, all of the earnest people who have conducted research and written major reports on the subject of homelessness, and are cited in this book, have my respect for attempting to elucidate the complex nature of this enormous social problem.

Nobody can produce a book without the help of an informed librarian. At the University of Southern California, we have the services of Ruth Britten, who continues to be a writer's dream of a good librarian. The same is true of Larry Lederman, typist, proofreader, editor and generally brilliant with details.

—*Madeleine R. Stoner*

Prologue

This book grew out of my personal frustration over the stubborn resistance of social and political leaders and service providers for the homeless to address the appalling phenomenon of mass homelessness from the perspective of prevention rather than remedial aid. Unlike other books that deal with this issue, this book is not written to arouse sympathy through a series of personal case histories and anecdotes illustrating the plight of homeless people. The one exception to this is the recent encounter described at the end of this prologue, because it so vividly demonstrates how the most stable among us can become homeless. I expect readers to bring their own observations and experiences with homeless people to the analyses presented in the book. Most people in America's urban and suburban areas can by now relate anecdotes about men and women who lie on their sidewalks, front steps, parks and beaches. These are the images that readers can evoke throughout this book.

I also assume that most readers are by now aware that the homeless have become an increasingly heterogeneous population who have begun to resemble ordinary American men and women, rather than earlier stereotypes of winos and bag ladies. The term "homelessness" as it appears throughout this book is the United States Accounting Office's definition of the homeless as "those persons who lack resources and community ties necessary to provide for their own adequate shelter." This term includes homeless people in shelters, in the streets, or temporarily resident with relatives or friends. These three usages of the term refer to the population served, the population in need, and the population at risk. The book adds a fourth classification of people, those living in homes who are at risk of becoming homeless for any number of reasons which may be beyond their control. I refer to these people as "homeless-vulnerable."

The dramatic increase in the number of homeless people in America has become even more intense as we recognize similar increases in homelessness in most advanced industrialized societies. This book refers to international homelessness in an effort to broaden understanding of the problem and seek preventive solutions.

Ralf Dahrendorf has commented on the growth of an underclass (and those balanced precariously on the edge) in all OECD countries:

> For many people in the OECD world, there is today — and has been since the 1970s — a sense of downward movement, or at least of the precariousness of what has been achieved. This is not incompatible with the spectacular success of a few: on the contrary, casino capitalism would seem a fitting concomitant of general decline. This negative propensity may well be one of the reasons why the underclass is so important. It represents, so to speak, the ultimate extrapolation of the fate of many. And indeed, it is growing in significance, if not always in size.[1]

The chronic and pervasive deprivation in the context of burgeoning affluence in all advanced industrialist countries gives rising homelessness a new and troublesome dimension. It is the prospect of permanence and containment of homelessness, rather than temporary disruption which faces many households.

The explicit purpose and compelling force of this book is the urge to formulate policies and programs designed to prevent any further increase in homelessness and eliminate many of the causes of the problem. The results of this policy analysis appear as a political agenda for eliminating poverty. This is true because, in many respects, American homelessness is the most tragic manifestation of poverty. It is the poverty of the 1980s.

A final note about causality is an important guide to the reader. Despite sophisticated quantitative methods, problems of reliability and validity in collecting data about homeless people remain. It is therefore more appropriate to substitute the concept of "antecedents of homelessness" for causes of homelessness.

With the decade closing in upon us, it has become self-evident to community leaders, social agency staff, scholars, the general public — and all of the homeless — that we must move beyond the "ain't it a shame" perorations that have aroused our conscience to questions of prevention rather than remedial cure.

The following article, written by *Los Angeles Times* staff writer Fred Muir, appeared in his "My Beat" column in March 1988:

Nattily Dressed Homeless Man Has a Mission

Homeless activist Ted Hayes was holding court in the lobby of Los Angeles City Hall recently when a man in a blue suit and trench coat stopped to listen.

Hayes declared that rich people are dying to give their money away for the cause. "I'll bet you could write me a check right now for $1,000," Hayes said to the man in the blue suit.

"Are you sure?"

"Well, if not $1,000, I know you can write a check for $500," Hayes said.

"As a matter of fact," said the man in the blue suit, "I sleep on the streets of this city every night. I am homeless."

And so he is.

Jerry Neuman — husband, father, registered Republican and former middle-class breadwinner — lives out of a black attache case, not a shopping cart. He wears a tie, shaves every day and somehow keeps a shine on his black loafers.

But he sleeps in the downtown Greyhound bus station or occasionally under a highway overpass and, more often than not, goes to bed hungry.

He doesn't drink or take drugs.

Neuman has one vice, however. He is obsessed with his plan to build group homes for those homeless who are willing and able to work and want to get back into society. That's what brought him to City Hall.

"Everyone is being asked for solutions and input except the people that are most concerned with the problem and that's the people living on the street," said Neuman, who developed his plan after he became homeless about 18 months ago.

The realistic answers, he said, must come from the homeless themselves. "It has to be someone who in fact is homeless that can see the problem with some degree of empathy and insight," he said.

They understand that the small things often mean the difference between being hungry or satisfied, being warm or sleeping on the sidewalk, finding a job or just waiting for the next soup line to form, he said.

"Little things, like telephone calls, become insurmountable," he said.

Most of us can make a local phone call for a few pennies, as part of our monthly rate.

"I make a phone call from a Greyhound bus terminal to someone who lives in Beverly Hills and it costs me 50 cents for the first three minutes and a nickel a minute after that," Neuman said.

Then you have to get to the job interview.

"A homeless person cannot [afford to] buy a monthly bus pass with un-limited transportation...He drops 85 or 95 cents or a buck fifty if it's out of the third zone each and every time he gets on that bus," he said.

"You can spend $10 and accomplish nothing," Neuman said. "And then it gets down to a matter of am I going to spend $10 to talk to this person [about a job] or am I going to go get something to eat and make damn sure I'm clean and make sure I've got enough money to sit in the bus terminal and drink coffee all night."

And, Neuman said, there is a growing community of formerly middle-class workers like him who spend nights on the hard chairs of the Greyhound station, afraid of the night.

"With me, it happened to be a bout with thyroid cancer and not being able to work for a period of time and getting divorced in the interim" that wiped out his savings and left him destitute, Neuman said.

"If you have not been [homeless] before, you're going to be optimistic. You're going to have this can-do attitude. It's only then that you begin to realize things like the phone calls," he said.

"You don't realize till you throw your luggage into the locker at the depot that they charge you $2.50 or $3 a day, because you've never done that before. Suddenly, when you go in to get your things you find out that you owe $20..."

And for every one of the homeless — regardless of their background or education or former social standing — there is the first night on the streets.

"The one thing I remember feeling is the fear of it getting dark at night. That's a very, very, very frightening feeling" because it means you have to find a place to sleep. "Late in the afternoon you get this anxiety and you still get it even after a couple of months."

But beyond the night, there's even a greater fear for some homeless, Neuman said.

Many fear the dawn and another day on the streets.[2]

Introduction

Responses to Homelessness

Policy analysts consistently characterize the United States as a reluctant welfare state. Despite the sweeping language of the Social Security Act, which proclaimed guarantees of economic security for all Americans from birth to old age, the nation's social welfare programs have retained the eligibility criteria and harsh judgments of the early Elizabethan poor laws which made it virtually impossible for able-bodied poor people to receive adequate provision in times of need. The saga of mass homelessness across the United States during the 1980s has tested the limits of this approach.

In the winter of 1981, Rebecca Smith, age sixty-one, died in New York City. She froze to death in the home she had constructed for herself inside a cardboard box. She preferred it to any other home. In a sense, many people watched her die: her neighbors, the police, the Red Cross, and finally a city-dispatched social worker and psychiatrist. In a larger sense, the nation watched too, because her death made the front page of the *Washington Post*.

The senseless tragedy of Rebecca Smith's death immediately prompted a nationwide concern for the plight of homeless people. It also stimulated the emergence of two movements. One movement was the growth of homeless advocacy, beginning with the establishment of the National Coalition for the Homeless in 1981. The second movement was the explosion of homelessness which may surpass the homeless population of the Great Depression in the United States by 1990. Rough estimates on the extent of the problem are hard to come by, but there is general consensus that the nationwide total is three million people.

Homelessness signals the failure of every component within the public and private human service sectors. Its persistence and predicted increase of as much as 20 to 25 percent each year up to the year 2000 illustrates the fact that homelessness is not a temporary crisis, but a social problem which has expanded to chronic and permanent status.[1] The immutability of this social predicament serves as a moral and political reminder to the nation that the basic system of entitlements to human survival and dignity articulated in the Social Security Act and other policy mandates such as the Housing Acts of 1937 and 1949 and the Employment Act of 1946, must move beyond present limits.

This book attempts to advance recent considerations about homelessness by arguing that primary prevention, rather than cure, offers the only promise of solving the seemingly insoluble problem of the growing and increasingly diverse population of American individuals and families who are becoming dislocated. A preventive approach to homelessness emerges from the frustrating awareness that once people are out in the street they may be lost forever. A prevention paradigm, as a strategy, would literally keep such deterioration from happening. Borrowing from public health concepts and practice, prevention of mass dislocation involves the common ideology that no condition has been controlled or prevented merely by treating its victims. The objective of prevention is to reduce the incidence of the problem by altering community institutions and systems that contribute to human problems, and by strengthening the competence of individuals and families at risk in communities where there is a high incidence of social and economic problems. Prevention offers solutions that are less expensive than treatment and more humane and dignified. To rebuild a non-homeless America, it is essential to design or rebuild communal and social welfare systems that stress prevention. A preventive framework for homelessness would shift from categorical programs for specifically needy populations to universal programs, and expand the concept of basic rights to include all people regardless of their "worthiness" as able-bodied, "new poor" or "old poor."

Social welfare analysts have repeatedly noted that programs for poor people are poor programs, and that only universal plans directed toward mainstream society produce standards of equity. Universal systems, such as Social Security pension benefits are also less vulnerable to political changes which can result in reduced benefits. A preventive orientation would reverse the current emphasis on expanding food and shelter provision to programs that keep people from needing such temporary support.

Perspectives on Homelessness

The spread of homelessness in the 1980s has prompted the development of a substantial body of advocacy literature. In general, this literature views the existence of so much homelessness amidst so much wealth as a moral indictment of American society. Advocacy literature, found in scholarly journals, impressionistic research publications, highlighted by Kim Hopper and Ellen Baxter's *Private Lives/Public Spaces*, countless media stories and photographic exhibits, has helped the homeless become one of the few constituencies among the poor to gain program benefits in recent years.[2] Government reports ranging from local departments of mental health to the Department of Housing and Urban Development fall into this category as they have attempted to identify who the homeless are and justify public expenditures — or their absence.

As a matter of public controversy, homelessness has forced

those who have written about it to take political and moral positions. Items published by advocacy authors fall into three categories: 1) They publicize the issue of homelessness for a particular audience, 2) They interpret its meaning and implications, and 3) They make policy recommendations to remedy its effects.

Of the items that publicize the issue of homelessness, none has evoked more sympathy and frustration than Jonathan Kozol's *Rachel and Her Children*.[3] Following the pattern of Randy Young[4] and John Coleman,[5] this widely heralded book and its predecessor in *The New Yorker* join the journalistic exposes that dramatize the problem of homelessness by writing of the author's personal experiences among the homeless for the purpose of social reform and consciousness-raising. Kozol's major hypothesis is that homelessness is immoral and that homeless families have lost all of their support systems, thus falling prey to victimization.

Other authors view the existence of homelessness more cynically, as a planned way of reestablishing the old charitable traditions of moral obligation. Patricia Sexton[6] and, more particularly, Mark Stern,[7] argue that the homeless are a favorite constituency among the poor in the 1980s because they permit the reemergence of the gift relationship. At a time when the bureaucracy of the welfare state is under siege, the homeless have seized the public's imagination because giving to them satisfies people's need to "do good" with minimal personal sacrifice and social change. William Vosburgh has noted that the homeless are particularly well suited to be served by charitable organizations because they are a population which poses dilemmas for conventional, large-scale service organizations. Charitable organizations act as mediating institutions which reduce large institutions to a human scale for individuals. Homeless people are hard to serve. As such they comprise an important arena for the efforts of volunteers for five reasons: 1) their needs are concrete and essential, and detailed training is not necessary to help them; 2) Help is essential to immediate physical survival and must go on no matter what major policy decisions are at stake, making homeless people attractive to those volunteers who wish direct contact with the people they are helping; 3) Because the voluntary organizations tend to be small and local, activity within them appeals to a number of motivations; 4) There is frequently a direct connection to religious and other institutional areas of the volunteer's life; 5) Small organizations exercising direct activities yield immediately perceptible results.[8]

Kim Hopper and Jill Hamburg also suggest that homelessness, while not a planned crisis, serves as a disciplinary function of relief, latently intended to keep direct costs to the state down and enhance the legitimacy of the established order. The degradation of life on the dole and in the streets serves to remind recalcitrant and dissatisfied workers of the rigors of the world of work, and stifles demand for higher wages or better conditions. Prospects of homelessness also force people to seek assistance from other sources than the public.[9] In this analysis, the humiliation and hardship that go with public welfare and homelessness edifies working people in general, and frightens them into passivity regarding their working and living conditions.

Tensions among commentators on the homeless relate to differing emphases on the causes of homelessness and ensuing recommendations for program and policy strategies. Two types of extreme views dominate explanations for homelessness. One focuses on individual pathology such as voluntary withdrawal from society, substance abuse and refusal to take advantage of opportunities to work. The opposite position emphasizes institutional or structural factors in the environment, or social pathology related to a lack of jobs, housing and flaws in social service systems. Both views are valid, but the environmental view offers the broadest explanation. Generally, homeless people lack some human competence resulting from inferior education common among members of minority groups as well as individual pathologies that render them uncompetitive in society. They tend to manage until their twenties, when some economic or social trauma forces them into extreme poverty. Such poverty frequently precedes homelessness. Kasinitz[10] and Sloss[11] stress the housing dimension of the crisis, arguing that homelessness is essentially a problem of the lack of low-income affordable housing. Others, like Rodger Farr[12] and Richard Lamb,[13] focus on mental illness and the deinstitutionalization of the 1960s. Hopper and Hamburg's *The Making of America's Homeless*[14] explores the structural factors in the American political economy that are prompting a growth in poverty and dependency as a correlate of homelessness.

Numerous writers have singled out special groups among the homeless population as the focus of their concern; e.g., women, children, veterans, chronic mentally ill people, and older people. Perspectives among these writers range from extremely sympathetic, viewing their subjects as ignored victims, to extremely harsh, attaching culpability to homeless people.

Kozol, Hayes, Hopper and most advocates for the homeless present a homogenized description of the homeless and resist any tendency to "blame the victim." In most publicity, including television docudramas, homeless families are portrayed as white, working class and victims, presenting the notion that most people are vulnerable to homelessness. In fact, every study of urban homelessness indicates that the majority are black or Hispanic, on welfare, and headed by a single mother.

Ellen Bassuk conducted the most detailed study of homeless families in fourteen Massachusetts family shelters. She found that many homeless mothers are incompetent parents who were abused by their mothers. Roughly one-quarter had a major psychiatric problem including substance abuse, and over forty percent of the children had already repeated a grade at school before arriving at the shelter. Most of the women had never worked or had held a job only sporadically. In general, they demonstrated an inability to function as adults and had either no support system or a series of destructive relationships with family and friends.[15]

Thomas Main, especially, expresses his disagreement with the advocates' claim of a right to shelter. With Main, the literature on homelessness signalled a return to the Social Darwinism that characterized the Reagan administration's approach to social welfare. From this conservative perspective, Main has argued that the homeless should be contained within a social service system that has a strengthened work component. Any public shelter program

program should be accompanied by a work program. However, Main is concerned that public services for the homeless have the potential to create a new bureaucracy, and that the primary resource for homeless services should be charitable institutions.[16]

The Hogg Foundation for Mental Health offers the most unbiased theoretical model for understanding the causes, mediators and consequences of homelessness. This book utilizes the Hogg model in all of its considerations. It posits four types of homeless people:

Type I comprises those who are new to homelessness after losing a job, getting evicted because of an inability to pay bills, and existing on temporary day labor which is too insecure to allow saving for rental and utility deposits. This person remains connected to friends and family, has few homeless friends and is psychologically functional. Type I is identified as a recently dislocated person.

Type II is also recently dislocated but is less functional. Like Type I, he continues to seek employment and has few homeless friends. Unlike Type I, he has fewer defenses against the perils of homelessness and weakened family and social ties. He is more of a social isolate and it is unlikely that he will find any stable job. He is more likely to remain alone.

Type III, the isolate, is among the walking wounded seen wandering the streets, isolated and disoriented. He has severe mental and physical handicaps and is likely to have spent some time in a mental hospital. He no longer looks for day labor and depends upon handouts. Given sufficient time on the street, anyone can become isolated like this.

The outsider characterizes Type IV. The outsider has been homeless for several years and has adapted himself to the harshness of street life. He may have begun as Type I or II, but external circumstances depleted his resources; he withdrew from family and friends, and found support among the groups of homeless people who band together to survive.[17]

Another perspective on homelessness requires attention when considering prevention. A large number of people are not yet homeless, but are homeless-vulnerable because of any variety of individual problems which force them to live under the threat of being fired, evicted, abused, abandoned or ill.

An equally impressive array of publications have described model service programs for different groups of homeless people. The general thrust of these publications has been a demonstration that such programs could help homeless people and, in some instances, alleviate homelessness if replicated on a larger scale. These authors and researchers have addressed the following issues: 1) the role of religious and non-profit organizations in helping the homeless, 2) health care programs, 3) special programs for special populations like women, children and families, 4) innovative local approaches to services and funding, 5) the role of the government in helping homeless people, and 6) comprehensive approaches.

This last category has prevailed among homeless advocates. Led by the National Coalition for the Homeless, advocates have consistently proposed an agenda which features three tiers of service. The first tier comprises crisis services delivered in emergency shelters and day treatment facilities; the second tier focuses on the need for transitional living facilities to aid homeless people in their efforts to stabilize their lives; and finally, the third tier calls for an adequate supply of low-income housing for those among the homeless who are capable of independent living.

It has become alarmingly clear that the third tier of resources has failed to emerge and that for many homeless people emergency shelters have become a permanent living situation. A survey of New York City shelters in 1986 indicated that one half of shelter residents had spent as much as one year in the shelters.[18] This startling evidence signals the urgent need to raise new questions about homelessness in America — questions that seek to prevent any further increase in its incidence. The immediacy of thousands of homeless persons in our midst has pricked the conscience of the best and the worst among Americans and compelled us to reach out to those in such dire need by providing and offering short-term and immediate satisfactions such as blankets in the winter, turkeys at Thanksgiving and Christmas, dance classes for homeless children and, of course, more demanding arrangements for shelter, case management for chronic mentally ill people, job training for the able-bodied and general relief checks to meet minimal survival needs.

Writers and advocates have long addressed broad questions underlying the problem of contemporary homelessness and have agreed on the antecedents of the problem in the United States. Their general consensus attaches homelessness to three major factors: 1) economics, 2) lack of low-income housing, and 3) mental illness. Variations on these factors can be repeatedly cited, but such differences can still be placed within one of the three categories. Unfortunately, too few program responses have connected causality to prevention. The emphasis on services and immediate assistance to people afflicted by the plight of homelessness has not resulted from unawareness of the importance of prevention, but rather from the urgency to act in the face of woeful need. Such responses to the immediacy of problems confronting the homeless have drained resources from prevention to crisis intervention. In their struggle to obtain crisis help, homeless advocates and planners have also diverted their energies to fanning flames without putting out fires.

By promoting the development of a three-tiered housing system, housing advocates have relied upon the metaphor of a line. Any plan for preventing homelessness must change the metaphor of the line to a circle. The circle would focus on retaining people in the circle of housing with all of the necessary social and financial supports. This metaphor emphasizes the notion that it is easier to keep people out once they have left than it is to get them out in the first place. The metaphor of a circle of housing combines dual concepts of prevention and stabilization.

The purpose of this book is to move beyond the crisis responses and worries about the homeless by recommending a wide range of strategies within the economy, the housing sector, and mental health service delivery system that would prevent the projected increase in the incidence of homelessness and offer long-term solutions to the structural problems which contribute to homelessness. Many of the proposed recommendations are practical and feasible. Others require a more serious commitment to an activist government that advocates social spending and social change than may be possible during this period of American political thinking which supports reduced public spending, privatization of human services, and priorities directed to reducing the federal deficit.

Methodologically, conceptualizing a non-homeless future seeks to shift from emergency and other limited responses to homelessness to a paradigm of prevention based upon assumptions and values that espouse universal entitlements to a basic set of decent human services and income. The nature of this paradigm involves a mixture of normative and descriptive content. Descriptive generalizations offer evidence for the theory of prevention presented in the pages of this book.

A review of services for the homeless across the nation identifies three themes underlying policy responses to the problem. The first of these themes calls for serving as many people as possible for as little money as possible. A second imperative has required local government to appease the private market system and business interests with stakes in land development in order to attract affluent purchasers. Finally, local governments have strengthened and expanded strict vagrancy and public nuisance laws designed to remove the homeless from public places and public sight.

The Shelter System

New York City, operating under the Carey v. Callahan[19] consent decree, has built the largest public shelter system in the country. It spends $30 per person a night to operate public shelters. Shelters sponsored by the Partnership for the Homeless, a voluntary network in New York City, rely on volunteer labor to cut costs and can provide shelter for as little as $2.60 a night.[20]

Applying the principle of serving as many as possible for as little as possible, elected officials, public and private social service agencies, churches, synagogues and concerned citizens have become increasingly competent in providing emergency services and bare necessities to those who need them. Nevertheless, homelessness continues to plague communities where even the most benevolent programs operate, and volunteers as well as professional staff have grown disillusioned with shelters. New York's Partnership for the Homeless and the National Union of the Homeless have been pressing for permanent solutions.

The Union's logo is "No More Damn Shelters." Those who have worked most closely with homeless people understand the need to move beyond the provision of emergency care and public nuisance laws to a point where people can move freely from shelters to independent living, or to shift the focus of problem-solving to its origins and prevent people from drifting into homelessness. Observers and activists involved with service provisions for homeless people are beginning to register their concern that sheltering has evolved into a new service system that provides counseling, job assistance and other services along with food and beds. This concern is based upon analyses that the shelter systems across the nation have grown into a broad layer of bureaucracy that features the problems and complexities of many dysfunctional public services but retains the capacity to implement the mandate to provide a safety net for the truly needy. As homeless advocates begin to focus on more substantive measures than emergency care, they note that the present network of services resembles the lower tier of a dual-class delivery system. This means that within the public welfare safety net programs, a subdivision of provisions has evolved for homeless people, who are considered the least deserving of the poor, and therefore less deserving of comprehensive quality programs. Characterized by uncertain funding resources and minimal direct services,[21] many shelters and their facilities meeting the crises of homeless people have begun to resemble the almshouses of earlier years. Many homeless shelters and service centers provide decent and humane services. They even succeed in helping the most stable homeless people reestablish themselves in homes and jobs, or with family reunification. Others retain the harsh judgmental standards characterized by large private missions or public shelters like those in New York City.

The prospect of inventing a non-homeless future challenges existing assumptions about entitlement in the American welfare state. The reluctant welfare state model has facilitated the present complex of inadequate shelter services and transitional living facilities for the "new poor," who have no prior history of homelessness, joblessness or mental illness. A bolder approach to inventing a non-homeless world would perforce test the limits of America's will to construct a social welfare model which aggressively guarantees security for all and abandons its reluctance to support individual victims of poverty, inequality and illness.

Despite the fact that homeless advocates have pressed for the shelter system that has evolved, a bolder contemporary advocacy position would aspire to close down that shelter system. Shelter as a remedy has clearly failed to eliminate homelessness. Quite the contrary! As shelters have proliferated since 1980, the homeless population has grown in numbers and diversity. New York City alone estimates that the winter of 1988 presented a peak of 11,700 single men and women in shelters, a number that is expected to increase by 1992. The number of homeless families is projected to rise by 1992 to 8,802 unless city programs to prevent homelessness effectively occur.[22] Similar data in Los Angeles indicate the same pattern of escalation. The shelter system in Los Angeles—the other "homeless capital of the world"—has doubled in the last two years and is estimated to reach 9,000 beds by 1990. This excludes the provisions of the 22 missions operating in Los Angeles County.[23] These data are replicated in communities throughout the nation. They demonstrate that emergency responses are no substitute for a coherent and consistent policy of prevention. Not only have shelters failed to stem the growth of homelessness, their existence has served to perpetuate the homeless condition by keeping many in a transient state. Examples of legislation, like that in New York City requiring homeless families to remain in welfare hotels for eighteen months before they become eligible for permanent housing, force families to yield to the resignation, despair and deterioration brought about by their condition. Screening systems in private shelters select the least troubled among homeless applicants and increase the concentration of the most troubled and uncooperative people at the larger public and mission shelters. The policy emphasis on helping families headed by one (usually female) parent reinforces the exclusion of the other (usually male) and frequently leads to family breakdown. Certain social control tactics, such as arrest and harassment, stigmatize homeless people, thus perpetuating their plight.

As policy analysts and service providers involved with homelessness have begun to voice their concern that the shelter system has failed to curb the problem, some are attempting to add provisions for more permanent solutions. Indeed, the increasing number of cities that have begun to designate themselves as the "homeless capitals" of the world, e.g., New York, Los Angeles and Washington, D.C., have devised so-called comprehensive homeless policies. The New York Partnership for the Homeless has become more involved in the search for permanent housing. It has been pressing the city, for example, to begin a crash program to get homeless families out of welfare hotels within one year by paying market rents if necessary. Kansas City, Missouri, which showed the biggest jump in homeless families (44 percent),[24] has been trying to persuade the state legislature to set up a statewide housing trust to develop low-cost housing. Many cities have designed plans to rehabilitate old downtown buildings into SROs, or single-room-occupancy units, for the homeless under a new federal program that allows HUD Section 8 funds to be used for that purpose. The McKinney Act, the homeless assistance act passed by Congress in July 1987, provides grants for competitive programs for rehabilitating old SRO housing for the handicapped homeless, transitional housing and some innovative programs, in addition to grants for shelters.[25] Finally, the House of Representatives passed the Urgent Relief for the Homeless Act in March 1988. The bill allocates up to $500 million for emergency shelters, health care and other assistance to homeless people in this fiscal year. The bill goes far beyond the Reagan administration's proposal for $70 million in emergency relief and will, no doubt, change measurably by the time it passes the Senate.[26] The bill is largely based on one drafted by the National Coalition for the Homeless. The House notably did not act on the Coalition's other proposals to prevent homelessness and increase low-income housing. Emergency assistance remains *the* response to what has become a permanent emergency.

Public opinion surveys repeatedly indicate serious concern for homeless people and support for better services. This public concern, however, is offset by public officials who have sought to cut costs and have viewed additional programs grudgingly. They cite competing claims on their limited budgets. This budget shortage is real only because local governments view their highest priority as stimulating the private market and creating a favorable climate for the conduct of business. This market imperative among city leaders ranks social programs as a low priority necessary only to maintain the dependent population at a minimal level and exercise social control through law and order programs and institutional arrangements for dangerous persons.

Local governments have money for investment, but most of this goes to the economic infrastructure. Cities build shipping terminals, industrial parks, sewage lines connected to new real estate development, and public parks in affluent areas. These acceptable investments are often made at the expense of social programs. Moreover, cities that spend more generously on social programs often become targets of criticism by the business community, which views such public expenditures as antithetical to a healthy business climate.

Given the constraints imposed upon cities by scarce resources, market imperatives and concerns for public safety, it is not likely that they have the bureaucratic ability or the political will and power to implement any comprehensive prevention plan without strong pressure from a broad interest base. Nor is there a likelihood that mayors and governors will allow their cities and states the embarrassment of closing down shelters, thus placing the epidemic of mass homelessness in full vision. Shelters serve the same purpose as other institutions for those in dire need — to keep problems out of sight, hence out of mind.

Prospects of closing down shelter systems are dim and politically dangerous, but it remains possible to halt any further growth in these systems before they settle into permanent institutional arrangements resembling historical precedents of indoor relief that lasted for as much as one hundred years in the different historical eras when they were established. Any consideration of constructing a non-homeless future shifts the focus of services for the homeless from shelters to explorations of permanent housing, adequate income and social services for large numbers of poor people who have drifted into homelessness or live on the brink of homelessness. But there remains an opportunity to halt the growth of the shelter system before it settles into a permanent institutional arrangement similar to the poorhouses of centuries past.

Beyond the Shelter System

In summary, economic insecurity, an inadequate housing supply and mental illness are the three basic antecedents of the homeless problem, despite the fact that the homeless population is increasingly heterogeneous and reflects a wide diversity of specific problems ranging from poverty to runaway youth. Devising strategies and programs to deal with problems of this scope daunts the imagination and invites critics to dismiss any proposal as naive or impossible in a nation of diminished resources. But Congress has authorized $1 billion for the homeless under the McKinney Act, and the State of California Emergency Shelter Program's budget in 1986-87 was $4 million.[27] The availability of these funds argues that they can be spent more effectively to eliminate the causes of homelessness and divert part of shelter budgets to affirmative prevention measures.

Homelessness has always existed in the United States, but it has never been worse. The rising incidence of the problem means that the future is even worse! Today's homeless are different from those of the past. They are even different from those of five years ago. Sixty percent are women and children, and the majority of these are children. The number of single people who are homeless in the nation comprises 25 percent of the homeless population; families comprise 75 percent. The highest and most recent estimates of the size of the homeless population in Los Angeles

County place the figure at 50,000 people. If the current rate of growth of homeless people continues, Los Angeles and New York, which also estimates 50,000 homeless, could have anywhere from 300,000 to 500,000 homeless people in twenty years. This would make these internationally important cities look like Third World cities.[28]

Formulating adequate interventions to deal with numbers and problems of such magnitude are neither as complex nor unmanageable as they seem. A reminder that the City of New York Human Resources Administration presently has an annual budget of $5 million, and the United States Congress has authorized $7 billion out of a $1 trillion national budget for the homeless argues that the money is there. What needs to be there is the political will to spend these monies more efficiently to eliminate the causes of homelessness as the problem mounts. Government need not bear the responsibility alone. The private sector represented by corporations and philanthropic and religious organizations can play important roles.

The Plan of the Book

The following sections of this book outline approaches to the economy, the housing sector, and the mental health system designed to ameliorate present homelessness and prevent further dislocation. Each section identifies the links between homelessness and economics, housing or mental illness and recommends a series of preventive strategies for each policy sector.

Few of the recommendations are original. Many have been tested and demonstrated on a small scale under the rubric of model programs which could solve the problems of homelessness on a larger scale. Others have operated at state and local government levels across the country. Similarly, attention to how each sector contributes to homelessness is important, but this book adds little to what is already known about the antecedents of homelessness. The important point remains that we now know enough about how people become homeless, who they are, and what they want. The moral and political imperative of the 1990s is to shift the focus of attention to the problem of mass homelessness from cure to prevention, from hand-wringing to action, and, to cite the familiar social welfare theme, from "putting old wine into new bottles."

The challenge of homelessness raises fundamental questions about the reluctant welfare state model adopted in the United States. It forces renewed thinking about human entitlement, public responsibility and private rights. The purpose of this book is to identify and synthesize a series of practical and logical measures and social goals which could move beyond the limits of the reluctant welfare state. Prevention of homelessness may be the critical event which could force a more willing welfare state in America.

PART I

THE ECONOMY

Chapter 1

Economic Factors
Related to Homelessness

Homelessness points to the failure of economic policies that favor an unrestricted free market, and is a natural by-product of organizing total production around the requirements of the private sector. After more than a decade of laissez-faire political and economic theory, poverty has increased, with homelessness reflecting the most extreme state of poverty. Two major economic trends have contributed to homelessness: the declining American economy and cutbacks in federal income security programs. A combination of reduced wages and welfare benefits has resulted in many empty safety nets.

Unemployment

A recent publication by the United States Conference of Mayors noted that 64 percent of the cities surveyed indicated that unemployment and other employment-related problems were the major causes of homelessness.[1] The Southern California Association of Governments found that lack of employment is the single most important factor leading to homelessness. A study of homeless people in Chicago, released in August 1987, showed that 39.3 percent of the respondents were looking for work.[2] Lengthy periods of unemployment compound the problem by leading to eviction and loss of unemployment benefits. People who become homeless in this process soon lose confidence, and frequently lack basic skills and stable records of recent employment to seek and retain employment. They rapidly shift from behavior associated with the recently dislocated homeless to the more chronic social isolates.

This employment picture becomes more fragile in the face of new data which identify the proliferation of full-time temporary jobs. The U.S. Bureau of Labor Statistics released data in February 1988 showing that the nation's full-time employment rate has grown by 10 percent since the 1982 recession. By comparison, the part-time work force, those who work 35 or fewer hours a week, has grown by four percent to 20 million. It is these part-time workers who help explain why the civilian unemployment rate fell to 5.7 percent in February, the lowest level since July 1979.[3] Many of these part-time jobs are highly fragile and are likely to disappear quickly when a recession occurs. They also pose dangers to their incumbents because they carry no benefits, or only limited ones. "This is a phenomenon we have not seen before, so we don't know what is going to happen in the next economic contraction," reports labor economist Orley Ashenfelter, "but the existence of many temporary workers could move the unemployment rate up more quickly than in the 1982 recession, if a recession occurs." [4] What is clear is that a 1984 Department of Labor survey showed that a majority of more than five million people whose jobs were eliminated remained either unemployed or in the lowest wage positions or in part-time work.

This alarming prospect of potentially high unemployment, despite claims of high employment, raises serious implications about the growth of homelessness. As the ranks of the permanently unemployed and the marginally employed grow, so will the ranks of the homeless. The 1982 recession contributed to double-digit inflation and permanent unemployment for many. Formal surveys, media horror stories, and countless anecdotes clarified the fact that many of those who lost their jobs during the early 1980s as the recession peaked never regained stable employment and became homeless. Men and women who were once ordinary and independent working-class people were slowly converted to a hopeless, unemployable and homeless underclass. They have become Type I and Type II recently dislocated homeless people.

The fragility of employment is more worrisome when we consider the phenomenon of the working poor. The nation's six million working poor, people who work full-time with wages at or near the federal minimum wage of $3.35 an hour, earn less than $7,000 annually. This is below the official poverty index for all but a family of three and $21,000 less than the median family income. Buying power of the nation's working poor has fallen 30 percent since Congress raised the federal minimum wage in 1981.[5] In Chicago, 32.2 percent of the homeless population work in low-pay full-time or day labor.[6] Many of these working poor cannot meet their rent obligations if they are faced by any one of many catastrophies that can befall them and force them into homelessness.

Even in those parts of the nation where unemployment is below four percent, such as the Northeast, wage increases have leveled off. Labor's power to command higher wages has greatly diminished for many reasons.

The most widely accepted reason for this wage decline is management's success in convincing workers that American companies and the jobs they provide cannot survive against lower-cost foreign competitors unless wages are kept down. Unit labor costs have risen much more slowly than prices. They have hardly moved, and when adjusted for inflation, are lower today than they were one year ago!

Job security has replaced higher wages as a top priority for workers, whether or not they are union members. A growing number of companies now offer bonuses and one-time payments in lieu of permanent increases in base pay. Many retailers choose to remain understaffed rather than bid up wages enough to attract more workers.

An equally compelling concern about homelessness and employment in a tight labor market is the growing shortage of highly trained workers to meet the need for skilled manufacturing and service jobs. On the opposite side of the ledger is a surplus of poorly educated and chronically unemployed people in the nation's inner cities.

This new form of unemployment poses particular peril for young people seeking to enter the work force. It also means that new workers, or older workers faced with the prospect of unemployment, will be compelled to work at lower-paying jobs and remain insecure for all of their lives.

Poverty

The growing number of women and children who are homeless, now comprising the largest part of this population, coincides with the most statistically important trend involving women. This is not the fact that over one-half of the labor force is female, but what has been called "the feminization of poverty." This means that two out of three adults in poverty today are women, and one-half of all households containing people in poverty are headed by women. The proportion of the poor who are members of female-headed households and single-person households rose between 1959 and 1986 from 30 to 60 percent. This increase resulted from the combined effects of changes in the family composition of the population as a whole and changes in the relative poverty rates of various household groups.

Mary Jo Bane estimates that 42 percent of the increased feminization of poverty over this 20-year period was due to differential changes in poverty rates. Even though the rate declined for female-headed households, it declined less for them than for other groups. The remaining 58 percent was attributed to changes in the household composition of the population.

Bane also argues that changes in family structure have less

causal influence on poverty than is commonly thought. She suggests that much poverty, especially among black families, is the result of reshuffling; that is, already poor two-parent households break up, producing poor female-headed households. Most poverty, even among female-headed households, comes about because of income or job changes.[7] For women this problem is compounded by their concentration on jobs at the low-pay end of the spectrum.

With the vision of 150,000 women in the United States entering the poverty population each year, it is no accident that women and children have become the majority of homeless people. The feminization of poverty has become synonymous with the feminization of homelessness.

These data should not indict all poor people as homeless. Most surveys of the homeless population have found that less than 3% of poor people are homeless. The comparable figure for poor families is less. Nevertheless, poor people and families make up one-third of the homeless, and non-homeless poor people are homeless-vulnerable. Homeless people appear to be different from other very poor people. They tend to be more isolated, have more serious mental problems, and lack competence in an increasingly challenging society.

Beyond poverty, demographic data from many sources tell us that the gap between the richest and the poorest in the United States has grown, resulting in a shrinking middle class. A widespread middle class is a requirement of any dynamic economy. Moreover, the existence of a substantial middle class remains the core of a modern democracy.

The Congressional Joint Economic Committee completed a study revealing that in 1983, the super-rich (defined as the top 0.5 percent of all American households) owned 35.1 percent of family-held wealth. This was up nearly 10 percent from the 25.4 percent figure of 20 years earlier. The distribution is even more skewed if personal residences are excluded. The top 0.5 percent then owns 45 percent of all the private wealth in the nation. The overall share of the national wealth held by the super-rich has increased 38 percent over the last 20 years, and has now reached its highest level.[8]

Income distribution has also suffered setbacks in terms of equity and the shrinking middle sector. The rate of job creation from 1980 to 1986 has been among the nation's fastest. The number of jobs increased by 10.1 percent. However, this rate of job creation has been marked by a sharp division between positions that pay and those that do not — the "good" jobs and the "bad" jobs. Bennett Harrison, Chris Tilly and Barry Bluestone[9] have shown that only 23 percent of all new jobs created between 1963 and 1978 paid poverty or near-poverty wages. Between 1978 and 1984, this figure jumped to 48 percent, according to Barbara Ehrenreich.[10]

What has become increasingly apparent is that those people who formerly occupied the lower levels of the middle sector with blue-collar jobs have fallen to the bottom level as the spread between the richest and poorest people has widened. Some of those who have fallen from the middle became homeless when they lost their tangible resources.

The universality of reduced personal economic security reminds us that many Americans are living precariously on the edge of catastrophe. William Ryan's claim that every American who depends upon a paycheck to meet all living expenses is two monthly paychecks away from poverty remains alarmingly valid. In 1988, he might alter this claim to two months away from homelessness.[11]

This analysis of the economy and its effects on homelessness views homelessness as the latest manifestation of poverty, the unavoidable result of organizing production around management imperatives of the private sector.[12] Emphasis on the supply side of the private sector, combined with reduced public sector spending, reflected the economic theme of the Reagan administration; however, general consensus on this broad theme emerged in the second half of the Carter administration as a means of reinvigorating the economy. Thus, the responsibility for homelessness spans partisan lines.

Government Reductions in Service and Income Programs

While there are clear drawbacks to having homelessness continue to grow, there are obviously some economic benefits as well. It may be that city governments and business managements that take advantage of the opportunities provided by widespread homelessness have no conscious intention of benefiting from its spread. They are simply taking opportunities where they find them. These may be identified as labor market opportunities and graft opportunities.

The labor market opportunities lie in the fact that some homeless people constitute a labor pool that can supply an inexpensive labor force. In New York City, for example, there are special shelters where companies are allowed to recruit scabs when strikes occur. During a recent strike of aircraft cleaners, large numbers of homeless people were taken by company buses from the shelter to the airport and back again. The workers slept on a different timetable than shelter residents are usually allowed to, and their schedule was protected by the shelter staff. Shelter residents have also been used by New York City to supplement or replace union workers in doing such tasks as cleaning subway cars and stations. The shelters themselves use these workers at the magnificent sum of $12.50 per week (for 20 hours' work, or 62.5 cents per hour) for menial jobs. If shelter residents decline to participate, they are transferred to less desirable shelters. While union-busting is not an announced policy of the city, it seems that its practices support such an objective.

In less highly organized labor markets, the availability of homeless people in the casual labor market may have the effect of driving down wages, since homeless people will often work for whatever they can get. Many shelter residents work regularly, leading some observers to speculate that they are saving large sums of money. It is more likely that they are working at exploitative wage rates in jobs that are not reported, earning little money and receiving no health coverage, disability insurance or pension credit.

Hamburg and Hopper make the point that another labor

market benefit is the cautionary example that homeless people represent to people who might be tempted to throw over their less-than-satisfactory jobs. Following this train of thought, it is helpful to management to be able to point to the dangers of homelessness as a stick to beat recalcitrant labor with.

The second major economic cause of homelessness is cutbacks in federal income security, service and resource programs. Four programs are most directly connected to the populations at risk of homelessness: AFDC (Aid to Families with Dependent Children), disability benefits, food stamps and SSI (Supplemental Security Income). Reductions in each of these programs added to the number of poor Americans who could easily become homeless, or actually became homeless. Job training programs have also been drastically cut, keeping some people homeless and unemployed.

The AFDC program consumes less than one percent of federal spending, but it was a special target of the Reagan administration. AFDC has also gained more prominence than it merits as a favorite target for welfare reform from the broad consensus of leaders who view it as the demoralizing culprit of the poor and an unnecessary national cost. Long a target, the current widespread attack on a program which uses one percent of the total federal budget best demonstrates the reluctant welfare state orientation of the United States and its citizenry.

Since 1981, AFDC eligibility and payment standards have changed three times, cutting a total of $3.6 billion and eliminating 442,000 people from the national welfare rolls.[13] Many of these reductions were specifically directed at working families, 250,000 of whom lost their eligibility. Another 200,000 received reductions in benefits.[14] These cutbacks came on the top of the long-term deflation in the value of AFDC benefits. In no state does the value of AFDC benefits amount to more than 75 percent of the official poverty level, and in half of the states, AFDC pays less than 50 percent. By cutting the deflated safety net of AFDC, Reagan further compounded the effects of this trend.

There is a well-documented relationship between cuts in disability benefits and the spread of homelessness. Public officials in

Denver, Columbus and New York City have attributed some of the new homelessness to the overly zealous enforcement of the 1980 removal of 491,000 recipients from the disability rolls. These cuts were most conspicuous among the homeless mentally ill, who comprised almost one-third of the terminated cases, although the mentally ill made up only 11 percent of all people receiving disability benefits.[15]

After great public outcry and court challenges to disability cuts, 200,000 people were reinstated. Moreover, while these cases were being adjudicated, Congress passed the 1984 Social Security Disability Benefits Reform Act (Public Law 98-640). This law forbids the termination of benefits unless it has been shown that improvements in recipients' medical condition enable them to work. One intent of this law was to warn the Reagan administration that Congress and its constituents would not tolerate such discretionary cuts for the disabled poor. Unfortunately, the fact that 200,000 people were reinstated meant that 291,000 others permanently lost their disability benefits. Among these were many who have become homeless.

Since 1982, the food stamp program has received cuts of $6.8 billion, eliminating one million recipients from the rolls and reducing benefits for another 20 million. Ten million more eligible people do not participate in the food stamp program. The net result is that the percentage of the officially poor population who receive food stamps has dropped from 68 percent in 1980 to 58-60 percent in 1988.[16] Like the AFDC program, the food stamp program barely meets the cost of food. The value of the average benefit is a meager 49 cents per meal. Even those who benefit from the program cannot rely upon it as a buffer against the pressures of meeting their basic necessities.

Common sense presumes that cuts in employment and job training programs during the Reagan administration have contributed to homelessness in much the same way that the cuts in income security programs have. However, the evidence to support this remains more complex. Research on the effects of government-sponsored employment and training policies on low-wage workers reveals only a few success stories. Laurie Bassi and Orley

Ashenfelter claim that "employment and training programs have been neither an overwhelming success nor a complete failure in terms of their ability to increase the long-term employment and earnings of disadvantaged workers." [17] Employment and training programs never covered a large proportion of their target group, but even if they had, there is little evidence to suggest that they could have reduced pre-transfer poverty.

The evaluations of employment and training programs generally find that gains are larger for women than for men. The programs have increased earnings for women chiefly by raising their hours of work rather than their hourly wage. Since women generally work fewer hours than do men, it is easier for them to improve their earnings. Individuals who benefited the most from programs under the CETA (Comprehensive Employment and Training Act) often were those with the least prior work experience. These findings demonstrate that greater benefits of employment and training programs are likely if they are targeted to poor youth and women. [18] Of the success stories, most focus on the social benefits of the programs. The Supported Work Demonstration, the Job Corps and the Youth Incentive Entitlement Pilot Projects produced social benefits measured in terms of goods and services produced by participants, increased tax payments on post-program income, reduced transfer payments, reduced criminal activity, and a decline in other federally provided services. Consistent evidence demonstrates that the most disadvantaged members of society have benefited the most from these programs, and this provides a solid basis for judging their social value as a buffer against economic catastrophe for some.

In 1982 the Job Training Partnership Act (JTPA) replaced CETA, the Comprehensive Employment and Training Act. The new program emphasizes combating structural unemployment rather than cyclical unemployment. It provides no funds for direct job creation in spite of the fact that the national unemployment rate had reached double-digit levels while JTPA legislation was being written. The Reagan administration opposed job creation in the public sector, arguing ideologically that the only federal responsibility is to provide training for disadvantaged individuals. In effect, this resulted in a mere $3.8 billion JTPA annual budget, compared to the much larger $19 billion annual budget for CETA.

Although employment and training programs have not been a panacea for disadvantaged workers, they cannot be dismissed. The mistake in most of the programs may have been investing too little too late, and expecting too much. What is clear is that funding levels of structural employment and training programs increased steadily from the early 1960s to 1979, when they dropped sharply. In examining empirical relationships between funding levels for those programs and unemployment rates, analysts have found that funding levels have been poorly coordinated with the unemployment rate.[19] Employment and job training programs have constantly lagged behind unemployment by at least five years.

The poor timing of employment and training programs has meant that the political system has been unable to respond quickly enough to unemployment rises. It is no accident that the sharp decline in spending for these programs occurred in 1979, immediately preceding the 1980/81 recession which hurled many into permanent unemployment. Some of the casualties of that recession are today's "new poor" homeless.

Structural Transformation of the Economy

Changes in the job market, conservative economic policy, and cutbacks in government social programs are inextricably linked to the major structural transformation that is taking place in the economy. As market demands have switched from manufacturing to services, they have promoted the emergence of an urban "underclass" whose labor is superfluous to the society's needs. Underemployed, undereducated and dependent on reduced social benefits, they meet all of the economic preconditions for homelessness. By themselves, or in combination with other preconditions to homelessness, these weaknesses in the economy have translated into homelessness.

The most apparent direction for preventing homelessness through economic interventions is the elimination of poverty.

There is no question that a world without poverty equates to a world without homelessness. Visions of poverty elimination or reduction remain central to notions of an equitable and humane society. They also point to the social costs of homelessness as the new and most unconventional form of poverty. The greatest cost is the public acknowledgment that the United States can no longer meet people's basic needs and that the appearance of prosperity is deceptive. There is a critical failure in the market-oriented economy. However, the proposals raised here do not solely rely upon the utopian goal of eliminating poverty. Instead, they rely upon efforts that are more readily manageable and provide adequate protections against economic insecurity and catastrophe that result from poverty.

The universality of reduced personal economic security, as evidenced by statistics on the distribution of wealth, citing the enlarged spread between the highest and lowest incomes in the United States, signals the necessity of a return to economic approaches like those espoused by John Kenneth Galbraith. He has never relinquished his claim that the economy must serve public purposes rather than those of the market planning system (that relationship between the government and large industries which manage the economy) which excludes participation from smaller firms. Galbraith argues that the free market is, in effect, a controlled market designed to serve the interests of the largest corporations and the government.[20]

A number of contemporary political and economic analysts are predicting a resurgence of liberalism in the 1990s. Among these are Robert Kuttner, Michael Harrington, Robert McElvaine, Arthur Schlesinger, Jr. and Galbraith.[21] Renewed liberalism need not recreate the programs of the New Deal or the War on Poverty with exactitude, but contemporary liberalism should reiterate those parts of earlier economic and social ideologies that articulate the concept that the economy should be based upon political and moral principles of equity and security, as well as less personal economic theories that focus on money supply, the value of currency, prime interest rates and efficiency.

In simple economic language, the New Deal committed the

federal government to provide for those who are unable to sustain themselves either because of personal incapacity or misfortune or the failure of the economy to guarantee sufficient employment. It established the principle that moral and humane considerations have a rightful place in the economy and that the government bears the responsibility to ensure such an imperative.

In the 1960s Lyndon Johnson sought to expand the New Deal by completing its agenda to provide economic security for every American and build a social and economic state that no longer stigmatized the disadvantaged or blamed the victims of poverty for their plight.

Despite those critics of the New Deal who argue that it is no longer relevant, and those who fault the War on Poverty for its failed policies, both programs resulted in the reduction of poverty. The combination of Keynesian economics and public employment programs did get the nation back on its feet after the Great Depression. Many data cite positive outcomes of the War on Poverty programs. The most illustrative are those which demonstrate that the percentage of people living in poverty was at least halved between 1960 and 1980. Some data estimate that the decline was actually greater — from 18 to 20 percent in 1960 to four to eight percent in 1980.[22]

The results of the New Deal and the War on Poverty should again become sources of pride for caring Americans in the face of the harsh inequities perpetrated by conservative economic politics and programs. Specific targets for completing the agendas of the New Deal and the War on Poverty require a movement away from the reluctant welfare state and a more aggressive public stance about protection against economic hazards. These targets go beyond the earlier "tax and spend" bromides and suggest new funding arrangements that incorporate all resources.

Chief among these economic targets are the following measures:

- The establishment of industrial economic policy that supports full employment at a living wage and protection of workers against economic downturns.

- The establishment of family economic policy that offers necessary supports for worker parents designed to help them stay in the labor force while meeting their responsibilities to their families.

- Changes in unemployment compensation that extend the maximum duration of benefits and eligibility to all workers.

- A reversal in taxation trends which have steadily increased reliance on regressive taxes to a reliance on progressive taxes.

- Welfare reform linked to the cost of living and work with dignity.

The following chapters develop these recommendations and cite their efficacy as measures for preventing homelessness. Much of the theoretical grounding of this economic analysis of homeless prevention rests on the work done by Robert Kuttner, who effectively disproved "the economic illusion that social justice is bad for economic growth." [23] By carefully studying how other countries provide social security, promote full employment, stimulate investment and economic growth and influence the distribution of wealth, Kuttner demonstrated that equality and efficiency can function together so that Americans can achieve a more humane middle ground that preserves political democracy and personal freedom from either too much market control or too much state intervention.

Chapter 2

Industrial Economic Policy

The economic event of the 1980s may well be the growing phenomenon of plant closures resulting from corporate mergers and acquisitions, foreign competition and advanced technology — all of which frequently create permanent unemployment. Amid the economic restructuring of America, an estimated two million workers lose their jobs each year by plant closings and mass layoffs.[1] Many of those laid off through closures are the dislocated Type I homeless people. Deindustrialization has played at least as large a role in producing homelessness as deinstitutionalization. The relationship between these events and homelessness lies in an explanation of how macroeconomics affect income distribution and poverty. Fighting homelessness is an uphill struggle in a deinstitutionalized urban society and declined agricultural sector. Without an economic upturn, we cannot anticipate substantial reductions in homeless people, but prevention is still possible if special programs are developed to provide tangible resources to those most seriously hurt by economic conditions.

Full Employment

Macroeconomists have attempted to measure the extent to which poverty rates among different groups respond to changes in economic growth and fluctuations in business cycles. Consistent findings demonstrate that the effects of the business cycle are borne unevenly across demographic groups. The relative wage structure is only slightly affected by cycles, but group-specific unemployment rates are affected differentially. Unemployment among the old and among women is less sensitive to overall economic conditions, while unemployment among the young and non-white male household heads appears to be more sensitive. Despite many denunciations of inflation as the cruelest enemy of the poor, there is little or no evidence to support this. Unemployment, not inflation, bears most heavily on the poor.[2]

Joblessness among young black men has increased dramatically since 1970. Official unemployment statistics do not explain this problem accurately because they exclude discouraged workers who have stopped looking for jobs. What needs to be measured is the number of men who are neither working nor in school or in the armed services. Using this definition, 21 percent of all non-white men were unemployed in 1984-85. This came down from 26 percent in 1980-83. However, the surge in joblessness among young black men reveals itself most vividly when we see that eight percent were idle between 1965 and 1969, and ten years later 20 percent were idle.

Young black men were not the only unemployed group after 1970. Idleness is half as common among young white males as among young black males; however, when the black rate rises or falls, the white rate for the same age group rises or falls at about the same percentage.[3]

Given the relative unimportance of inflation and income distribution, the emphasis on preventing poverty-related homelessness must rely on the maintenance of employment during cyclical variations. At the present time, the United States has no formal policy to protect workers against long-term unemployment. In 1946 Congress passed the Employment Act setting maximum employment production and purchasing power as goals of government policy.[4] After 42 years, no evidence of the law's implementation has surfaced. Job security and maintenance of employment has emerged as a major concern of Americans as they increasingly fear the nation's vulnerability in a changing world market.

The optimistic political climate has changed dramatically since the Republican resurgence in 1980. In the early years of the decade people still believed in the strength of the American economy and market. Americans also still believed people were responsible for their own economic problems: Black youth were unemployed because they were lazy; white ethnic steel and automobile workers got what they deserved because of selfish and exclusionary unions that priced them out of the market; family farms failed because of faulty management practice; and homeless people preferred life in the streets.

Today, it is less possible to blame the workers. The promise of a bright economic future has faltered, and American workers, including those with college educations, have begun to view corporate greed, bad management and government incompetence as the source of their troubles. When Americans still believed that economic conditions were largely controlled in Washington, they accepted the idea that people should get ahead on their own. This free market rhetoric has been challenged by the shifting global economy. As Americans have learned that they live in a world where their economic security depends upon decisions made by other countries, they have begun to demand that their own government better represent them in the world marketplace. McElvaine describes the growth of the Springsteen Coalition (based upon the theme popularized in the song "Born in the USA") as a response to this concern.[5]

The employment picture of the 1980s has been marked by two troublesome characteristics. The first is a shortage of jobs in the total labor market of all advanced industrial nations, including the United States. The second problem is the growing shortage of good jobs. In America there is substantial evidence that job opportunities and pay scales have declined, leaving a reduced middle class in the labor market.

Contemporary national industrial policy responses to these concerns require renewed emphasis on job security. It is no accident that the basic thrust of labor-management negotiations in the 1980s has been on the maintenance of jobs rather than increased wages. Full employment policy requires strategies to save jobs as well as create new ones.

Among these strategies would be strict anti-trust monitoring of corporate mergers and acquisitions that set limits on the number of job dismissals related to proposed reorganizations. A simple test of the impact of a change in corporate ownership on employment seems to be fair and logical extension of federal anti-trust regulation.

Any consideration of full employment goals must take into account the reality that full employment no longer causes celebration on its own merits. The current economy, operating at less than six percent unemployment for one year, has not resulted in a secure economic environment. Full employment has become a muddled concept. Contemporary economists generally view the term as the lowest possible unemployment rate that will not set off inflation.

Under today's version of full employment, many unskilled workers still lack jobs. Depressed regions or industries remain. Economists warn that these problems are too persistent and local to be cured easily by traditional economic policies designed to stimulate the economy — lower interest rates, tax cuts, more government spending. Higher inflation would be the main result as scarcities of skilled workers and goods drove up wages and prices.

Even the term "full employment" has been re-invented by economists as the "non-accelerating inflation rate of unemployment." That is, the level of unemployment that will not increase inflation.

Most economists do not think that this level is permanently fixed. For example, if more unskilled workers can be trained, an expanded labor force of better workers would lower the rate. Most estimates of the safe non-accelerating inflation rate of unemployment vary between five and six percent.

The double-digit high unemployment rate of the 1980s is said to have frightened workers. Even in labor markets that are tight they are less inclined to demand high increases in wages because they fear they could lose their jobs in the next downturn. In addition, the aging of the baby-boom generation promotes slightly lower unemployment because the older workers change jobs less often than do teenagers or young adults.

Job polarization and real or potential unemployment cannot be solely attributed to the technology resulting from a shift in manufacturing and industrial jobs to service jobs. The problem is not a simple economic one; nor is it the obverse of advanced technological skills. In the final analysis, the issue is political, and raises critical questions about who benefits from the distribution of gains.

In a society that places value on its workers, a full-employment climate would mean that the replacement of productive workers by machines would not result in heavy losses on the displaced worker. There is nothing intrinsically superior or more demanding in manufacturing jobs than service jobs. Both can pay equally high, moderate or low wages. The crucial factor determining wage scales is political choice about the amount of money workers should receive. In a full-employment atmosphere, service workers responsible for computer programming would earn as much as auto assembly mechanics.

It is no accident that the higher wage scales in the manufacturing jobs went to unionized workers. The contemporary decline in union membership and power has resulted in a largely non-unionized service industry sector — and in depressed wages.

For Western European countries such as West Germany, Austria, Sweden and Norway, where strong labor organization exists in new service jobs, along with a union, management and government commitment to egalitarianism, wage spreads are much more even at no cost to efficiency. With or without unions, this commitment to equal outcomes must become a feature of American employment.[6]

The Minimum Wage as a Strategy for Full Employment

The matter of a decent wage remains a key element in full employment policy. Many threatened industries have attempted to maintain full employment by depressing wages. The spreading policy of two-tiered wage structures, whereby new workers are entering companies at lower wages than their counterparts who perform the same jobs at higher wages based upon their longevity with the firm, is counterproductive to the goals of full employment. Underemployment is not full employment; two-tiered employment is also reflected in the proliferation of permanent part-time jobs. Both of these practices require serious attention and measures to protect workers from losses in work and benefits. References to opportunities in the expanded service industry often tend to overlook the fact that jobs in this sector fall heavily at the lower end of the wage scale.

Any reference to decent wages raises the issue of the minimum wage. Necessary legislation to raise the federal minimum wage has failed passage in the Congress. For nearly six million workers, this setback legislation means a seventh year without a pay raise and another year of failing to keep up with inflation. Objections that raising the minimum wage would cost jobs, especially for those who are young and seeking entry-level opportunities, persist with some validity. Advocates of a higher minimum wage argue that any loss would be outweighed by positive aspects of enhancing the self-esteem of poor people and increasing chances for breaking out of poverty. Raising the minimum wage is not just a benefit for the poor. It also helps many families who are near poverty.

Most minimum wage workers earn $3.35 a hour, which is the federal level. This adds up to less than $7,000 annually — below the poverty level for a woman with two dependent children, and less than what she would receive on welfare. In six states, minimum wages are higher than the national average. California's new minimum wage, which took effect on July 1, 1988, is $4.25 a hour. Legislation sponsored by Representative Augustus Hawkins (Democrat-Los Angeles) and Senator Edward Kennedy

(Democrat-Massachusetts) would have provided a boost in the federal minimum wage to $5.05 an hour as of December 31, 1991.[7] This rate would have finally made a paycheck worth more than a welfare check, and stifle those critics who insist that people choose welfare over work because they are too lazy to work. It would have added necessary income to help working people pay for housing and other basic human needs.

Because the buying power of the nation's poor has fallen 30 percent since the last raise in the minimum wage in 1981, any new raise should include built-in guarantees of wage stability through indexing to provide automatic pay raises, allowing low-wage earners to keep pace with inflation.

Proposals to establish a subminimum wage for teenagers and for trainees in their first few months on the job offer little to the working poor. They merely encourage firing workers as they turn 20 or enter their post-training period in the interest of maintaining a subminimum labor force.

One way out of the "jobs vs. income" dilemma is to raise the neediest workers' pay without raising employers' labor costs. The federal income tax code has already built such a wage subsidy into its provisions through earned-income tax credits. In 1987, married workers with children and incomes up to $6,080 a year received a 14 percent earned-income tax credit which is refundable. Workers who file a federal form can have the extra cash added to their paychecks. This wage subsidy phases out, gradually disappearing for families with income over $15,000.

If this tax credit were raised and linked to family size, it would have no adverse effect on employment. A boost in the maximum credit to 35 percent of wages up to $2,500 for families with four or more children would increase the take-home pay of a full-time breadwinner earning the minimum wage by 82 cents an hour.[8]

Besides boosting take-home pay without reducing the number of jobs, such an increased earned-income tax benefit would focus on those in need. On the other hand, a teenager would get the full benefit of the minimum wage but would not be eligible for the tax credit. Those eligible for the earned-income tax credit are not a small category. The Congressional Budget Office estimates that in

1985 fewer than 20 percent of the minimum-wage workers were members of families living below the poverty line.

Despite these apparent advantages, the tax credit suffers two flaws: First, the working poor need a steady, respectable wage, not three dollars and thirty-five cents an hour plus a windfall every April. Although they can have the tax credit added to their paycheck by completing a tax form, few of them do.

The more serious problem with the earned-income tax credit is that it is a handout, and this discourages employers from raising wages and employees from seeking higher-paying jobs. If we are to seriously consider full employment policies, we must view full employment as stable jobs that pay above the official poverty level. An economy which supports too many low-pay, marginal, high-turnover jobs keeps workers dependent, discourages incentives to advance, and forces people to live on the edge of disaster.

The Kennedy-Hawkins minimum-wage legislation was consistent with historical benchmarks. In 1991 a wage of $5.05 would be approximately 45 percent of the average manufacturing salary. This is where it stood during the Eisenhower through Carter administrations. Nevertheless, Kennedy's proposal to link the minimum wage to average pay may have been misguided. In a strong economy, when companies have extra cash, a minimum wage does not cost too much in jobs. In weaker economies, the minimum wage can cost more jobs and should be raised more cautiously.

In the past, it was estimated that a 10 percent increase in the minimum wage would result in the loss of 600,000 jobs for teenagers. The 1980s, however, are different. There are currently three million fewer teenagers than during the 1960s and 1970s. Also, the minimum wage is less of a percentage of the average than it previously was. Another factor is that some states have higher minimum wages than the national minimum. Taking all of this into account, a University of Michigan study put the job loss at only 70,000 from a ten-percent increase in the minimum wage.[9]

There is no such thing as a free lunch, and there are inevitable compromises in the formulation of social and public policy. Despite a loss of jobs from a raise in the minimum wage, millions of people would be better off.

Protections Against Plant Closures and Industrial Restructuring

Other directions for industrial policy involve national legislation requiring companies to give notice of an impending factory shutdown. Such notice would include specific provision for education and job retraining, both for the young and for workers who need new skills in a changing economy, and for the benefits they need to find new jobs with decent wages. Recent trends indicate a growing collaboration between the nation's junior and community colleges and businesses in providing customized job training and technical education to meet changing technical demands in the workplace.

This new role for junior and community colleges has been financed by government revenues and private contributions. It involves a cooperative strategy between state and local political leaders, labor unions and manufacturers to improve workers' skills and make local communities more efficient and competitive. As an innovative resource for job training, this strategy can create more jobs, more employees and, therefore, more people in communities who will pay more taxes. This benefits all and involves no act of charity.

Because many employers have shifted to lowering wages and relying on part-time workers to allow greater flexibility in adjusting to economic conditions, they need encouragement to participate in full-employment schemes. Such incentives could come from federal, state and regional economic development funds allocated around the concept of public and private sector investment in workers as human resources, through research into new products and technologies, and regional development projects. Examples of this abound in the New England states which have converted from textile, leather and manufacturing to advanced high-technology industries. Pittsburgh offers another example of conversion from a steel industry city to a region of technological excellence, most notably in the medical field. Sadly, Homestead and similar towns adjacent to Pittsburgh have not fared as well.

Michael Harrington emphasizes that full-employment planning should not require that "obsolete industries and technologies be maintained in place. But it should work to see to it that the transition from one technology to another should not be made at the expense of the workers and their communities." [10]

One illustration of such planning can serve as a useful model of public/private initiative to save jobs and communities. Governor Robert P. Casey of Pennsylvania established the Governor's Response Team in February 1987. The team consists of nine people who negotiate with private entrepreneurs to assemble financial packages to help save faltering industries or to help attract out-of-state companies. In slightly more than one year, the team has handled 214 cases, and, while it is too new to evaluate its impact, the team claims that its efforts have led to the creation of nearly 10,000 jobs, either actual or projected, and the saving of 10,000 more. [11]

The ability to move in fast and avoid red tape is the essential characteristic of this effort, in contrast to many other state aid programs for private industry. For example, the team secured a $6 million low-interest loan for J&L Structural, Inc. in Aliquippa that enabled the company's new owners to save the last functioning steel mill of the LTV Corporation and preserve 130 jobs immediately, with the expectation of returning another 100 workers over three years. The team also provided $500,000 for retraining workers. All of this took place in just 60 days, which is record speed in the world of government planning. It also demonstrated how the 60-day warning in the newly enacted federal trade bill could be applied to its fullest advantage.

A second characteristic of the Governor's Response Team is that it is proactive. Members of the team are constantly looking for companies that are in trouble in an attempt to save them before they close down. Of the 214 cases taken on by the team, only 52 have been closed. The rest are still in negotiation.

President Reagan's veto of the weakened Omnibus Trade Bill marked a serious setback for worker protection. The law would have required companies with at least 100 employees to give 60 days' notice to employees and local community officials when they plan to shut down a factory, move out of town, or lay off more than one-third of their work force for more than six months.

The modest bill had solid support among liberals and many conservatives in Congress. The Senate passed the measure by a 60-40 vote. Despite this support and the limitations of the bill, the President vetoed it on the basis of the 60-day warning requirement. He subsequently signed a revised bill requiring 60-day notice.

Even the 60-day time period is far too brief to allow workers and their communities to adequately cope with the impact of massive layoffs. There were also more loopholes in the 60-day warning law than there are in the tax code. Faltering companies, for example, do not have to give advance notice if they have a reasonable belief that notice would cause a shutdown that might otherwise be avoided.

A variety of proposals to protect workers and their communities from the ravages of unemployment have been considered by the Congress over the past 15 years. All died in committee. The idea of notification time is far from radical. It is common in Europe, and a recent survey showed that 87 percent of Americans approve of the advance-warning system. Even President Reagan and almost all employers, as well as the most conservative members of Congress, agree that workers and local communities should receive advance notice of massive layoffs. However, many of these same people object to legally requiring that employers give such notice to their workers. They argue that the best way to achieve the goal is through the acceptance and promotion of voluntary standards of business ethics that provide for adequate notice of plant closings and mass layoffs.

That voluntary plan has not worked for most companies, so the 60-day warning legislation was needed.

Many unions and companies in the steel, auto, rubber and other industries have negotiated contracts with advance notice provisions, and several of those are far superior to the 60-day-notice bill signed by the President.

Federal law should include, as several union contracts do, such provisions as mandated consultation with workers, their unions and community officials, in addition to simply warning them about imminent mass layoffs so they can prepare for pink slips.

Such consultations can help, as they did for most of the 2,000 workers at United States Steel's Geneva Works in Provo Utah, after they were told that the plant was going to be closed.

A spokesman for the United Steelworkers of America explained that the union put out "feelers" for prospective buyers of the plant. Some Provo investors concerned about the future of the town formed a company, negotiated a union contract and put the plant back in operation with 1,400 workers.

Those who did lose jobs are receiving reasonably good early retirement benefits or severance pay and government help in finding and getting training for new jobs.[12]

An adequate plant closure law, itself, is insufficient, although it would end the widespread cruel practice of telling workers on a Friday that their jobs end when their shift does. The best solution lies in industrial policy designed to guarantee that viable companies can survive. Industrial policy could assure that assistance is available for a community's workers and not leave them entirely dependent on the judgment of a handful of corporate executives for their survival.

A national industrial policy approach to economic justice and full employment does not justify protectionist trade practices. Restrictions against foreign competition can dangerously redound against American workers and owners in the form of higher prices on consumer goods and reduced international markets for American-produced goods. The emphasis on international trade should be to monitor fair trade. Only in situations involving troubled industries, some temporary protective measures to invest and modernize to become more efficient may be justifiable. The real issue related to foreign markets is labor. American-owned companies must stop exporting high-paying jobs to foreign countries where workers make little money and work under substandard conditions.

This reference to foreign competition raises a different approach to the concept of competition, that of vying with the full-employment security policy in Japan. Large employers provide lifetime employment guarantees to their employees. One-third of the Japanese labor force with these jobs may be requested to change their jobs or be loaned to other organizations, but their paychecks never stop. When times are bad, annual bonuses shrink, but wages remain. Thus, Japanese corporations keep people working by cutting income from bonuses and benefits. This system also controls inflation and recession.[13]

Weitzman proposes that the Japanese model would work in General Motors. Lester Thurow describes this plan as the "share economy," [14] but argues that such planning fails to account for the steady increase in management salaries in the United States. When sales and profits fall in Japan, management and executives take cuts in their compensation. This has not been the case in the United States. The embarrassment of the 1980-81 United Auto Workers / General Motors negotiations remains a blot on our memories. It was those negotiations, taking place during a recession, in which management extracted major concessions from the union while simultaneously announcing new and lucrative bonuses for top management. Since 1980, the number of corporate executives earning $1 million and over has multiplied despite uncertainty in the economy. An authentic share economy requires both management and labor to accept their shares of gains and losses. Without this equity, reduced wages as a strategy of full employment will only exacerbate the growing distance between the poorest and the richest in the nation.

International Business Machines (IBM), long recognized for its full-employment policy, provides an instructive case study of how firms can retain personnel when corporate performance is down. The company boasts that it has not laid off employees for almost 50 years.

One method used by IBM is redeployment of workers to new jobs needed to boost its performance. A company report issued in June 1988 announced that IBM would redeploy and move thousands of workers into new jobs. The move is intended to shift personnel from manufacturing and administrative positions into revenue-producing sales jobs. This move occurred at a time when the Armonk, New York company was generally suffering from slow domestic sales. To recover sales, IBM developed seven new personal computer models and disclosed a trade-in plan for owners of older IBM machines. The next logical step was to enlarge its sales force to promote the new equipment, along with other standard products. This combination of new product development and maintenance of jobs resulted in a net gain for the corporation and its employees.

Some industry analysts criticize this kind of redeployment as a method of cutting staff without actually laying off workers. In any massive redeployment, some workers are bound to quit rather than move to a new job. This pattern does not obviate the value of worker redeployment as a mechanism for maintaining full employment.

IBM has utilized other mechanisms to strengthen corporate overall performance without firing people. Since 1986, it has cut its payroll largely through early retirement plans, cutting back on temporary employees, and reducing hiring. These steps are legitimate examples of balancing the profit requirement of corporations with a responsibility for full employment.

The preceding full-employment agenda relies on private corporations to protect jobs and build new service technology industries in areas of high unemployment and poverty. The only role for the government in this part of the agenda lies in tax subsidies, tax deductions for employer-sponsored job retraining, or other incentives such as economic development funds and protections against underemployment by a raise in the minimum wage.

Public Sector Responsibility for Full Employment

Any full employment agenda must involve the public sector, if only because the corporate sector has consistently demonstrated its unwillingness to invest in social need and human resources. Indeed, it may be too much to expect market-driven companies to sacrifice margins and profits, given their separate mandates from investors and shareholders.

Because the least skilled workers, employed at the lowest wage levels, are the likely candidates for homelessness, special job-training programs are necessary for those people who are the most difficult to train. Included in special work-training programs for the least skilled homeless-vulnerable people would be an opportunity for a secure life with a place to stay, food and psychological counseling.

A secure life would free those people who live precariously from survival concerns and enable them to pursue more long-term gains in the job market. By emphasizing work in contrast to welfare, work programs — as distinct from workfare programs tied to welfare — would require federal support for vocational rehabilitation. In particular, this support should focus on the long-term unemployed and the many poor who are most likely to become homeless.

Few economists on the left, right or center have retained faith in public employment strategies like the failed Humphrey-Hawkins Balanced Growth and Full Employment Act of 1978. Fully implemented, the law would provide sufficient public employment to fill the gap between willing and able workers and the number of jobs available in the private sector. Concerns of economists focus on the undisciplined nature of public activity and its potential for intruding in free market competition. In addition to charges of inefficiency, economists relate public employment activity to inflation and possible recession.

Harrington offers a series of measures designed to assuage such concerns. These steps start with the preparation of a national needs inventory to be prepared by local and national planning bodies and presented to the Congress for acceptance as a national industrial planning data base. One example of possible public sector employment is the creation of new regional rail systems under decentralized public ownership. This would create a service that would pay for itself, provide jobs, and be socially useful.[15]

Harrington and Robert Lekachman both advocate the establishment of a national health insurance system in the context of full employment planning. National health insurance bears on full employment in several significant ways. As people lose employment, they lose health coverage. The new shape of the labor force, with its concentration of low-paid, temporary, non-union, low-benefit jobs lodged chiefly among women and minorities, has created a stratum of medically needy people. Simultaneously, the proprietary health care sector which has proliferated treats fewer chronically ill and medically needy people. Health care has clearly become an arena in which public full-employment planning can be combined with universal human service.[16]

Finally, Harrington does not call for a return to the government-run full-employment prescriptives of the 1960s and 1970s as embodied in the Humphrey-Hawkins bill. The bill, however, retains its integrity as a commitment to full employment within the framework of a mixed economy. Because the term "public-private partnership" retains its appeal in the American mixed economy, the goal of full employment, as exemplified by the Pennsylvania Governor's Response Team, must be sought through this combination. Public-private arrangements as a conceptual framework for industrial economic policy do not obviate the selection of certain industries for nationalization. Hence, the suggestion for nationalization of health.

Commercial and residential construction are among the most obvious industries that could contribute to full employment and prevent homelessness. Development projects can serve social as well as profit needs because their tremendous multiplier effect creates new business opportunities, jobs and housing. Partnerships between the government and business to develop housing and commercial projects have been the mainstay of the federal government's housing policy in the past, and the state and local government have adopted the same arrangements to fill the voids left by reduced federal involvement in housing. Renewed emphasis on public-private partnerships designed to stimulate full employment through the construction industry promises to serve the interests of all and contribute to a non-homeless future.

Kuttner offers another direction for full employment regulated by the government. He recommends a series of devices to shorten working time and spread employment and available jobs. Arguing that millions of workers are involuntarily unemployed, millions more are working harder and longer than they wish.

Foremost among these unemployed workers are those near retirement and working parents.

Kuttner recommends an extension of the Social Security retirement concept to cover workers who voluntarily drop to a 20-hour work week at age sixty. This would reduce the sudden trauma of forced retirement and open up jobs for younger workers. The combination of a paycheck and a partial pension would net the retiree 85-90 percent of his or her previous full-time wage.

Overemployed working parents, permitted to drop to half-time work for nearly full-time pay through a system of family allowances or parental leave, would benefit from the opportunity to spend more time with their children. It would also reduce unemployment by spreading jobs and available work to more people.[17]

Ultimately, whatever strategies are selected are less important than the goal of distributing wages and job security more evenly and equitably throughout the economy. The promise of a good job that one can count on over time can keep people in their homes and encourage those without homes to make rental or purchase commitments.

Industrial policy need not exclude social justice. The American assumption has not supported this principle, but there is nothing intrinsically contradicting the coexistence of both goals.

## Chapter 3

Family Economic Policy

Full employment is impossible under the present organization of the American labor market. Feminists and other minorities have taught us that social rights are empty without economic rights. With this understanding, family economic policy must become a reality as a protection against the growing marginalization of a low-paid full- or part-time labor force whose incumbents live on the edge of unemployment and ensuing homelessness.

All public officials and homeless advocates note that the largest-growing homeless population is families with children. They estimate that over one-half of the homeless are now such families. Homeless mothers need assistance in all basic life matters like budgeting, child care, jobs, obtaining child support and welfare benefits, housing and psychiatric services. The Urban Family Center, a non-profit agency in New York City, provides all of these services. It reports that the problems of homeless families are so severe that the average stay of one homeless family at the Center is nine months.

The goal of family economic policy has gained ascendance among American policy imperatives because of the dramatic changes in the composition of the labor force, nearly half of which is female, with married women with young children comprising the majority of all new labor force participants. Most of these new jobs going to women are low-paid, menial and lacking in dignity.

The U.S. Bureau of Labor Statistics reports that there is a direct positive correlation between salary level and the percentage of males in a particular occupation. Most women work in jobs where the majority of employees are female; 80 percent of all employed women work in only 20 of the 427 occupations listed in the Bureau of Labor Statistics, and in those fields dominated by women— secretary, sales clerk, bookkeeper, waitress, household worker— the wage structure remains low.[1]

It is predicted that about one-half of the labor force in 1990 will be women under 18 at home. By 1995, the proportion may be two-thirds.

The convergence of a female labor force, dominated by low-wage jobs, the feminization of poverty, and the growth in the number of homeless women and children may or may not be accidental. It is nonetheless compelling as the basis for forming a national family policy that would strengthen the foundation for the family and the competitiveness of the economy by providing a supportive infrastructure that would enable working parents to successfully mediate the demands of jobs and family. Only the United States and South Africa have failed to implement policies to accommodate families in a changed economic and social environment.

Family economic policy designed to maintain economic security for worker parents would include the following items: 1) maternity and parental leaves and benefits, 2) child care, 3) maternal and child health care, 4) a flexible workplace, 5) divorce and child custody reform. These changes would not only offer job security, they would profoundly change the character of work to acknowledge that workers are parents, spouses, children and neighbors. They would also rely upon non-welfare strategies to maintain a decent level of human services.

This chapter offers theoretical and factual considerations as the basis of recommendations of family policy initiative with direct implications for protecting families from homelessness.

Maternal and Parental Leave Benefits

In the United States only 40 percent of working women are entitled to a leave from work for childbirth that includes partial or full income replacement and a job guarantee for six to eight weeks. Fewer parents are entitled to additional leave. Childbirth and caring for young children at home have compelled American women to interrupt their work more frequently than men.

These employment breaks, no matter how brief, are too often unprotected and result in a decline in the long-run earnings and benefits for even the higher-earning women. For low-wage earners, these breaks frequently result in the loss of employment and ensuing poverty. Employment breaks also partially explain the earnings gap between the male/female labor force.[2]

Federal legislation should be enacted requiring public and private employers to provide temporary disability insurance (TDI) to all employees. Currently, only five states require this. The Pregnancy Discrimination Act of 1978 requires that pregnancy must be treated as any other disability. The term "disability" can be questioned as an accurate description of pregnancy, but even with this disclaimer, the 1978 law has not been implemented in the vast majority of the states. Legislation, the Family and Medical Leave Act, is presently moving through the U.S. Congress. This Act would provide 18 weeks of unpaid leave for parents of newborn or adopted children, medical leave, and leave to care for a seriously ill child.[3]

Disability leave should be fully job-protected for all employees. The wage-replacement ceiling should also be raised and the standard leave for pregnancy should be extended from six to eight weeks. This is not even bare minimum time for healing of the mother, nursing and bonding, according to medical and psychosocial experts. Employers should provide parenting leave to all workers, with their job or a comparable job guaranteed. This leave should extend to at least six months, which is the minimum amount of time required for physical recovery from pregnancy and childbirth.

Child Care

In the United States there were more than 20 million children under 13 years old with working mothers in 1984, including nine million under the age of six. In one survey, 23 percent of working parents admitted that they left their children alone. Other parents are not working because they cannot find child care. A recent survey of low-income mothers found that one-half of those who had never worked and more than half of those who were recently unemployed were not working because they could not find, or could not afford, child care.[4]

Recent estimates reveal that there may be as few as one million center care slots available nationwide. Approximately one-half of these are in the 11,000 child care centers funded federally through Title XX of the Social Services Block Grant, which has received funding cuts of 21 percent. Although employer-sponsored day care is viewed as the wave of the future, only 2,000 of the nation's six million employers provide any kind of child care assistance.[5] The most common form of out-of-home child care is in informal family care arrangements. Pre-school part-time arrangements and Head Start enrollment account for the next largest set of arrangements of child care, but this is only partial coverage.[6]

The states, with the encouragement of federal financing through Title XX, should provide expanded appropriate child care services, improve the training of child care workers, and enforce quality standards. The largest current form of federal expenditure on child care, the Dependent Care Tax Credit, should be expanded beyond the Tax Reform Act of 1986 provision of $720 for one child and $1,440 for two or more children, and be credited to non-working parents.[7]

Federal, local and state government should encourage employers to structure benefits programs to include child care assistance through, for example, Dependent Care Assistance Plans (DCAPs) which allow companies to subsidize child care assistance because they allow employees to make choices that are consistent with their personal circumstances.

Head Start programs and the Child Care Food Program should be restored to pre-1981 levels because they offer the widest form of child care and family economic security for low-wage working parents by providing education and nutrition.

Community institutions offer a major resource for child care. Churches, synagogues, "Y"s and other non-profit civic organizations are attempting to develop child care services within their communities. Similarly, public kindergartens and secondary schools should begin to acknowledge that in their efforts to ensure excellence in education they also have the capacity to provide quality child care for children whose parents work. These organizations cannot undertake child care independently. They require financial support and incentives from public sources and corporate sponsors, as well as contributions from their constituents. In the past, publicly funded child care was viewed as un-American and anti-individual in a nation which only reluctantly embraces welfare. This is no longer the case. Approximately 70 day care bills have been introduced in the Congress, demonstrating mainstream support for child care.

The current momentum of support for child care across ideological partisan lines offers an opportunity for linking child care to the wider range of concerns in family economic policy. Beyond this, the fact that higher wage earners are pressing for child care means that this family support, at minimum, can be designed as a mainstream service for those who can afford to pay as well as those who are too poor to pay. The history of social services demonstrates that mainstream, or universal, services are more effective than categorical programs targeted at poor people. For many women, the availability of child care can make the difference in their ability to sustain a stable family and avoid the omnipresent threat of eviction.

Equal Employment and Pay Equity

More than 20 years after the passage of the Civil Rights Act, Title VII, the effects of discrimination in the workplace remain visible. Women workers still earn only 64 percent of what their male counterparts earn, although 54 percent of all American women are in the labor force and 44 percent of the total work force is female.[8] This earnings disparity has a negative effect on total family income, and the impact is particularly serious on households headed by women.

Most women work, including 61 percent of married women with children, and most of these women work out of economic necessity. In 1984 the median family income for all two-parent families with children was $34,668 when the mother worked, $23,582 when she did not. In single-parent families headed by women, average earnings are $11,400, or one-third of the earnings of two-parent worker families. Forty-three percent (2.8 million) of black families are headed by women, and 13 percent (6.7 million) of white families are female-headed. As a result, 35 percent of all female-headed households fall below the poverty index. Two-thirds of all poor adults are women, and nearly one in four children in the nation lives in poverty.[9] Discrimination in the workplace against women is compounded for homeless families because the majority of them are black or Hispanic, which further depresses wages and employment opportunities.

Some of the disparity between male and female earnings can be accounted for by differences in education, training, socialization and preferences. Some is the result of a history of discriminatory practices affecting access to higher-paying jobs and compensation levels for female-dominated jobs. The present reality and past history of an underpaid female work force poses a constant threat of economic disaster to women in the form of job loss, spousal desertion, lack of resources to leave an abusive relationship, eviction and, ultimately, homelessness.

Employment barriers and occupational segregation must be eliminated. This would require initiatives in vocational education programs to encourage women to enter "non-traditional" fields dominated by men and to encourage male acceptance of women in these fields. As discussed earlier, poor women have been one of the only groups to benefit from public employment and training programs. New initiatives in this direction could help today's enlarged population of poor women.

Given the existence of protective legislation, the federal government should strengthen the enforcement of the Equal Pay Act, Title VII of the Civil Rights Act, and Title IX of the 1972 Educational Amendments. The passage of the Civil Rights Restoration Act in the face of President Reagan's veto may be a force for such renewed drive. Similarly, the federal government should strengthen enforcement of Executive Order 11246 which requires federal contractors to guarantee equal employment opportunity.

Finally, federal, state and local governments should adopt the controversial "comparable worth" policies in occupations where women predominate. Arguments that "comparable worth" would be too expensive make sense to employers who logically maintain that their firms are not social agencies. Again, encouragement in the form of tax incentives or subsidies from government sources could meet this objection.

Maternal and Child Health Care
and Health Care for the Elderly

In the United States, the largest source of health insurance is through employee benefit plans. However, with escalating insurance premiums and declining employer contributions, many employees are receiving reduced insurance coverage. Most part-time employees receive no health benefits. There is evidence that at any one time, up to 25 percent of the United States population has no health coverage. Moreover, dependent-care coverage is disappearing in many health insurance programs. Most families pay most of the costs of pediatric care. Approximately 33 million Americans are completely without health insurance. Thirty percent of divorced women lose coverage when they are dropped form their former spouse's plan, and one-third of all working women do not have basic medical coverage. Homeless families, confronted with the need for food and shelter, generally forgo all but the most acute emergency health care.

Medicaid reaches only 40 percent of the eligible poverty population, which is comprised primarily of children and the elderly. Medicare Parts A and B cover 55 percent of the total health costs of the elderly.[10]

The Minimum Health Care for All Bill, sponsored by Senator Edward Kennedy and Representative Henry Waxman, would require all employers to provide at least a minimum degree of uniform health insurance to employees.[11] Similarly, new Medicare provisions covering catastrophic illness promise to ameliorate some of the problems with limited Medicare coverage, but they do not go far enough in fulfilling Medicare's commitment to ease the largest cost item of older Americans, meeting their health expenses.

In the absence of the ideal national health insurance program, the following agenda would provide health security for Americans, many of whom are subject to permanent bankruptcy and debt in the event of serious illness:

- Complete prenatal, maternal and child health coverage should be extended, through Medicaid, to all low-income women and children not otherwise covered.

- Private health insurance plans should offer an option that covers all expenses associated with prenatal care and delivery, and employer-provided insurance plans should offer the option of coverage to the employee's immediate family.

- The Special Supplemental Food Program for Women, Infants and Children (WIC) should be expanded, at a minimum, to its pre-1981 funding level.

The Flexible Workplace

The workplace, like most other institutions in America, has not been organized in a manner that helps mediate the competing demands that job and family responsibilities place on working parents. Most working parents find that the pressure of their dual roles can affect their ability to perform at home and on the job. A growing number of corporations are beginning to recognize this problem and take steps in these directions. These changes are encouraging. It is noted that they are in the best interests of the organization, parent workers, their children, and the society at large.

To further insure accommodation of working parents, employers should uniformly permit greater flexibility in scheduling time. For example, vacation time need not be limited to two weeks in the summer, but may include shorter periods that coincide with children's schedules such as Christmas school vacation, special holidays and a range of individual special needs. Inclusion in the workplace of flexible schedules (flextime), compressed work weeks like those routinely scheduled for nursing staff at many hospitals, job-sharing, and voluntary reduced work time would abet the efforts of worker parents to meet their work and family obligations. Care should be given to all flexible arrangements so that salaries and benefits do not suffer if employees participate in such options.

The flexible workplace model would incorporate the implementation of flexible benefits packages. Most traditional benefits plans were designed for the employee who is the male head of household. New benefit packages should allow carry-over of unused credits and benefits at year-end in flexible benefits/employee spending account programs. Currently, the biggest obstacle in the way of flexible benefits is the "constructive receipt" problem. This occurs because many benefits, no matter how flexible, are considered income and, therefore, subject to tax. Increases in the number and categories of benefits frequently lead to increased taxation, obviating the efficacy of the benefits plan.[12]

Divorce and Child Custody

The divorce rate has risen precipitously up 115 percent since 1965. In 1986, 1,187,000 divorces were granted in the United States. Most divorces create strain. Within the first year after divorce, women and children suffer a 73 percent drop in their standard of living, while men experience a 43 percent rise.[13] Under community property and no-fault divorce laws, women do not fare as well as men, whose greatest asset is their higher earning capacity which results in larger pension and retirement based upon earnings accrued after the divorce and property settlement, as well as before.

The economic power of men also translates into power in child-custody contests. Fit mothers are losing custody at an alarming rate. Weitzman and Dixon[14] completed a study showing that fathers win two-thirds of the time in contested child-custody cases. While it may be egalitarian to legally avoid presumptions about the fitness of mothers or fathers relative to child custody, mothers and fathers are not coming into courts as equal contributors to their children's welfare. Fathers enter court with greater evidence to prove their competency to support their children. Because men remarry more quickly than women, they are also more able to re-create the appearance of a traditional family with a new wife who can provide the stability of the nurturing figure while the father pursues his higher-paying occupation. The harsh reality of economic inequity means that mothers are not receiving what the Constitution provides – "equal protection under the law." The "bag lady" who frequently alludes to what seems like imaginary children may very well be the woman who yielded to the economic power of a husband at the time of divorce, desertion or abandonment. Many women abandon their children because they feel compelled to leave their husbands, but recognize that they cannot support their children, and their husbands can.

Despite the high cost of divorce for all women, it is far costlier for women with limited schooling and job skills than for upper-middle-class women. Couples with neither money nor education have always had more trouble keeping their marriages together than more privileged couples. This is more true now that marital breakups are viewed as normal. Poorly educated ex-husbands can seldom afford to support two households, and they seldom make adequate child support payments. Nor are poor divorced women in a competitive position if they want to remarry. Poor children have suffered the most as divorce has grown increasingly acceptable and the two-parent norm has diminished.

Prevention of the new social phenomenon of the "displaced homemaker" calls for divorce law reform that includes earning capacity as a fixed asset to be divided equally under community property and equitable rights settlements. Pension benefits incorporating future payouts should be included in property settlements as a law, rather than an item for litigation.

Private insurance companies could consider offering divorce insurance to ease the unequal financial strain of divorce. Even the simplest divorce involving two lawyers and a modest amount of property can cost from $5,000 to $15,000.

Stricter enforcement of child support payments has become an issue embraced by Democrats, Republicans, feminists, the middle class and the poor. Not only can child support enforcement programs save states money on welfare, but they can also provide a needed service to families. Despite the increased attention to this issue since passage of the 1984 federal child support amendments, there has not been sufficient improvement. This is most evident when one encounters a homeless mother (and her children) who frequently has lost all contact with the children's father and is unable to locate him for purposes of child support. Of women who were supposed to receive payments in 1985, less than half (48 percent) received the full ordered amount. Another 26 percent received only partial payment, and another 26 percent received nothing.[15]

Several states, led by Wisconsin, require automatic withholding of support payments from an absent parent's paycheck. Wisconsin is beginning to test a program that would guarantee children a minimum support payment whereby the state makes up the difference if the parents cannot meet the standard.

Several other innovative plans for payroll deduction of child support obligations by public and private employers are being set up. In Los Angeles, city employees may participate in payroll deduction. County employees of the Los Angeles Department of Water and Power are using the same program, and the Transamerica Insurance Company has introduced the plan for its employees. According to the Los Angeles District Attorney's staff, there may be as many as 200,000 cases in the county in which parents are either ignoring or are in arrears on their child support payments.

These plans are simple and effective and could become a model for every government and private business. In California, 80 percent of the poor could be removed from the welfare rolls, or at least have their payments reduced, if they could get the child support that is due them.

Last, but certainly not least, the courts must preserve the custody rights of fit mothers. This requires legal reforms because lawyers in contested cases demand large fees which women, with their 64 cents to a man's dollar, cannot match. Judicial reform is equally important because judges tend to be dominated by traditional male values. Too often, rather than meting out justice, they are punitive to mothers. "In the best interests of the child," the adversary system should cease.

Just as consideration of industrial policy invited international comparison with Japan, an international perspective on family economic policy offers important data for Americans.

Many Western European nations have well-articulated family policies which recognize the need for family support to meet the socioeconomic needs required to facilitate productive labor force participation of all members in society. Recent demographic and employment trends in Europe parallel those of the United States, and family policies and support structures have grown with changes in family structures and women's labor force participation.

More than one hundred countries, including every industrialized country except the United States and South Africa, guarantee all employed women the right to a fully protected leave from work at childbirth for an average duration of five months, accompanied by a cash benefit generally equal to the maximum insured wage.

Every other advanced industrial country provides free medical services to cover prenatal care, childbirth and postnatal care for infants and mothers.

Sixty-seven countries provide a cash benefit—a family allowance to supplement the income of adults rearing children.

Many countries allow parents leave time to care for sick children. Sweden guarantees all parents the right to a six-hour work day until their child is eight years old.

Child care is more available in Western Europe than it is in the United States, especially for the three-to-six-year-old group. France provides free public schools for 95 percent of this age group; West Germany provides 75 percent; and Italy 70 percent. After-school programs are more common in Western Europe than in the United States, as are family day-care spaces and center care places for infants and toddlers.

What is convincing about these policies is the fact that the countries that have responded supportively to women's labor force participation have eased some of the tension between work and the family. This is best reflected in the narrowing gap between male and female earnings. In Sweden, women earn 90 percent of male earnings; in Britain, women's wages increased from 63 percent of men's in 1970 to 73.5 percent in 1969. Women's wages in Italy rose from 70 percent in 1962 to nearly 84 percent in 1986.[16]

All nations, regardless of supportive family policies, continue to experience the problem of women who carry the double burden of work outside of the home and primary responsibility for household work. This is a social problem rather than an economic issue. However, the implications for homeless families, especially women and children, are great. The double burden often means that fathers, under the strain of poverty or financial burdens accrued through underemployment or unemployment, desert their families, leaving women with the sole responsibility for sustaining themselves and their children.

Family Policy as a Non-Welfare Approach to Helping the Poor

The family policies recommended herein have the additional advantage of bridging current welfare programs by providing income and services that would help people leave the welfare rolls, or never enter them in the first instance. By introducing family economic policies that include child support assurance, child care, health insurance, pay equity and equal employment, government and business might reduce the welfare rolls and poverty at a lower cost than present welfare reform strategies based upon work requirements.

It is important to note that strengthened support for all families, recommended here, would translate to homeless-prevention. A recent study of homelessness in Chicago reported that among the new poor, those who have experienced homelessness reported a similar family background to those who have never been homeless. The study further reported that the modal response was that 42 percent of all respondents come from families with "average" incomes.[17] What is clear is that homeless people are primarily either single and living alone, or one-parent families.

Non-welfare strategies, rooted in family support systems of entitlement, can add a strong measure of security to all American families. They can provide the most solid grounding for maintaining people within the circle of their families and their homes.

Chapter 4

Income Policy

Inadequate unemployment compensation and a steady erosion on the progressivity of taxes, along with social insurance programs, offer insufficient protections against unemployment, illness or age. Recent changes in the tax code, resulting from the Tax Reform Act of 1986, have also eliminated major incentives for construction of low-cost housing. These weaknesses in social insurance and taxation both contribute to homelessness and offer slight support for those in economic need.

Anecdotes, case histories and surveys clearly demonstrate that unemployment compensation has been too limited to provide any substantial support for people who lose their jobs so that they can retain the security of paying their rent or mortgage. Similarly, the trend away from income taxes to value-added taxes has resulted in a disproportionately higher tax bite for poor people. Changes in both unemployment compensation and taxation would add protections against homelessness in periods of economic downturns.

Unemployment Compensation

None of the major social insurance programs in the United States—Social Security Old Age and Survivors Insurance, Medicare or federally supported unemployment insurance— were specifically designed to stave off poverty. Clearly, social insurance provides protections against several important causes of poverty, but it ignores other sources of poverty. A worker or new labor market entrant, after a period of long-term unemployment, can expect to receive little or no help under social insurance. Workers who are steadily employed, but at low wages, also receive minimal, if any, aid for their families until they reach age 62, become disabled, or die.

While Social Security, Medicare and the high pre-retirement incomes of Social Security and Medicare recipients have reduced poverty among the elderly and the disabled, unemployment insurance has been less effective as an anti-poverty program. A higher proportion of jobless benefits is received by families whose annual incomes would be above the poverty line in the absence of social insurance payments. Eligibility criteria under Unemployment Insurance (UI) include a recent and stable work history. This precludes many classes of the poor: the nonemployed, the erratically employed and the chronically underemployed.[1] Most homeless people in the labor force have employment that resembles these unstable patterns.

The major difference between UI and Social Security is that unemployment is viewed as temporary, while retirement and disability can last indefinitely. All of the social insurance programs are generally perceived as mainstream, middle-class benefits. Only one-quarter of UI funds are distributed to people who would otherwise be poor. Nevertheless, the significance of UI in aiding the poor cannot be underestimated. Three-fourths of those formerly poor who receive UI are moved out of poverty by this income.[2]

Blank and Blinder have demonstrated through regression analysis that when the general economy declines, certain workers experience much larger increases in unemployment than others. The patterns in their regression coefficients confirm that the burden of unemployment is distributed unequally across age, race and sex groups. "In particular, non-white and young workers are more severely affected than female and older workers who receive such low wages that they are not as sensitive to changes in unemployment rates."[3] Some older women workers have other sources of income from transfers or other family members, allowing them to drop out of the labor market more easily.

Unemployment Insurance is the largest government program designed to cushion the effect of unemployment. It is available to all workers in covered industries who have worked a certain length of time and who are involuntarily terminated. The percentage of jobs covered by UI has expanded from 58 percent in 1950 to 93 percent in 1980.[4] However, newer service industry people are less likely than industrial workers to apply for unemployment benefits. Earlier service workers stayed in their jobs longer. Part-time work was less dominant. The frequent shifts in jobs and preponderance of part-time work render service workers ineligible for jobless benefits.

On the other hand, many of the new entrants or re-entrants into unemployment have not worked long enough to be eligible for UI. Others cannot draw benefits because they quit rather than being fired, or their unemployment period lasts longer than their eligibility for benefits. The ratio of unemployed people receiving benefits to the total number of unemployed stayed between 45 and 55 percent during the 1950s and 1960s, peaked to 78 percent in 1975, and fell precipitously to 43 percent in 1982. Today, fewer than 32 percent of the unemployed receive jobless benefits — the lowest level in the program's 53-year history.[5] This recent decrease in UI recipiency appears to be related to legislative changes in eligibility rules and the duration of benefits. In 1976 the maximum duration of unemployment benefits was 65 weeks, varying in each state, and in 1983 it was down to 34 to 55 weeks.

Unemployment Insurance is less frequently available to the low-income workers who are likely to be found among the homeless or potentially homeless. The eligibility requirements mean that those who are most likely to experience unemployment are least likely to receive UI. The United States Bureau of Labor Statistics records the distribution of Unemployment Insurance. Data from 1979 demonstrate that unemployment benefits were disproportionately received by whites, males and prime-aged workers.

Private forms of unemployment insurance are also available to laid-off workers, primarily to unionized workers. Unfortunately, this form of protection is also unlikely to help low-wage workers because most of these jobs are not generally unionized. The United States Bureau of Labor Statistics showed that 37 percent of the work force earned less than $200 per week on their primary jobs, but only 15.2 percent of all unionized workers were in this earning category.[6]

Income protection designed to aid people in transition from one job to another and prevent personal disaster, which could result in eviction and homelessness, compels several fundamental changes in the present Unemployment Insurance system. Eligibility criteria for benefits need extension to include new workers and those who have a less stable work history. Contemporary economic uncertainties and massive plant firings have rendered such work histories more common than in the past, and new policies must respond to these new problems.

It is difficult to avoid commenting on the ludicrous fact that legislative changes intended to reduce eligibility and the duration of UI benefits were introduced in 1983, immediately after the 1980-81 recession. This pulled the cushion of economic support out from those who most needed it during the most serious economic downturn of the decade. Many of these people became Type I homeless people. It should never be allowed to happen again. This means that measures to extend eligibility and the duration of benefits must be put back in place if we are serious about preventing homelessness.

Instead, many local governments have turned to the welfare system to replace Unemployment Insurance by introducing requirements that unemployed people who receive general relief, the lowest amount of public assistance available, produce written evidence that they have sought one or more jobs during the month as a condition of their relief. Failure to produce such evidence can result in the reduction or loss of benefits. Such laws place the burden of unemployment insurance on the unemployed. Insurance, in this context, means seeking employment. This policy makes the ludicrous changes of 1983 seem sane by comparison.

Unemployment insurance is, was, and always has been a program of short-term, partial wage replacement for those between jobs. It is not and never has been a program of long-term income maintenance.

The proportion of Americans with jobs has never been higher, even though the wage structure may be lower. Over 16 million new jobs have been created since 1982.

The unemployed want these jobs, not Unemployment Insurance or welfare. Fifty-five percent of the unemployed are either new to the work force or re-entering the labor force with no recent work qualifying them for Unemployment Insurance. Others are long-term unemployed who have exhausted their Unemployment Insurance benefits.

The level of benefits payable in each state is determined by the state, not federal law. In most states, it is pegged at about one-half what the claimant earned on the job. There has also been a sharp drop in the resources of the UI system, which has made it less efficient and responsive to people in need. The number of workers who process unemployment claims has been cut from 54,000 to 40,000 since 1981. Since that time, claims dropped over 40 percent.

Federal legislation mandating companies to give advance notice of plant closings and layoffs, plus increased jobless benefits is the clear direction for helping the unemployed. In addition, immediate adjustment assistance on site, when a plant facility is closing or laying off a substantial number of workers, provides another avenue for relief, in combination with other steps.

Tax Reform

Where the poor are concerned, the main pattern in postwar tax history has been the rapid and continuing growth of the payroll tax. Over the 1950-1983 period, the poor paid higher state and local sales taxes and higher state and local payroll taxes. Changes in personal income taxation have been minor for the very poor, but the near-poor have paid higher income taxes as well.

Numerous changes in the tax code have occurred since 1950. Those relating to corporate income tax are irrelevant to the poor. Changes in excise taxes and customs duties are too disparate to permit any generalization. In effect, payroll and personal income taxes and sales taxes most directly affect the poor.

The payroll tax is considered the most regressive because it taxes only income from earnings, not assets. Because maximum taxable earnings have grown much faster than average earnings since 1950, a larger portion of non-poor workers have paid payroll taxes on every dollar earned, thereby making the payroll tax less regressive. However, the payroll tax has more than quadrupled since 1950, which leaves little doubt that the tax burden on the poor has substantially increased in the past 33 years.

The federal personal income tax is more complex than the payroll tax. Those provisions of the income tax which are most relevant to the poor are the personal exemption, the standard deduction, and earned income tax credit.

The personal exemption remained $600 for 20 years between 1948 and 1969, and was steadily eroded by inflation. During the 1970s it was raised to $1,000, where it remained until the Economic Recovery Tax Reform Act of 1986 which set the rate at $1,900. Thus, the real value of the personal exemption has fallen to about one-half of what it was in 1955, reducing progressivity at the low end.[7]

The lowest tax bracket was 17.4 percent in 1960 and rose to 22.2 percent by 1972; since then it has fallen and is now only 14 percent. This decline in the lowest bracket rate has helped reduce the tax burden of personal income taxation on the poor.

Inflation has reduced the value of the standard deduction substantially since 1979. It increased from six to 10 percent of adjusted gross income until 1969, and decreased thereafter to five percent for an individual and eight percent for a married couple. However, the increase in the standard deduction in 1977 removed many poor and near-poor people from the income tax rolls.

There are basically three categories of low-income families who can be affected by personal income taxes: those in abject poverty with earnings at or below one-half of the poverty index; those who earn the equivalent of the poverty index; and those who earn one-half of the median income.

The first group of families would never have been subject to income taxation and would have received a negative income tax rate of 10 percent starting in 1975. This family's tax burden, including income and payroll, has changed little since 1950.

The second family of four has paid an increasing share of its earnings in taxes since 1965, and by 1983 paid 16.5 percent negative tax based upon earned income credit.

The third family, which some poverty analysts cite as the most identifiable group of relatively poor people, has experienced an average income tax rate up from zero in 1950 to five percent in 1983.[8]

Between 1950 and 1970, state and local taxes grew much faster than the gross national product, and federal taxes and their structure have also changed in important ways. Personal income and payroll taxes are now much greater sources of revenue than they were in 1950. Sales taxes have greatly expanded. The largest reduction in revenue source has come from property taxes. U.S. Department of Commerce data reveal that the share of personal income taxes increased as much as the share of property taxes decreased.

Most states have personal income taxes, and a number of large cities also have them. Most of these taxes have a progressive rate structure, including a zero bracket which effectively removes the poor from the tax rolls. Although the shift from property tax to income tax remains controversial, it has resulted in increasing the progressivity of the state and local tax structure.

For the poor, income taxes are basically irrelevant. Sales and payroll taxes matter, and in some instances, property taxes. Over the 1950-1983 period, the poor paid higher state and local sales and payroll taxes, thus experiencing an increased tax burden from these sources.

Citizens for Tax Justice, a research and advocacy organization sponsored and funded by labor unions and liberal social organizations, claims that the nation's poorest families, with incomes averaging less than $8,600 a year, pay five times as much of their earnings in state sales and excise taxes as those who earn more than $600,000. This unfairness is especially hard in states that impose heavy taxes on food, utilities, tobacco and fuels.

It is not just the poor who spend disproportionately on sales and excise taxes. A four-member family earning $31,000 a year spends three times as much of this income on these taxes compared to the richest Americans.

Citizens for Tax Justice opposes such consumption taxes because they are not based upon ability to pay. The organization advocates tax reforms which, if enacted, would ease the tax burden of the poor and near-poor. For many homeless people, sales taxes and other consumption taxes are the only tax they pay. For them the tax on a package of cigarettes represents an onerous amount of their general relief check. According to the Citizens for Tax Justice, the worst income tax is far fairer than any state sales tax.

Data produced by Citizens for Tax Justice demonstrate that the poorest families pay five times as much of their earnings as the highest-earning families. Their study found:

- The poorest 20 percent of four-member families, averaging income of $8,581, paid 5.4 percent of their earnings in sales and excise taxes in 1987.

- The second one-fifth, averaging $20,535, paid 3.9 percent.

- The third, averaging $31,497, paid 3.3 percent.

- The fourth, averaging $44,910, paid 2.9 percent.

- The top-earning five percent, averaging $187,316, paid 1.6 percent.

- Four-member families averaging $612,122 a year, the richest 0.7 percent of Americans, paid 1.1 percent of their incomes for sales and excise taxes.[9]

Tax reform intended to preserve the purchasing power of the poor requires that states begin to rely more on income taxes, which place the least negative burden on poor people. Sales taxes can also be made less unfair by extending rebates to the poor. These taxes could also be applied disproportionately to services that are generally used by the more affluent, such as club memberships and home-improvement services.

Only six states have sales tax credits for the poor, and only in New Mexico does the credit offset more than half of the burden for low-income people. The other five states are Kansas, Vermont, Idaho, Hawaii and North Carolina.

Sixteen states, including those with the heaviest sales taxes, all tax food — one of the most onerous burdens on the poor. The poor also spend 6.2 percent of their income on electricity bills — more than twice the rate of the middle-income family. But the middle-income family pays three times as big a share for electricity as do the rich.[10]

The presumption underlying the Economic Recovery Tax Act of 1987 is that it will abolish inequality and is an example of populist tax reform. This is blatantly inaccurate. Some tax shelters for the rich have been eliminated, but the singular fact that begs attention is that the maximum tax rate for the rich has been drastically reduced. Some minor tax reductions for the poor, mainly in taxes which were very recently raised for them under the 1981 and 1987 tax reform laws, have reduced the maximum rate for the rich from 50 percent to 28 percent, which used to be a middle-income taxation level. We have also reduced inheritance taxes which, combined with reduced income taxes, means tax reform for the rich at a time when the middle-class lifestyle is disappearing and mass poverty, reflected at its extreme in mass homelessness, is growing. Real tax reform must reverse these priorities if there is any real intent to prevent the spread of income problems which result in homelessness.

Tax reform remains a useful strategy for encouraging investment in low-income housing. Unfortunately, the Tax Reform Act of 1986 has changed depreciation allowances and restricted the availability of passive-loss deductions for individuals. In addition to restricting individual tax incentives for housing construction, the Tax Reform Act also issued strict limitations on the amount of tax-free bonds that states can issue. Housing bonds are restrictively regulated and lumped together with all other tax-free bonds, forcing state officials to choose between housing, roads, schools, sanitation, and so on. These restrictions, designed to insure a more neutral tax code, have wielded serious disincentives for the much-needed construction of low-income housing.

To offset this, the tax code offered a new tax incentive for rental unit production. The new plan was only a three-year tax credit program scheduled to expire in 1989. It allows each state to allocate a limited amount of tax credits (calculated at $1.25 per citizen) providing a maximum nine percent annual tax credit for ten years for the construction or rehabilitation of low-income housing units not federally subsidized for up to 80 percent of the value of the unit, a maximum four-percent annual tax credit for ten years for the acquisition of low-income housing units without any rehabilitation, or for units that receive other government subsidies, including tax-exempt bonds. However, expenditures must exceed $2,000 per unit for an owner to claim either tax credit. Although tax credits are extended over ten years, the set-aside for low-income units must be maintained for a "compliance period" of fifteen years.[11]

It is too early to assess the effect of this tax program on the construction industry. State agencies and administrators are trying hard to make it work. Intermediaries like the National Income Housing Coalition are trying to find investors. On the other hand, state agencies are also reporting that they can only expect to allocate a small portion of tax credits, and national surveys of housing developers show that only a few builders believe they can make the tax credit work.

All agree that the new tax program will require state or local subsidy appropriation on top of the tax credits to provide low-cost rental units. The reality is, therefore, that the tax incentives are part of a decrease in federal involvement in housing.

Expanded unemployment insurance eligibility, benefits and duration, coupled with a renewed reliance on progressive taxes, carry the potential to protect the poor against catastrophes and preserve their basic survival needs. Finally, recent tax reform needs to be adjusted to renew earlier incentives for the construction of low-income housing.

Chapter 5

Welfare Reform

Welfare reform efforts aspire to two different goals. The first goal would alter the system to one which provides more adequate and less demeaning benefit schemes designed to help people live with dignity. A second goal would change the system to reduce welfare expenditures by limiting the size of benefits, restricting the amount of time people can remain on public assistance, and attaching strict eligibility requirements for such assistance.

Prevention of homelessness would be abetted by pursuit of the first goal. Unfortunately, the consensus around welfare reform that presently exists derives from the second goal. Arguments espoused by liberal and conservative supporters of the Family Security Act, authored by Senator Daniel Moynihan, the long-time advocate of welfare reform, all focus attention on the promise of the "workfare" provision in the Act to lead people off the welfare rolls and ultimately reduce the cost of operating the system.[1]

Unless higher standards are established and benefits increase, there is little possibility that homelessness can be prevented or ameliorated. It is also clear that welfare rules contribute to this situation, and that changes in certain rules, as well as in administrative and supervisory systems that contribute to homelessness, would prevent some of the problem. Many homeless people have been forced into their circumstances because of excessively rigid requirements that have been the basis for denial of welfare benefits. Proof of residency, including birth certificates, social security cards and other documents, is generally a problem for people to obtain, and result in the denial of applications for welfare.

The Reagan administration pronouncements that all people could rely upon a safety net as last-resort assistance have provided the rationale for federal and state cuts in income maintenance, service and resource programs. There is ample evidence that the safety net has large holes in it, causing many people to fall out of the net and into the streets. Much of this gap derives from welfare reform efforts specifically designed to reduce the operating costs of welfare programs.

Los Angeles County data dramatically demonstrate this disaster. Each month, about 10,000 people apply to Los Angeles County for cash assistance. About 5,000 are homeless when they apply. General relief is the lowest level of the safety net. Funded entirely by Los Angeles County, it provides recipients with a monthly allowance of $280. Persons who have any resources, or who are eligible for any other form of benefit, are ineligible for general relief.

About one-half of the people who receive general relief are physically or mentally disabled and are not required to work in exchange for the money they receive. The other half are required to perform menial tasks at county facilities to "work off" the $280 grant. Such jobs include cleaning beaches, mopping hallways in county facilities, digging graves and tending the furnaces at the county crematorium. One prerequisite for all jobs assigned to those on general relief is that the jobs are not unionized, so that the destitute cannot take away jobs from union members.

Workfare labor is the least of the burdens of being on general relief. The real struggle is survival in Los Angeles on $280 a month. The grant is supposed to be based upon objective criteria of what it costs to survive in Los Angeles County. This sum has not been increased since 1981.

The $280 total is the sum of three components of a basic budget index which provides $74 for food, $11 for clothing and all other personal needs, and $143 for housing. There is no housing at $143 a month in Los Angeles. Even the smallest room on Skid Row costs an average of $240 a month.

The result is that the 35,000 people now on general relief are either homeless at least a part of each month because they cannot pay a full month's rent, or they spend all of their money on rent, forgoing other necessities like food, clothing and health care, unless they can get them free through soup kitchens and volunteer used clothing provisions.

For those forced to live in the street for a week or two each month, the result is illness, violence, and sometimes death. Despite its mild climate, Los Angeles' coroners report deaths from hypothermia at the same rate as New York City.

Men and women who were once ordinary and independent working people are slowly converted by the general relief program into a hopeless and unemployable "underclass." With their entire existence consumed by finding food and shelter, they become unlikely candidates for employment. The general relief system in Los Angeles, and its counterparts in counties throughout the nation, are a dismal failure that blatantly contributes to homelessness, as compared with some of the more indirect practices that relegate poor people to hardship.

At a minimum, general relief programs must provide benefits that meet the cost of one month's rent in the least expensive available housing.

For women with children, the welfare department has become such an unwieldy system over the last 20 years, that even those who seem obviously eligible for their services must go through not just hours and days, but weeks of standing in lines, filling out forms, making and keeping appointments, and waiting for paperwork to be processed. This is an arduous and overwhelming task for the most sophisticated of people. The failure of every state to keep pace with the increases in the cost of living has made the allotment a mother may receive a sad commentary on the way we care for the poor in our country. In California, a single parent with two children and with no income is eligible for a maximum cash grant of $633 per month, or $7,596 per year. This AFDC benefit equals 83.7 percent of the 1987 poverty line for a family of three. (The estimated poverty line for a family of three was $9,069 in 1987.)

The tragic scenario of women who, because of circumstances beyond their control, have had to apply for AFDC, debilitates even the strongest among them. After making all of the necessary efforts to complete the application process, they must wait for approval and processing through the system. With no resources, they can rely on good friends and family for small loans, food and temporary lodging. But these resources and the patience of family and friends are soon exhausted. One month after applying for AFDC, a check may not have arrived. This results in eviction from a dilapidated $400-a-month apartment, ensuing long waits at emergency shelters, many of which do not take children, and sleeping and begging wherever possible.[2]

When the first AFDC check does arrive at the old apartment, it is not much money, but it can pay for two weeks in an old hotel that does not require first and last months' rent. It is enough to buy a hot-plate, some diapers, toilet paper, toothpaste and soap — all items not covered by food stamps.

Food stamps last for two weeks if people are careful and lucky. More than one out of four AFDC households in California do not even receive food stamps. Survival in the welfare system is a perpetual struggle. Work is a problem because of the cost of adequate (or inadequate) child care.

Although these welfare programs are designed to aid the needy, even the aggregate of income and in-kind services and resources is insufficient to raise poor families even to the poverty level.

Similar problems exist in the Social Security disability program, which is the primary resource for mentally ill people. Rules governing this program, as well as the Supplemental Security Income program, result in strong work disincentives. People who earn more than $300 a month for nine months lose their benefits. This benefit cutoff level is simply too low for people to meet basic needs, including housing, which can hardly be found for $300 a month rent. These rules hurt rather than help recipients, who are either afraid to work because they will lose their higher benefit levels or leave jobs when they cannot earn enough to afford the loss of disability or SSI. The two programs combined serve approximately six million people. If recipients could continue to receive the difference between their earnings and the maximum allowable benefit for their disability status, work incentives would be strong, living standards would be more decent, and homelessness would be less ominous.

In the last five years, while hundreds of thousands of women and their dependent children have slid into poverty, the public response has been to decimate the few limited programs that provide any help. Aid to Families with Dependent Children (AFDC), housing subsidies, food stamps and Medicaid have served as the last resort of residual help for families. Attacks from the conservatives on AFDC, which is the most stigmatized program despite the small percentage of the federal budget that it occupies, have spurred further discredit to social programs ranging from Unemployment Insurance to Social Security, Medicare, and nutritional programs for infants.

Analysis of Welfare Dependency

Conservative attacks, predicated on the arguments of Charles Murray, claim that welfare hurts recipients by undermining their work ethic, thus demoralizing them; welfare also destroys their families.[3] This argument is 400 years old, dating to the Elizabethan poor laws. Murray further claims that generations of families receiving AFDC has resulted in a permanent "underclass" of culturally homogeneous people.

Barbara Ehrenreich, in challenging the component myths about the welfare population, initially questions the term "underclass."

Developed by the University of Michigan Social Research Institute, the term emerged from an empirical study that followed a randomly chosen group of American people over a ten-year period. The researchers found that during that period, one out of four subjects became poor enough to make use of AFDC, food stamps or other means-tested programs for more than six years. Those one out of four were labeled the "underclass."[4] Sociologists have recently grasped this term as the new description for poverty that seems unsolvable.

Ehrenreich and other poverty analysts deny that these people comprise a permanent underclass. Their supportive evidence lies in the composition of those who circulate in and out of welfare programs. They are predominantly white, and the next largest group are black. They are single-mother families. Many are families whose breadwinner was a laid-off industrial worker. Some grew up in poverty and others grew up in comfort. Most depend upon AFDC for a relatively short period of time as an aid in transition from life crises and episodic need. Most studies of welfare dependency conclude that one-third of the recipients are chronic, or on welfare for six-plus years; one-third use welfare episodically; and one-third are one-time users seeking temporary aid to restabilize their lives. This means that two-thirds of welfare recipients cannot be properly described as an underclass. Even the Michigan study identified only one out of four people as "the underclass."

The term "underclass" poses a series of problems for those attempting to plan programs for the poor. The popularity of the term signals a political shift to blaming poverty on the poor instead of on society, as we did in the late 1960s. "Underclass" clearly refers to the undeserving poor: those who live on the streets, winos, criminals, unemployed men and women on welfare. The deserving poor — the elderly, two-parent families, and the working poor — are not a part of this underclass. As in the past, new programs are being targeted to the deserving poor.

Widespread acceptance of the term "underclass" arouses concern among compassionate liberals who argue that such terminology blames the victim. An even stronger argument of liberals is that acceptance of the term spells a willingness on the part of society to accept the status of "underclass" as a permanent structure of American life and abandon its moral obligations to this part of the community. William Wilson has struggled to respond to analysts who accept the permanence of an underclass comprised largely of black men and women living in inner cities who reflect social pathologies and behavior that contrasts with that of mainstream America. His response attributes three key factors that explain the rise in the "underclass" in black urban communities. These are:

- Joblessness has increased among young black men because there are fewer unskilled and semi-skilled blue collar jobs in urban areas where most black people live. The essence of this explanation is structural unemployment.

- The two-parent black family is disappearing because male joblessness has made marriage less attractive.

- Single parenthood and male joblessness have increased among poor black people because the black middle class has been moving out of the urban ghetto. This means that there are fewer role models for black youngsters in the ghettos.

Wilson's emphasis on the neighborhood in shaping the lives of the poor may be his most important contribution to the underclass debate. He argues that the departure of the black middle class has made it more difficult for the poor to escape poverty. As poor areas have lost populations, their housing has been abandoned; black women are more likely to become pregnant at an earlier age; and black men work fewer hours and earn lower wages than black men from similar families who grew up in richer neighborhoods, if they work at all.[5]

Many liberals claim that even Wilson's structural approach to black ghetto culture blames the victim. Wilson has been interpreted as portraying victims who are not innocent because they make obvious choices based upon self-interest, and their leaders have abandoned their struggle to assert morality and limit destructive behavior.

This debate serves little purpose. What is critical is that we expect more of the poor and the larger community, and reassert a moral contract between the poor and the rest of society.

Wilson outlines what America's social obligations should be under such a moral contract. He calls for tighter labor markets, more job training, children's allowances, subsidized child care for working mothers, and other programs designed to help bring the underclass into mainstream society. These institutional reforms, complemented by a conscious effort at cultural change among poor urban black people, can improve the lot of the so-called underclass and remove the specter of instability, dependence and forced transience.

On the other hand, the conservative position that welfare is demoralizing rings of truth. AFDC, as it is currently administered in the United States, does demoralize those who must depend upon it. The program was designed to be demoralizing. The long waits in welfare offices, frequently with impatient small children, the demeaning treatment often meted out by public welfare staff, the stares directed at food stamp users in the supermarkets, the condescending attitude of many Medicaid physicians are all demeaning. What is most demeaning is that people undergo such shame for so little money, always less than the official poverty index. That is because welfare was designed to discourage any use except by those who are so desperate that they must tolerate demoralization for survival.

In rebutting the conservative myth that welfare destroys the work ethic, Ehrenreich uses two themes. In talking about AFDC and the work ethic, conservatives are actually describing single mothers with small children — the largest proportion of AFDC recipients. These women may not be employed in the labor market, but they are raising children, and that is work. If the conservative right believes that raising children is an appropriate occupation for middle-class women, the same should apply to poor women. The feminist slogan "Every mother is a working mother" demands renewed attention in the welfare context.

The second theme refuting the work ethic myth is based upon empirical evidence, or the lack thereof. There is still no strong evidence that welfare at current benefit levels reduces anybody's interest in seeking paid employment. At current levels people are still eager to find work. Indeed, benefits are so insufficient to cover family needs that children in welfare families can be removed to foster homes as dependent and/or neglected children. Welfare departments throughout the country require service agencies to report all homeless families. Investigations of these reports frequently result in separation of children under protective services. This only perpetuates the tragedy of homeless families.

A Welfare Reform Agenda

Specific items for welfare reform are the restoration of cuts in social programs during President Reagan's administration and increases in benefit levels indexed to meet basic survival needs. McElvaine describes the welfare programs established in the 1930s as economic vaccinations against illnesses in the economy. When any downward spiral started in the economy, increased payments of unemployment compensation, AFDC, food stamps and Medicaid sustained people who were at risk of financial disaster and prevented demand from falling off so precipitously that the nation did not sink into a deep depression. McElvaine uses the metaphor of immunization, and claims that the Reagan cuts in social programs have weakened the nation's immunity to the contagion that resulted in the Great Depression.[6] Any reference to immunity serves as a reminder of the public health model which requires prevention of disease by attacking its causes. This public health model remains a sound approach to preventing personal and collective loss attributable to economic downturns.

Because it is clear that many people became homeless when they lost their benefits derived from disability, AFDC, food stamps, Medicaid and child care programs, restoration of these cuts would be a first step in eliminating a large part of the homeless population and returning them to their earlier status.

The new State of California Homeless Assistance Program, launched on February 1, 1988, offers promise as the vaccination needed by homeless people to move them back to permanent housing. The program has two major components: temporary shelter assistance and permanent housing assistance.

Under the temporary shelter assistance plan, such shelter must be provided on the same day that it is requested, or the following day, if the welfare department arranges for shelter in the meantime. Temporary assistance consists of $30 per day for a family of four or less (plus $7.50 per person per day for each additional person up to $60 per day). Temporary shelter can be provided for up to three weeks and extended another week if the family has made a good-faith effort but has been unable to locate permanent housing, or if the permanent housing will not be available until then.

The second kind of special assistance for permanent housing actually guarantees that the welfare department will now pay the total amount of move-in costs, including security deposits. They will pay up to two months' rent for security deposits and/or last month's rent, and up to the actual cost of gas, electricity and/or water. The new program will not pay the first month's rent, which must come out of the family's welfare grant.

To qualify for such assistance, the family must find permanent housing with monthly rent that is less than 80 percent of the family's AFDC grant. If the AFDC family will share housing with others, then its share of the rent must be less than 80 percent. The new program also requires that current AFDC recipients who are homeless must be given permanent housing assistance within the rental cost requirements. Families that have not been approved for AFDC must be approved and given permanent housing assistance within one day after they bring in necessary proof-of-eligibility documents and proof that they have found a place.

The final and problematic requirement is that eligible families must not have more than $100 in savings or funds from the current AFDC grant. They must "spend down" this money in order to qualify for security deposit assistance. This means-testing component of the program compels people to make a destructive choice in order to qualify for housing assistance.

The program is too new to evaluate. It also has several minor flaws, e.g., a homeless family should be eligible for a special-need payment of $100 in addition to the $30 a day in temporary shelter assistance. But no other public welfare program has taken steps to move families into temporary shelter and permanent housing; so that families have suffered from the anomaly that once they lose their homes, they cannot afford first and last month payments to regain housing, even if they earn above the poverty level. The California Homeless Assistance Program does have the potential to become a model for preventive welfare reform for the nation. The funding for this program is half state and half federal, and its cost is estimated at $34 million.[7]

One other attractive feature of the Homeless Assistance Program rests upon its coordination between the housing, income and service needs of beneficiaries. As many more women and children become poor, a new and expansive housing policy must offer shelter plus social and income service programs. Welfare policies and housing policies must be integrated. No housing policy can substitute an adequate welfare and income support system; neither can an income policy that only addresses the financial pressures that put families at housing risk ignore the non-economic problems that confront families on welfare.

Emergency aid to welfare recipients cannot address all of the problems that lead people to homelessness because the low level of benefits creates many of the crises that result in the loss of housing. Also, the provision of help for people on welfare who are at risk of homelessness can be viewed as an incentive for some individuals to face eviction so that they qualify for emergency aid. If homeless-prevention programs ultimately expand to large-scale projects, they might be most equitably administered through a system of rationing that sets a percentage limit above the welfare benefit level for emergency assistance.

Homeless-prevention programs targeted to people who receive welfare would also be more effective as preventive measures if they were extended to General Assistance recipients.

Welfare and Workfare

No discussion of welfare reform can ignore contemporary versions of workfare programs. In a rare consensus, conservative and liberal political leaders and policy analysts are embracing workfare as the largest single attack on welfare dependency in the country. Conservatives, best represented by Lawrence Mead, support workfare as a condition of receiving welfare. Mead argues that the programs of the Great Society exacerbated poverty and the persistence of an underclass because nothing was demanded in return for benefits — no schooling, no work, and no obedience to the law.[8] On the liberal side, proponents of workfare like Senator Daniel Moynihan view it as an opportunity for poor women to gain the skills they need to be competitive in the job market, helping them to take advantage of women's expanded role in the labor force.

The history of earlier workfare programs is instructive in the current drive for workfare. Most earlier programs have been guilty of "creaming," putting most of the resources into finding jobs for the 20 percent of the people who are easiest to place — people who were probably going to find jobs on their own — so that the program would look good.

Today's workfare schemes presumably put most of their resources into the people who are the hardest to place, but there is no evidence to support this. Forty states have work programs for welfare mothers, and the Moynihan Family Security Act, passed by Congress in June 1988, attaches work, training and child care to AFDC at the federal level.

The biggest problem with new-style workfare is that it is coercive. At best, it would provide opportunities for the most qualified top 20 percent of participants as in the past. At worst, it would force a new rationale for employing women in menial and demeaning jobs at the lowest end of the pay scale. This does not create new opportunities, it merely insures that AFDC mothers will meet their social obligation to work off their welfare. Nothing in the new law can guarantee to maintain welfare families within their circle of housing.

Undoubtedly, well-funded voluntary programs offering high-quality child care and job training would help certain people. The Massachusetts and Michigan experiences of voluntary workfare have demonstrated this. However, the likelihood is that most public welfare programs would be unable to offer either acceptable child care or well-paying jobs. The cost for child care in a licensed, professionally run center can be as high as $100 a week per child. This is more than most states now pay in welfare benefits, and for two children, more than most welfare recipients would be able to earn in the work force. Staff and participants in the Michigan and Massachusetts programs alleged that the day care allowance was too meager to solve the critical problem of care for children of working mothers.

The alternative is family day care, or leaving the child of one welfare mother with another welfare mother who will, in turn, be paid as a home child care worker. In effect, this merely circulates low-wage jobs and services among the welfare population. In New York City, home care workers for the elderly earn less than the poverty level for a family of three. Those home care workers who find full-time employment through the Human Resource Administration can help AFDC recipients become competitive in the work force.[9]

Wilson agrees that the new-style workfare is better than having no strategy at all to enhance employment experiences, but emphasizes that the effectiveness of such programs depends upon the availability of jobs. This is not a new position, but it does underscore the futility of any version of workfare in an economy where unemployment remains high in many regions of the country.[10] Estimates are that the Family Security Act's provisions will result in jobs for one in 50 welfare cases annually.

Workfare which forces millions of impoverished women into an already overcrowded, underpaid labor force will not cure their poverty; nor will it improve conditions of the working poor who earn wages at or near the poverty line; nor will it prevent poverty-related homelessness. Poverty cannot be cured with poverty-level jobs, and this concern becomes more troublesome in light of predictions that the United States is going to be a country of increased low-wage jobs. This trend has already been set in motion, and there is no reason to believe that it will be reversed.

In the seven congressional hearings on the Family Security Act, only one welfare-rights group was invited to testify, and no welfare recipient was included, despite the fact that many advocate groups have opposed this legislation. The result was that little was reported about why women and children are receiving AFDC benefits. The focus on "workfare" diverted attention from the effect of Reaganomics, underfunded and understaffed schools, lack of economic alternatives to poverty, drug trafficking and the government's role in that, and racism, among other things.

Racism remains a pervasive factor. Although most people on welfare are white, in proportion to the general population, a greater percentage of black people and other people of color are on welfare. This results from our legacy of racism and injustice that the presence of a black middle class cannot hide.

The basic premise of workfare is that parents are responsible for their children. There is no quarrel with this. However, workfare proponents interpret "responsibility" only as working for wages outside the home. Full-time homemaking and child-rearing are not considered work. The irony that more affluent mothers are being applauded for leaving their jobs to become full-time mothers at the exact time when welfare mothers are about to be forced to leave their children and seek employment cannot be lost. Workfare does not value the work that the wheels of the economy through government, industry, commerce and community life would halt.

Those who support workfare ignore the fact that it has not proved to work. The effect of existing mandatory workfare programs on job placement has, at best, been questionable. Even before full implementation, California's model program, GAIN (Greater Avenues for Independence), has failed. It lacks the funds to mandate full participation and has reduced the number of people who will be included in the program.

Workfare proponents dangle carrots like child care, educational programs and medical benefits as incentives, but these services are limited and vastly underfunded. Welfare reform proposals are weighted toward the creation of a second, lower tier of social service programs paid for out of public funds. Welfare recipients will participate because they have no other choices.

Understanding the nature of the workplace and the changing needs of workers could make a significant difference to public deliberation on workfare. The shift from an industrial to a service economy demands skills that stress communication, interaction and literacy. Requiring people to work without preparing them for long-term employment will, in the long run, fulfill the worst expectations of welfare reform.

For workfare programs to represent an important policy offering structural reforms in welfare, they must become part of a more comprehensive program of economic and social reform that encompasses the dynamic interplay between societal organization and the unequal opportunity structure for disadvantaged minorities. Industrial and family economic policies relying on non-welfare strategies offer greater promise of work and employment reform than workfare schemes. They must be designed to offer opportunity to work in ways that enhance human lives and offer social mobility for those locked into unequal life chances. Since most of the 3.7 million adults on Aid to Families with Dependent Children are not qualified for such employment, the government would have to subsidize private sector jobs, or serve as the employer of last resort to achieve this goal.

Finally, workfare is unlikely to overcome the demoralization associated with welfare dependency because existing programs and proposals before the Congress relegate workfare clients to a marginal employee status unprotected by federal labor and civil rights legislation. To improve the morale of welfare recipients, a more direct approach would be a raise in welfare benefits at least to the poverty level of $12,000 for a family of four, and a reduction in the bureaucratic harassment that is routinely inflicted on welfare recipients and, in the case of homeless welfare recipients, creates endless despair and frustration. Lessons from the 1980s workfare programs operated by state and local governments demonstrate that workfare can encourage independence and self-sufficiency among some women and children only when they are part of a larger anti-poverty strategy. Ultimately, non-welfare provisions offer the greatest promise for welfare reforms. Congress must consider the nature of the workplace, not just the motivations of the workers. Work, not workfare, is the key to welfare reform.

The preceding agenda for adjustments in the economy through protection of employment supports for families, equity in unemployment benefits and taxes, and dignified welfare comprises an agenda for primary prevention of homelessness. Primary prevention refers to strategies targeted at larger social and institutional problems that threaten special populations and result in structural disadvantage.

The remaining sections of this book offer prescriptives for more direct preventive measures through strategies for housing and the institutionalization of community mental health services.

PART II

THE HOUSING SECTOR

Chapter 6

The Erosion of Low-Income Housing

The national deficit may not emerge as the critical problem of the 1980s. The dwindling supply of affordable housing promises to affect more people than the deficit, and solutions pose greater dilemmas for public and private homebuilders. Many homeless advocates claim that homelessness is a housing problem. Others counter that the problem is broader. Regardless, homelessness is the most graphic symbol of the drastic shortage of affordable housing. David Schwartz et al. identify five housing trends which evidenced a downturn in the living conditions of millions of Americans in the 1980s. These trends have affected middle-class, working-class and poor families.

The first trend is the decline in home ownership, nationally. This follows a steady increase over the preceding 35 years. The percentage of Americans able to buy their own homes has decreased annually since 1980. This trend was particularly marked among young families and first-time homebuyers.[1]

Robert Kuttner claims that housing has become the great divider of the haves from the have-nots. The haves are those who own their homes and effectively increase their net worth as inflation adds to the value of their homes. The have-nots are tenants of moderate means who are vulnerable to a shrinking supply of rental housing, the escalation of rent costs, and the threat of condominium conversion.[2]

The second trend has been the explosive proliferation of homelessness. When homelessness became visible in the early 1980s, most of the homeless were deinstitutionalized mental patients or voluntary transients. Today, an increasing number of people on the streets or in shelters are ordinary Americans who are not mentally ill but have fallen out of the middle class. It is a useful reminder that most people started out their lives in houses and lived in houses for most of their lives. For most people on the streets, homelessness is a recent experience.

A decrease in affordability, availability and quality of the nation's rental housing stock marks the third major housing trend of the 1980s. A majority of the nation's 30 million tenants live in rental units that the federal government considers to be inadequate, overcrowded or cost-burdened. The National Low-Income Housing Coalition has calculated that seven million Americans were paying more than 50 percent of their income for their housing in 1980. In the same year the median rent for the 2.7 million households that earned less than $3,000 was $179 a month, leaving $71 of their monthly budget for other expenses. Since 1980, rents have risen at a rate 14 percent higher than prices generally. In a report, "The State of the Nation's Housing," prepared by the Harvard-MIT Joint Center for Housing, it was disclosed that single-parent families are paying an average of 58.4 percent of their income for rent, up from 35 percent in 1973.[3]

Fourth, the shortage of affordable housing for poor people has reached crisis proportions. Only 28 percent of renter households at or below poverty level live in public or federally subsidized housing. This means that the remaining 5.4 million households at poverty level are competing for a dwindling supply of low-cost housing in the unsubsidized rental market.[4]

Finally, the quality of the existing housing stock has declined, relegating 10 million families to inadequate or overcrowded dwelling units, and 24 million families to units that the government classified as having a "housing problem." [5]

Uncounted numbers of families are doubling up in apartments where 10 people live in space designed for four. Still others are living in garages with inadequate heating and ventilation.

Bureau of Labor Statistics data document a steady decline in basic wage rates, which compounds the scarcity of decent affordable housing. Basic wage rates over the past 12 months have risen 2.6 percent for union workers and 3.5 percent for non-union employees. When benefits are included, the overall hourly cost of labor in private industry increased at three percent for non-union members and four percent for union members. In effect, the cost of housing has escalated at a disproportionately higher rate than wages. [6]

These data support Michael Stone's formulation of the concept of "shelter poverty" to denote those people who do not have enough money to pay for non-shelter necessities after paying for housing. Such people live continuously on the brink of poverty and homelessness. They are not presently homeless, but they are homeless-vulnerable and comprise a growing number of people for whom preventive measures could make the crucial difference. [7]

At the same time that the status of low-income rental housing and affordable home-ownership manifested themselves as matters of crisis proportions, the federal government virtually eliminated all but minimal housing aid after 40 years of active involvement in the construction and subsidization of housing.

Public Housing Programs

The critical turning point in the national housing crisis began in 1981. The Reagan administration was the first since the New Deal to withdraw the federal government from building or subsidizing low-rent housing. Public housing, mandated in the Housing Act of 1937, protected inhabitants from shelter poverty, even though it was a flawed program. It stigmatized inhabitants through means-testing and rigid eligibility procedures. The urban highrise units have attracted damaging publicity and have been designated as poor housing for poor people. Since the 1950s, however, most public housing has taken the form of garden apartments and is quite decent. As troublesome and unattractive as public housing seems, more people are on waiting lists for public housing than are living in it. In Los Angeles, the waiting lists are a minimum of two years.

Today even this housing has disappeared. The federal housing budget has been more severely cut than all other discretionary domestic programs combined. It has dropped from a peak of about $30 billion in the late 1970s to about $7 billion in 1988. The federal government is now subsidizing about 90,000 rental housing units, down from 300,000 in the peak years of the late 1960s and 1970s. The general thrust of the Reagan administration's approach to housing was to halt construction of new public housing units, issue vouchers for housing aid and devolve public housing to tenants by offering incentives to purchase their apartments.[8]

None of these strategies have worked. Housing vouchers are not generous enough to purchase shelter, and most reports claim that only a few people use their vouchers. Purchase arrangements are less plausible because public housing tenants are too poor to buy their apartments under any type of incentive scheme. The public housing tenant of the 1980s is very poor, and getting poorer relative to the rest of society. Public housing once served the working poor. Since the 1960s it has become the housing of last resort and serves the hardest core of the poor, mostly single mothers and children, and the elderly. Incomes of families living in public housing average $6,000 per year; elderly tenants (38 percent of all public housing tenants) have even lower annual incomes, averaging about $5,000 per year. The overall average income of public housing renters in 1983 was $5,360, or 24 percent of the national median.

There are currently about 1.4 million public housing units operated by local public housing authorities receiving subsidies from the federal government. The public housing stock represents a public investment valued at an estimated $75 billion, but it faces serious problems. A Department of Housing and Urban Development (HUD) report prepared in 1986 identified the fact that public housing projects require $20 to $25 billion in renovations. Much of this housing stock is not 40 or 50 years old.[9]

With public housing in disrepute for many reasons, ranging from the behavior of tenants to the poor quality of highrise construction, the Congress shifted public housing policy to public/private housing. The 1968 Housing Act was one of the first examples of public/private partnership. The law represented a compromise attempt to publicly finance the construction of low-rent housing by paying private developers to build the projects. This housing partnership marked the beginning of public policy designed to attract private developers who, through tax incentives and subsidies, could yield profits from building at the low end of the market.

The program, known as Section 236, gave developers government-guaranteed one-percent mortgage loans, tax breaks and rent subsidies. It was possible for a developer to produce a Section 236 project without putting up any personal money. Approximately one-half million such units were built, and HUD repossessed over one-third of them.[10]

By the early 1970s, many Section 236 buildings were found to be in default. As defaults spread, President Nixon froze the Section 236 program. Despite the failure of the first public/private partnership in housing, Congress opted for a stronger "market-like" approach to such a partnership and provided Section 8 as a new program. Section 8 housing is the voucher system which provides a poor household with a housing voucher to pay a landlord the difference between market rent and the rent that a family could afford. Some Section 8 contracts also went to developers of new housing to replace Section 236 construction.

Section 8 did succeed in avoiding defaults, but it had two major weaknesses: It did not build enough new housing, and it also bid up rents because it armed poor people with more purchasing power. The second major flaw was that the program favored landlords. Under the law, they could accept Section 8 tenants as long as their neighborhood was depressed, but as soon as the neighborhood became a prospect for gentrification, the landlord could quit the Section 8 program with no obligation to keep the apartment available to low-income tenants. The current shortage of housing has meant that only 56 percent of Section 8 voucher certificates are used.

There are presently three million housing units subsidized under Section 8 or Section 236. However, even this stock is under jeopardy. When the original contract expires, after 20 years in the case of Section 236 and as few as five years under Section 8, developers are free to remove their buildings from low-end housing. In strong housing markets like New York, Los Angeles and Boston, this means that tens of thousands of subsidized apartments will be eliminated and rented to higher-paying tenants, leaving the low end of the rental market with more severe shortages. The National Coalition for the Homeless estimates that 2.5 million people are evicted every year and that one-half million units of low-income housing units are lost every year.[11]

State Housing Supplies

During the past 20 years, the states have moved into providing housing for tenants whose incomes are between 40 percent and 80 percent of the area median. States have produced more than 635,000 rental units using tax-exempt bond authority. Most of these units were produced in conjunction with Section 8 or Section 236, but approximately one-third were built without federal assistance. The production of non-federally assisted state housing has increased in response to federal cutbacks and local needs, but the 20-year average production of low-rental units is less than 15,000.[12]

Because of their limited fiscal capacity, the states need partners to become more active in building or subsidizing low-rent housing. Such partners can be local housing authorities, the federal government or private developers.

Private Low-Rent Housing

The erosion of low-cost housing has been exacerbated by the disappearance of single-room-occupancy (SRO) hotels. SROs, despite their horror tales, provide housing as a last resort for the casual laborer, the unemployed, the elderly and many single men and women, as well as the mentally ill. Homeless families are increasingly turning to SROs. Most of these people cannot afford rent in the least expensive public housing. Most SRO occupants have incomes below $3,000 a year. SROs provide the only housing resource for these people. Without them, their only alternative is the streets.

Many homeless people today were former SRO occupants. Although media reports about welfare highlight the unsafe and unsanitary conditions and high cost of these dwellings, they mislead the public into thinking that there is an oversupply of such places. The opposite is true. Between 1970 and 1982, New York City lost 110,000 units of SRO housing, or 87 percent of the existing stock.[13] Similar trends exist in all major cities.

The disappearance of SROs occurred because normal private market processes took place that rendered the land value more profitable through conversion to higher-income-producing usage such as condominiums, office buildings and other commercial space.

Incentives for conversion of dilapidated housing occurred as an unanticipated consequence of a well-intended program designed to encourage landlords to improve the living conditions of tenants in cold water flats. This law, initially passed in New York City in 1955, gradually became transformed into an all-purpose tax abatement for every conversion in the city. It enabled the upgrading of hotels, commercial spaces and multiple dwellings. More significantly, the distribution of these abatements was unevenly slanted toward the richer communities and developers, resulting in the widely publicized gentrification process, and the practice spread to most cities across the nation.

This economic restructuring of the cities, supported at all levels by government, has contributed to the now-drastic housing shortage and to homelessness. Skid Row areas all over the nation have been eliminated as downtown areas expand and improve.

As discussed in Chapter 4, the Tax Reform Act of 1986 reduced or eliminated major incentives for private production of low-cost rental housing. Capital gains are taxed at a higher level than in the past. Depreciation schedules are lengthened, reducing the attractiveness of investment in rental units. Losses on real estate no longer balance other taxable income for private investors traditionally interested in rental housing. Finally, the rigorous limitation imposed on the number and size of tax-free bonds issued by states reduces the availability of housing bonds. Although these tax reforms are intended to reduce tax advantages for the rich, they do so at the expense of depleting opportunities for private investment in housing.

Tax reform related to housing incentives contradicts the widely held conservative myth that the private market is the best supplier of housing. Liberals have equally subscribed to this myth, so that the net result of the nation's housing policy for the past 40 years has been a reliance on the market instrument to achieve the social goal of housing. Under the new tax reforms, even this resource has all but disappeared for the low end of the housing market. What remains is a market that caters to the most affluent home buyers and landlords. Low-rent tenants and homeless people can no longer contribute to landlords' profits or to builders' sales through indirect incentives via subsidies and taxes. Government housing policy, predicated on a privatized market approach, now supports a private market that, in fact, has contributed to the growth of homelessness through soaring rents, gentrification, and the conversion of marginal buildings.

Two other factors have contributed to homelessness and the shortage of low-rent housing. Both arguments are tenuous and speculative, but they do merit consideration. Rent control and the emerging slow-growth movements designed to limit commercial and residential development in localities throughout the United States carry serious implications for low-cost housing.

Critics of rent control argue that it is a major contributor to homelessness. They claim that there is a higher correlation between rent control and homelessness than other factors thought to contribute to homelessness, such as unemployment and poverty, the availability of public housing, weather, and rental vacancy rates.

William Tucker, writing for the *New Republic* and the *National Review*, compared estimates of per capita homeless populations in 50 cities with the above factors. He found that rental vacancies showed a high correlation with homelessness. Approximately 15 percent of the homelessness in and among cities can be explained by differences in rental vacancies. Cities with lower vacancy rates have higher homelessness, suggesting that homelessness is basically a housing problem.[14]

The largest correlation identified was with rent control. Eight rent-control cities were included in Tucker's study: New York, Yonkers, NY, Boston, Hartford, Washington, San Francisco, Los Angeles and Santa Monica, CA. All eight ranked among the top 17 cities for per capita homelessness. Cities with rent control had, on average, two and one-half times as many homeless people as cities without it.

Over 200 communities have adopted rent control since 1970. Most of these cities previously had healthy vacancy rates of six to seven percent. Their present vacancy rates have fallen below three percent and may decline further.

The obvious concern of rent control opponents who are also homeless advocates is that rent controls are allowing people who can afford higher rents to live in lower-rent units, thereby keeping out those who most need the protection of rent control. Others argue that rent control prevents more people from becoming homeless.[15] This housing gridlock and the respective strengths and merits of rent control as a preventive measure will be further examined in Chapter 8, "The Rental Market."

Forces Against Housing Development

The slow-growth movement, spreading throughout the nation, promises to be another major detriment to low-cost housing. Less than two years ago Los Angeles emerged as a national leader of the slow-growth movement when the voters approved Proposition U, the ballot initiative that cut in half the maximum permissible density on most of the city's commercial and industrial land. In the past two years, dozens of local measures halting growth have become law. In the June 1988 primary elections, 13 measures were on the ballot aimed at controlling growth; seven of them passed in the State of California alone.

Ironically, while many of these new initiatives imposed no comparable limits on commercial or industrial building, home construction was the target of restricted growth. For example, the metropolitan area surrounding San Jose generated 24,000 new jobs in 1986 and 1987. But only 7,500 new houses were built. Similarly, in the greater Oakland area, there were 45,000 new jobs but only 17,800 new houses. This biased ratio of jobs to housing has produced such a scarcity of affordable homes that Californians are reporting all-night vigils and competing in lotteries for whatever new housing becomes available.

One of the most serious problems with slow-growth measures is that they encourage only the most lucrative form of development. Perhaps the most blatant example of this problem occurred in the wealthy residential community of Indian Wells near Palm Springs. Property owners, business leaders and politicians sought to boost the tourist trade there with a 640-acre hotel/retail complex comprised of 4,500 hotel rooms, a 400,000-square-foot convention center, two golf courses and 100,000 square feet of shops and restaurants.[16]

State law in California requires the city to channel some of the tax revenue from this project into low- and moderate-income housing. But Indian Wells countered that it could not find the space. Instead, it proposed to build the housing in neighboring communities. Of course, these affluent cities did not want the housing either, and they have responded by suing Indian Wells. In the meantime, the people who will clean the hotel rooms, caddy for the golfers, wait on tables, wash dishes and punch the cash registers will have no place to live near their work and will be forced to commute long and expensive distances to their low-pay jobs.

By voting for slow-growth measures, most citizens believe that they have made a worthwhile trade-off: less development and economic growth in return for less traffic congestion, noise and pollution. This is not the case in today's heavily urbanized California, or anywhere else.

Growth is not the real problem; it merely exaggerates the transformation of residential communities to commercial and industrial centers. In the course of this transformation, jobs are locating at the emerging urban village core centers in order to be closer to the work force which has already moved to the metropolitan area's outskirts. But the jobs are not moving out quickly enough. As a result, workers still face long and frustrating commutes into more centrally located urban village cores.

In planning new urban village cores, government and developers are not fully considering the housing needs of the metropolitan area's moderate- and low-income workers. Most of the new urban village cores growing up around central metropolitan areas are emerging into largely white upper-middle-class areas. This arrangement is time- and energy-efficient for executives and business owners who live nearby, but it creates unnecessary hardships for the clerical, light assembly and service employees who face long car, rail or bus commutes from the few neighborhoods where they can afford housing.

If too many slow-growth measures are enacted in protest to contemporary development trends, metropolitan areas could lose much of their future economic growth to other, less restrictive regions and states. Worse, the already scarce low and moderate housing stocks could further diminish, and in some cases, like Indian Wells, never be built. Slow-growth began as a conscientious effort of middle-class environmentalists to protect and preserve healthy communities. It has unfortunately shifted to a barrier against housing for the poor.

Another potent anti-development force is the "not in my back yard" movement. This protest movement, known as "NIMBY" among planners and developers of everything from hotels and airport extensions to shelters for the homeless and low-income housing are active, powerful and pervasive. The number of

NIMBY organizations is growing dramatically as citizens' groups use the political system to cripple development projects.

Politicians, planners and scholars allege that NIMBYs have created total deadlock on government and private business decisions about projects that the economy and society need to function. Whether NIMBY concerns are about property values or the quality of life, they are important enough to the people involved to turn them into formidable adversaries.

Participatory democracy, a long-cherished ideal of American life, remains a worthy value, but the entry of neighborhood organizations into development decisions has complicated planning and construction decision-making. It has also biased planning away from any development that might have the potential to reduce property values or threaten middle-class quality of life such as low-cost housing, halfway houses, and even human service agencies designed to serve local communities. In attempts to halt the construction of nuclear power plants and toxic waste sites, neighborhood organizations have confused all development projects as posing the same threat. They therefore wage strong battles against large-scale dangerous developments and less ominous housing projects with the same force and energy.

Demographic Trends Relative to Housing

In classic economic theory, real estate is supposed to "trickle down." Historically, rich people have bought new houses at full market prices, leaving older properties to the poor. Several unique characteristics of the housing market have jammed the trickle. Housing markets are singularly affected by location, thereby segmenting housing by neighborhood, race and class. Two buildings of equally good quality yield different value, depending upon their location. One building, located in the finest neighborhood of a city, will be far more desirable and valuable than its counterpart located in a deteriorated section of the same city. Occasionally, the deteriorated neighborhood is gentrified into a good community, but that does nothing for the supply of low-rent housing; it only diminishes the supply further. Even an apartment with zero value costs a minimum to maintain — approximately $300 per month. This is beyond the reach of somebody earning the minimum wage, or poverty level.

The Future of Affordable Housing

Until the Reagan administration, every administration — whether liberal or conservative — acknowledged the unique problems of the housing market and supported measures to narrow the gap between purchasing or renting power and the housing supply. The American housing market has historically adapted well and quickly to the needs of relatively affluent families. Unaided, the market responds less quickly or adequately to the non-affluent.

To be convinced that the shortage of affordable housing is serious now, we need only look forward. "Homeless" does not simply describe thousands of low- and moderate-income families that have no suitable place to live today. Under existing law, thousands of homes occupied by poor families will soon soar in price, driving even more people to the streets.

Two million apartments are currently affordable through federal rent supplements. Under existing law, as many as 500,000 of these will lose their supplements between now and the year 2005. Tenants in an additional 330,000 apartments, built with special low-cost mortgages, may also become vulnerable to higher rents — perhaps twice as much as what they can afford — as owners exercise their right to pay off the original mortgage and refinance with conventional mortgages.

Approximately 80,000 such apartments are located in areas where owners could be expected to do so. The Reagan administration's proposal to sell public housing apartments would make the crisis even worse. Although the prospects of selling them are dim, even a five-percent loss in this inventory would cost 65,000 more families their homes.[17]

The expiring subsidies and the threat of dispossessions from privately owned low-rent housing pose two major crises in the supply of low-cost housing. Housing experts and demographers agree that further problems will arise in the next decade, con-

tributing to further erosion in the availability of affordable housing. General consensus exists that the 1990s are likely to be years
in which the gaps and mismatches between housing needs and
the housing supply will increase.

Young families will continue to experience financial obstacles,
and the pent-up demand of the 1980s will spill over into the 1990s.
Over two million young families will enter their prime home-
buying years, but will not be able to achieve home ownership unless home purchase rates return to pre-1980 levels. Based upon
current trends, the housing market is not likely to be building
homes at a size or price that first-time young homebuyers can afford. Trends in median income and personal savings have been
mixed or declining for the average American throughout the
1980s, especially for younger families, offering little encouragement that they will be better able to afford larger down-payments
or the high interest rates predicted for the 1990s.

The growth of the elderly population confronts housing policymakers with major challenges. Households headed by persons
aged 65 or older grew steadily in the 1980s, reaching 17 million in
1987, and projected to be 21.4 million by 1995. The number of "old
elderly" is expected to grow from an estimated seven million in
1987 to 1.9 million by the year 2000.[18]

The incidence of housing problems among the elderly in the
1980s has been lower than for the population as a whole. This is
likely to be true into the 1990s.

One special problem of older homeowners is that they are likely to be "house rich and cash poor." Although three-quarters of
older people own their own homes, and 80 percent are mortgage-
free, they lack the income to maintain their homes and themselves.
Equity conversion programs, or reverse annuity mortgage interests, are beginning to be used as a mechanism to enable older
homeowners to remain in their homes.

Some senior citizens will need housing help in the 1990s to
avoid unnecessary or inappropriate institutionalization. National-
al studies on the needs of older Americans estimate that 15 percent (about 3.5 million senior citizens in the 1990s) will need
support services, modifications in their dwelling units or new

housing designed to meet their physical functioning. The 3.5 million estimate is low because it does not include the 300,000 people who, at any given time, live in nursing homes but could be discharged if these units were available. Gerontologists and housing analysts estimate a 1990s need of about 1.7 million new or substantially rehabilitated units designed for the frail elderly, and about two million more units with support services but not major structural modifications.

As in the rest of the housing market, the private housing market is beginning to respond well to the needs of upper-income frail elderly persons. However, the growing proportion of senior citizens who have low and moderate incomes will probably need some government help in order to live in the appropriate housing units.[19]

The 1980s witnessed the first time in America when so many people were poor. It was also the first time that more poor people with less money sought fewer available apartments of inferior quality, paying higher rents. These problems will worsen in the 1990s. Given the existing housing need of poor American families, the anticipated increase in the number of low-income families, and the continuing loss of low-income housing stock to abandonment or gentrification, there is a need for at least 350,000 new and rehabilitated low-income rental units each year for the rest of this century.[20]

The enormous growth in female-headed households in the past 40 years, from 3.5 million in 1960 to over nine million in 1980, is expected to increase by about one-half in the 1990s.[21] Single-parent families disproportionately live in inferior housing with little resources to improve their circumstances by moving or housing rehabilitation. With their low median incomes, under the official poverty level, they have difficulty coping with the maintenance of their rent and are shelter-poor or homeless-vulnerable.

Because of mounting evidence that the proliferation of homelessness is occurring among families, most of which are headed by single women, the future demands special attention to their housing needs. Housing policies and programs are needed to help these women and children live in decent housing which they can afford.

Access to Affordable Housing for Minorities

The fair housing laws that were enacted in 1968 failed to include provisions to enforce the law. This has resulted in continuing housing discrimination against black families, Latinos, disabled people and families with children.

Survey data from multiple sources demonstrate the extent of unfair housing practices. The Department of Housing and Urban Development surveyed 3,000 brokers and rental agents in 40 metropolitan areas and found that 48 percent of black families seeking to buy homes faced discrimination. In addition, 72 percent of black families seeking to rent dwellings encountered racial discrimination.

Latinos are far more likely than non-Latinos to live in substandard, overcrowded housing and much less likely to own their own homes, according to a study released in June 1988. The study, "The Hispanic Housing Crisis," cited a disparity in the way housing funds are distributed to minorities, reporting that black renters were somewhat better served than are Latinos. Among poor renters, 39 percent of blacks were able to secure subsidized housing, compared with 22 percent of Latinos and 23 percent of whites who are poor.[22]

Strengthened enforcement provisions allowing civil penalties up to $50,000 for offenders of fair housing laws promise to remedy some of this problem. By adding the physically and mentally disabled and families with children to the list of people falling under protection of anti-discrimination laws, the bill has expanded coverage as well as enforcement mechanisms.

Minority group representatives are calling for stricter laws to strengthen access to fair housing, along with a tripling of subsidized housing, greater protection of residents displaced by urban renewal, and major outreach programs that include bilingual staff for Latino people.

Under the House bill, HUD can initiate an enforcement action on every complaint in which the department finds reasonable cause to believe that discrimination occurred or was about to occur. HUD then has 100 days to investigate and require conciliation between the parties. The bill also authorizes administrative law judges to assess penalties of up to $10,000 for first-time violators, $25,000 for second offenders in a five-year period, and $50,000 for those with a third offense within a seven-year period. In federal court cases, the losing party is also required to pay court costs and punitive damages.

Summary

There is clearly a broad consensus that the United States is in the midst of a national housing crisis. Declining home ownership, huge losses of affordable rental units, and large deteriorating housing stock, combined with reduced economic capacity resulting from changes in wages and the national employment structure, all demonstrate that the 1980s have been disastrous for affordable housing. It is small wonder that homelessness continues to rise at a rate of between 20 and 25 percent annually. Homelessness has become the most graphic symbol of this drastic lack of affordable housing at all but the most affluent levels. This housing crisis has turned into a true national emergency, one that merits full attention by the public and private sectors.

The demographic trends cited above mean that there is a need in the 1990s to encourage the supply of affordable starter homes for about 3.3 million young families. New or rehabilitated units, appropriate for 1.7 million frail elderly people are needed. Low- or moderate-income people will need about 3.4 million new or rehabilitated units.

Creative housing analysts addressing this crisis are offering solutions ranging from returning to earlier public/ private arrangements to build and subsidize public housing to solutions that reject such a market-based housing economy. All agree that we need policies intended to stop homelessness before it starts.

The following chapters in this section will review and recommend approaches to meeting the nation's housing needs.

Chapter 7

Approaches to
Building Affordable Housing

The American dream of "a decent home and a suitable living environment for every American," articulated in the Housing Act of 1949, persists. This has been a basic priority of American government with deep historic roots going back to the Homestead Act in the nineteenth century. It was only the decade of the 1980s that witnessed a nearly complete federal withdrawal from housing. During this period, state and local governments, business leaders and non-profit organizations have attempted to pick up the slack left by the federal government. These efforts provide encouragement and lessons for those concerned about innovative approaches in an otherwise dim arena.

It is clear, however, that the most successful alternative approaches to housing require federal resources if they are to be replicated on the required scale. The magnitude of the problem simply cannot be met by local governments, well-intentioned business people or energetic non-profit organizations. What these efforts have accomplished is the demonstration of new models of financing and partnerships among a broadly expanded group of community activists, state and local legislators, clergy, labor, foundations, and business people in the drive for affordable housing and care for the homeless.

Some of the most critical housing analysts argue that nothing short of abandoning current conservative and liberal perspectives on housing based upon the market economy can resolve the crisis in affordable housing. One proposed alternative advocated by these housing experts is the social ownership of housing. This alternative would reinforce the concept of treating housing and land as a socially owned resource and would reject America's highly privatized housing system. Closely connected to social ownership is the idea of the public sector taking more responsibility for the financing of housing for people who are not poor. Under this scheme, the federal government would become more involved in providing direct financing for tenants, cooperatives and non-profit community-based organizations that would both own and manage housing. The agenda for converting housing to social ownership also stresses equality, social and collective ownership, and self-help on the part of disadvantaged people.[1]

Whether one subscribes to liberal, conservative or socialist perspective, there is a clear consensus that Americans are ready to return housing to the nation's agenda. Few, however, are willing to return to the big-spending housing programs that offered private developers large tax breaks, low-interest mortgages, and rent subsidies as inducements to build low-income housing.

New flexible and cost-effective approaches are necessary. The current challenge is to identify examples of housing development that avoid the wasteful programs of the past but that move beyond today's hands-off approach. Fortunately, such examples have emerged. This chapter analyzes and describes the most innovative and promising programs. The core of this analysis is that the programs deserve attention as models for a new national housing policy, and that none of these programs can meet the nation's housing needs without major enlargement of federal responsibility for housing.

State and Local Government Housing Initiatives

Affordable housing offers communities more than shelter. It is a key component in economic development and revitalization. The most precise assessment of the relationship between housing development and economic development was established in a 1980-81 study by the Bureau of Labor Statistics, cited in the December 1981 *Monthly Labor Review*. That study found that 25,400 jobs were created for each billion dollars of multi-family construction contract expenditures. Similarly, for each billion dollars of single-family construction, 22,000 jobs were created.[2]

Because housing equals new jobs, it equals new economic activity through wages, profits and commerce directly associated with the construction of new dwelling units. This multiplier effect becomes extended through the additional impact of spending the dollars resulting from construction in other areas of the economy. In 1979 the National Association of Homebuilders (NAHB) gauged the overall economic impact of 1,000 new single-family homes at $110 million and the economic activity generated by 1,000 multi-family units at more than $50 million. This analysis suggests the opportunity costs incurred by the United States by not investing in housing. It adds yet another critical dimension to the elements of industrial economic policy.[3]

Thus, viewing affordable housing for workers as a key component in economic revitalization, local governments are setting up revolving funds for housing assistance, encouraging public-private partnerships for developing low-cost housing, and earmarking certain taxes to finance housing programs.

While federal programs faded, the states and localities were developing new approaches to housing assistance. By 1972, they were providing housing subsidies to about 600,000 units a year.[4] No current estimates are available, but this number has increased rapidly since 1982 and new programs are being enacted with an expanding variety of resources. State and local initiatives have become so prevalent and diverse that their influence on federal involvement may be as strong as the federal influence on local housing and community development activity of the earlier period from 1934 to 1980.

Homelessness-Prevention Programs

Three states have adopted homelessness-prevention programs that make timely interventions through short-term loans and grants to ward off eviction or foreclosure. These states are New Jersey, Pennsylvania and Maryland. Massachusetts has adopted a more limited homelessness-prevention program for welfare mothers. At the local level, Allegheny County in Pennsylvania, St. Louis, New York City and Los Angeles County have developed sound prevention programs. All of these warrant replication because they have demonstrated their efficacy.

New Jersey's Homelessness Prevention Program provides temporary assistance as a last resort to households facing eviction or foreclosure because they lack money for reasons beyond their control. Such reasons include loss of employment, medical emergency, government-imposed and fault-free loss or delay in benefit payments, crime victimization, natural disaster, forced illegal eviction, non-payment of child support, loss of income because of divorce or separation, and threatened eviction. The program requires strict documentation of imminent homelessness and further proof that all reasonable efforts to obtain alternative funding have been made and exhausted.

Clients who prove their eligibility can receive loans or grants for rental security deposits, rent arrearages, forward rent payments and second mortgage loans. Most program assistance is organized in the form of loans, but poor families who pay more than 50 percent of their income in rent receive grants.

The program began in 1984. Between December 1984 and June 1987, 6,000 households, or about 15,000 persons, were helped. The average cost to the state was approximately $1,000 per household on a total expenditure of $6.5 million. Preliminary evaluations indicate that the program has about a two-thirds success rate in keeping families in their dwellings for one year after the termination of assistance, and is two to three times more cost-effective than shelters and 10 to 20 times more cost-effective than the use of emergency or welfare motels. On the negative side of the ledger, the program needs improvement in collecting its loans. Anecdotal data suggest that housing assistance helped program beneficiaries return to economic stability and independence from public welfare.[5]

Seventy percent of the households helped by the New Jersey program have not been on any form of public welfare. They have been poor and hard-working people who struggle from paycheck to paycheck and sometimes cannot make ends meet. They are the people whom William Ryan describes as "two monthly paychecks away from poverty."[6]

An important finding in the New Jersey program is that some homelessness is caused by government delays in benefit payments. Families living on the edge of poverty cannot make rent payments while waiting six weeks to six months for their checks, whether they are unemployment benefits, disability payments, Supplemental Security Income (SSI) checks or AFDC payments. Streamlining check disbursement and eligibility analyses would reduce homelessness. This would not even constitute welfare reform. It would merely force welfare systems to function efficiently and meet the same responsibilities for integrity required of welfare recipients.

Similar lessons have been demonstrated in Pennsylvania. The Commonwealth initiated the Homeowner's Emergency Mortgage Assistance Program in 1983 when the legislature appropriated $75 million to help delinquent homeowners. Between its inception and July 1987, the program helped 6,200 families maintain home ownership through the provision of loans averaging $9,430 at nine percent interest with flexible repayment schedules.

As in New Jersey, the program is available only to those persons who can document imminent foreclosure and financial hardship beyond their control. Applicants are also expected to indicate a reasonable likelihood of renewed ability to assume full mortgage payments within 36 months, and a favorable previous credit history. These requirements add assurances to the fiscal viability of the program, but they limit eligibility to about one out of three housing-vulnerable applicants.

Pennsylvania added two other programs to its homelessness-prevention efforts. It started 17 new or rehabilitated SRO apartment buildings using $5.5 million of appropriations to the Pennsylvania Department of Community Affairs. The second was a housing assistance program, similar to that in New Jersey, in the state's Department of Welfare. This program pays up to $750 in rent, security deposits or bills to keep tenants from becoming homeless. As of this date, the program is a demonstration effort and is not yet operating on a statewide basis.[7]

Maryland operates two smaller prevention programs, one for homeowners and one for renters. The eviction-prevention effort for renters is located in the Department of Welfare and is oriented to public assistance recipients. The Homeowner's Emergency Assistance Program, launched in 1985, assists homeowners who have been unable to keep their mortgage payments current because of loss of employment. This is the only condition for eligibility. The program provides last-resort loans and financial counseling.

Massachusetts provides child welfare payments, for a time, to poor women whose children have been temporarily placed in foster care to avert homelessness for the mothers and permanent breakup of families. Most states are beginning to adopt this practice by using federal welfare payments under the "emergency assistance" provision of the Social Security Act in ways that would help to prevent homelessness.[8]

Successful preventive innovations can also be found at the local level. The most successful efforts involve state and local governments and non-profit community groups working as partners in the prevention of homelessness.

Allegheny County's ACTION-Housing reported that several housing assistance programs, created by local non-profit housing and social service agencies, have helped lower-income families, unemployed people, and other at-risk populations resolve specific problems that threatened their dislocation from their homes. The Urban League of Pittsburgh has established a rental assistance program with state, county and FEMA funding that helped more than 2,000 people pay delinquent mortgage bills and forestall mortgage foreclosures. The organization has also developed a Dollar Energy Fund, through a coalition of 31 religious groups, to help families pay delinquent utility bills.

Pittsburgh and Allegheny County claim that the successful implementation of these preventive programs has enabled the area to avoid the larger homeless problems of other urban areas.[9]

All successful city and county-level prevention programs stress timely intervention by identifying families who are at risk of homelessness. Chicago has a security-deposit pool so that the homeless can overcome one of the major barriers to getting an apartment. Some cities and county welfare departments pay the first month's utilities, as in the case of the California Energy Assistance Plan.

In New York City, social workers are stationed in landlord-tenant courts as part of a $2 million experimental program called Housing Alert. They have the authority to pay a family's back rent, if necessary, to keep them in their apartment. New York's Human Resources Administration has also begun to use computers to predict families at risk of homelessness and try to prevent it.[10]

Housing analysts have identified certain clear risk factors for becoming homeless. Two of the most prominent of these are multiple moves within one year, and having one's public assistance terminated more than twice in one year. Computers now flag these families and send social workers to their homes to ascertain what support services are needed to prevent eviction. Some solutions are as simple as purchasing a sofa bed to keep a family in a relative's home. Because the program started in the summer of 1987, there are no data available about its results. But city officials estimate that if only 35 families are kept off the streets, the program will pay for itself, compared to the high cost of keeping one family in a welfare hotel.

St. Louis' city government established a Homeless Reception Center, accepting requests from housing-vulnerable as well as homeless people. Center staff classify visitors and callers into three groups: those already living on the streets, those at immediate risk of homelessness (0-48 hours), and those likely to be at risk within two to 30 days. Of the first 6,500 cases, two-thirds fell in the second and third categories. Staff provides crisis intervention and counseling, cash, and in-kind assistance which comes from church and other non-profit groups.[11]

All of these efforts are worthwhile but seriously underfunded in relation to need. The largest efforts in New Jersey and Pennsylvania are coping with 10 percent of the documented need. Their merit rests upon their successful demonstration that they work and, if funded on an adequately large scale, could prevent more homelessness.

State Home-Ownership Programs

Since 1980, at least 11 states have adopted 24 separate programs to stimulate new construction of affordable homes for low- and moderate-income families. Twenty-two states have initiated efforts that focus on the purchase of homes rather than construction of new homes. The construction programs typically provide lower-rate financing to builders, but some states also provide incentives to buyers in the form of deferred-payment loans, direct grants and mortgage insurance. Most of the state programs that do not stimulate new construction rely on offerings of reduced-interest and first mortgage loans to low- and moderate-income families. These programs use state revenues to buy down the interest rate. Many states target geographical areas especially in need of affordable housing.

Schwartz et al. cite five state-level home-ownership programs as models for new national housing policies. These are:

- Connecticut's Downpayment Assistance Program

- New Jersey's lease/ purchase plan (also operating in Colorado)

- Massachusetts' Homeownership Opportunity Program

- New York's Nehemiah Plan

- California's Shared Equity Mortgage Program

The Connecticut Downpayment Assistance Program provides a low-interest (six percent) second loan linked to a Connecticut Housing Finance Authority first mortgage. The down-payment loan can cover up to 25 percent of purchase costs and may be paid back over 30 years. This program is targeted to first-time home-buyers of low or moderate income. It began in the mid-1980s and has helped over 1,400 homebuyers on aggregate loans of less than $13 million.[12]

New Jersey's lease/purchase program offers low-interest mort-gages and an option to save the amount necessary for a down pay-ment. Under this plan, a potential homebuyer rents a unit in a project with an option to buy it at the end of the lease term. Poten-tial homebuyers place a portion of each month's rent in an escrow account. Lease/purchase agreements can work. The program began in New Jersey in 1986, and a 72-unit condominium project has been constructed in Atlantic City for moderate-income fam-ilies, of which 24 units have been allocated for low-income fam-ilies. A 108-unit development has been built in New Brunswick with one-third of the units designated for low-income families.[13]

The Massachusetts Homeownership Opportunity Program, be-gun in 1986, stimulates production of new housing for purchase by moderate-income families at low-interest, long-term rates. In this program, cities and towns combine with profit or non-profit developers for state funds to subsidize construction and mort-gages for affordable homes.

New York's Affordable Homeownership Development Pro-gram is similar to the Massachusetts program. In its first two years of operation, this program granted funds to approximately 70 projects, providing nearly 3,800 new or rehabilitated units.

New York's Nehemiah Plan is a far more comprehensive and complex partnership, combining several resources into an innova-tive financial arrangement to produce single-family homes at moderate prices in large quantity. The Nehemiah program has gained national publicity for combining church money with vacant city land and interest-free construction loans provided by private-sector lenders to build 1,000 low-cost homes in abandoned neighborhoods. The waiting list for new Nehemiah homes includes over 5,000 families.[14]

California's Homeownership Assistance Program (CHAP) relies upon a deferred-payback, shared-appreciation feature. This is also included in the Nehemiah program. California's program, begun in 1981, is targeted to income-eligible first-time homebuyers. It has helped about 500 families. The program utilizes two financing components: a primary loan made by a participating lender that conforms to its normal lending criteria; and a second, shared-appreciation loan with deferred interest. The primary loan is eligible for sale in the secondary market. The second trust financing, or CHAP loan, is funded by the state.

The second state-funded loan may cover up to 49 percent of the property's purchase price. These loans do not bear interest in the usual sense. Instead, the borrower, upon resale of the home, is obligated to pay the principal amount of the loan plus a part of the property's appreciation proportional to the original loan-to-value ratio of the CHAP loan.[15]

State Rehabilitation Programs

At least 24 states have adopted a combined total of 44 new housing rehabilitation programs. Most of these aim at helping low- and moderate-income homeowners or the owners of low-income rental units bring their properties up to code through low-interest loans. The financial arrangements reflect new thinking. In addition to first, second and third mortgages, states have tried deferred-payback plans, forgiven loans, joint city/ state loan programs, shared-equity loans and resale controls.

The states have targeted their money to the efforts and geographic areas perceived as most needing assistance. These range from rehabilitating units for the frail elderly, to neglected and blighted geographic areas, to promotion of energy conservation.

Massachusetts and New Jersey are experimenting with more

massive rehabilitation projects designed to revitalize entire neighborhoods, as well as help low-income people remain in their homes and communities. These projects involve the rehabilitation and conversion of factories, office buildings and warehouses to mixed-use projects, including commercial and residential facilities. Mixed-use projects can ensure the success of housing rehabilitation efforts by creating jobs and profit centers which, in turn, minimize the risk on housing rehabilitation loans.

State Programs for Non-traditional Housing Needs

More than 35 programs have been adopted in 19 states to meet non-traditional housing needs since 1980. Among these programs are homeless shelters, group homes with support services for disabled people, single-room-occupancy facilities for single people living alone, apartment complexes for single-parent families with support and child care services, temporary housing for battered women, boarding homes for mentally disabled people, transitional housing for the homeless, house-sharing programs, and housing located adjacent to hospitals to serve the handicapped. Most of these programs are concerned with special populations such as the elderly, disabled or homeless families. States have found that provision of housing for these populations is insufficient without a wide range of support services. "Housing plus" has become the key phrase in considering the needs of non-traditional populations.[16]

State Mortgage Bond Revenue Programs

The largest number of state housing programs utilize revenue bonds to subsidize home ownership and stimulate the production of rental units. These state programs have been financed by the federal treasury, which credits bondholders with tax-free status. Nearly every state has used the revenue bonds to facilitate housing reduction. As cited in Chapter 4, the Tax Reform Act of 1986 severely curtailed this program. On December 31, 1988, states lost their authority to issue mortgage revenue bonds for single-family ownership programs.

The elimination of state authority to issue bonds for home ownership is a counterproductive and contradictory policy. It reduces home ownership possibilities, diminishes housing construction and forgoes tax revenues on housing and related economic activity. It contradicts the policy choice in the Tax Reform Act to retain the mortgage interest-rate deductions for primary and secondary residences. These deductions were retained to encourage home ownership. But in its present state the Tax Reform Act encourages home ownership only for upper-income taxpayers and discourages the same for everybody else.[17]

State Housing Trust Funds

States have established housing trust funds which are a source of revenue designated to funding a specific program. There are a variety of ways to finance these trust funds. California established a fund that raises about $20 million annually by taxing offshore oil production. Maine has allocated about $2.2 million from a real estate transfer tax to a fund entitled HOME (Housing Opportunities for Maine). In New Jersey, the trust fund known as the Urban and Balanced Housing Fund raises $20 million annually. Other states have developed contributory, non-tax sources of revenue to finance trust funds. Massachusetts restructured taxation on life insurance companies, negotiating a lower tax in exchange for contributions to the Massachusetts Capital Resource Corporation. Several states have successfully negotiated with banks that hold public deposit notes.[18]

Non-Profit Housing Programs

Many housing analysts assert that the brightest spot in recent years has been the innovative efforts by local non-profit housing developers. The Nehemiah Plan frequently receives citation as the best example of non-profit initiatives. City and state governments have come to rely on non-profit organizations to develop and manage low-cost housing.

To be sure, the emergence of hundreds of community-based non-profit housing developers in cities across the country has provided encouragement when the federal government and private developers abandoned low-cost housing. These non-profit entrepreneurs have patched together financial support from state and local governments based upon the innovative structures described above. They have also attracted support from financial institutions, religious organizations and private foundations to construct and rehabilitate low-income housing and to rebuild urban neighborhoods.

Two large national foundations — the Local Initiatives Support Corporation, started by the Ford Foundation, and the Enterprise Foundation, created by developer James Rouse — are working with a growing network of community-based housing developers across the country.[19]

Another recognized example of non-profit housing efforts is Habitat for Humanity, the organization that has gained special publicity because of the active involvement of former President Jimmy Carter. Operating under Christian principles, but without any connections to an organized religious group, Habitat for Humanity claims to mix "sweat equity" with biblical economics, and is responsible for moving thousands of working poor families out of substandard housing into their own basic but adequate new homes.

Habitat operates in 280 cities in the United States and Canada, plus 25 Third World countries. It has built more than 4,000 homes since its founding in 1976, including 1,200 in 1987. Its goal is to reach 2,000 American towns and cities and 60 countries by 1996.

Habitat projects, operated by committee, select homeowners based on need, willingness to work and ability to repay. This eliminates the very poor, but keeps most low-income families eligible.

In general, most Habitat recipients work but are too poor to go to a bank for a housing loan. Families must include children, and able-bodied members of the family are expected to help build the house, while others pay only the value of the land and material at no interest over 20 years. Payments average $150 to $180 a month, including taxes and insurance. This money is recycled by Habitat to finance future homes.

With only a few skilled carpenters and numerous volunteers, wood-frame houses with up to three bedrooms can be completed in less than one week at from $25,000 to $28,000, including land costs in the United States. The cost is far less in developing countries.

Habitat operates on repayments and donations to its revolving fund and by resale of donated materials. The organization raised $18 million in 1987 and projects $30 million in 1988. Of the 150 workers at Habitat headquarters, 100 are volunteers receiving $25 a week and a room in one of several Habitat-owned-and-built houses. Volunteers who stay over three months get $300 a month and a place to live. Workers overseas, (approximately 100) get the same, or $500 for a married couple.[20]

Habitat provides clear direction for federal, state and local governments in building and rehabilitating low-cost housing.

These builders combine social concern with hard-nosed business skills. Through their access to relatively inexpensive "social capital" from foundations, union pension funds and other benevolent financiers, and because they do not try to make profits, they have created thousands of units of affordable housing that otherwise would not have been built. Once built, moreover, the housing is more likely to stay inexpensive, because non-profit builders are not averse to measures that limit rent increases and resale prices.

While the non-profit housing sector is the most interesting development on the urban horizon, it has grown unevenly. Some regions have small fledgling groups with little experience or resources. Others have community-based groups that are becoming highly professional.

Cities with sophisticated non-profit developers, including Boston, Baltimore, New York, Chicago, Cleveland and San Francisco, have formed umbrella organizations of community-based housing developers to improve efficiency and expand the scale of development. For example, the Boston Housing Partnership, a consortium of 10 neighborhood-based community development corporations, private-sector institutions and government agencies, just completed the renovation of 700 low-income apartments (a $38 million project) and have begun rehabilitation of another 950 units.[21]

The non-profit developments have demonstrated that affordable housing construction also has the multiplier effect of additional jobs, expanded local property tax revenues, revitalized commercial districts and stronger neighborhoods.

All of these efforts are working well, but local governments, churches and foundations lack the resources to convert these small successes into a major new nationwide supply of affordable housing. Only the federal government has these resources. A partnership between the federal government and these community-based housing efforts, in concert with state and local governments, signifies the only direction for structuring the resources necessary to fill the need for affordable housing.

Linkage Development Programs

"Linkage" has become a familiar term in reference to low-cost housing. Linkage practices are based upon the impact that commercial development has on a tight housing market. Substantial agreement exists that new office space increases the market demand for housing, and this forms the rationale for linkage requirements. Linkage assessments are based upon different formulas, but they typically pose a development fee on large commercial developments in the form of a requirement to build a fixed amount of low-income housing proportional to the size of the project.

Since 1980, linkage programs have been established in San Francisco, Hartford, Jersey City, Boston and Santa Monica, California. Other municipalities are considering linkage programs. Boston, San Francisco and Jersey City have the most experience with linkage. Typical features of each program involve the establishment of a per-square-foot appropriation for the construction of low-cost housing. The programs exempt small developers.

The first linkage program began in San Francisco in 1981 when it passed a linked development ordinance which requires that commercial developers either build or renovate a specified number of units or pay a fee of $5.40 per square foot in lieu of units to offset the increased demand for housing caused by downtown office construction.

By the spring of 1986, the San Francisco program had collected funds from 35 office projects and created about 3,800 units of low- and moderate-income housing. Housing advocates criticized the program for not building more affordable units. In response to this criticism, the San Francisco Planning Department revised the program to require that 62 percent of all the units be affordable to residents whose incomes were less than 120 percent of the area's median. The "in lieu of" fees were further designated to projects containing 100 percent affordable units.

The Boston linkage program, administered by the city's redevelopment agency, charges $6 per square foot for commercial projects larger than 100,000 square feet, with the fee payable over 12 years. The fee was disallowed by the Massachusetts Superior Court, and Boston is seeking new authority to exact the fee under its home rule powers.

Jersey City relies upon voluntary linkage agreements. The Jersey City Office of Economic Development has established mitigation formulas for each new type of construction in the city. Developers can choose set-aside units on or off the development site, or they can contribute money directly to other developers of affordable housing.

Linkage, although a popular idea, is fraught with weaknesses and charges of inequity. It can only succeed in areas where development pressures are strong and competitive enough to overcome the additional costs and constraints on the project. Cities trying to attract developers are not in strong enough positions to impose linkage requirements. There are also serious questions as yet unanswered concerning the effect that impact fees have on development. Developers claim that linkages can add unfair cost burdens to projects, especially in areas where the economy is weak. They also argue that new businesses which start as a result of development should also be expected to participate in linkage schemes. Linkage can be made equitable if it is based upon a cost formula that is sensitive to all development costs and changing market conditions.

Only San Francisco has successfully managed to assure that linkage actually achieves the goal of adding low-cost housing units. Much of the housing derived from linkage programs has been mixed, which usually means a mix of low, moderate and middle-income units, with more of the last than the first. Even units identified as low-cost are generally assigned to families with incomes as high as $15,000.[22]

Zoning Changes Aimed at Affordable Housing

Inclusionary and high-density zoning laws that reverse earlier exclusionary and low-density zoning restrictions are as important as new money in the search for affordable housing.

Inclusionary zoning reverses the practice of exclusion by setting aside land and specifically designating a portion of newly developed units for low- and moderate-priced housing. Most inclusionary programs set aside optional or mandatory requirements in exchange for special permits or other actions by zoning and planning boards. Development of new low-cost units is thus driven by demand for luxury and commercial units.

Massachusetts and California explicitly outlaw exclusionary zoning practices. California also requires affirmative action to preserve or replace low-income units affected by development in Coastal Management Zones. In Massachusetts, an anti-snob policy, Executive Order 215, links approval of federal and state discretionary grants to a community's willingness to provide low- and moderate-income housing.

By far the most experienced state in inclusionary zoning, New Jersey operates under the Mount Laurel and Mount Laurel II State Supreme Court decisions. These decisions made inclusionary zoning a key component of the state's efforts to provide affordable housing. In the Mount Laurel II decision, the court held that all municipalities have a constitutional obligation to "protect the general welfare of the municipality — and general welfare also includes the housing needs of those residing outside of the municipality but within the region that contributes to the housing demand of the region."[23]

New Jersey's legislative response to the court is the Fair Housing Act of 1985. The law gives the state a mechanism for assigning affordable housing goals and requirements to each region and municipality. The Act also established a planning and implementation process, including the Council on Affordable Housing, which defines housing regions and establishes each region's fair-share housing obligation. This provision of the Act attempts to forge public/private financing and alliances between local governments, non-profit organizations and private developers.[24]

Higher-density zoning methods are important tools for lower-income projects because land is one of the major components of housing costs. Density works to reduce the per-unit cost of land. It also reduces the infrastructure costs such as sewers, water and electricity.

Typical of higher-density zoning provisions are the accessory apartments, known as "mother-in-law" apartments, that have been added to properties zoned for large-acre building. Suburban communities with such large-acre zoning have increasingly come to find accessory apartments attractive as ways to provide housing for older parents and younger children who could otherwise not afford to live in their communities. Because many of the large homes in low-density areas are owned by elderly homeowners, accessory apartments offer a way to bring in extra income.

Accessory units also have the appeal of keeping multi-generational family units together. Opportunities for multi-generational living are largely missing in America's suburbs, and this scheme can create new and healthier communities.

Inclusionary and high-density zoning offer solutions that are practical, making low- and moderate-cost housing economically possible. They also provide strategies for mixed-use development that would commingle residential and commercial development and low-, moderate- and high-cost housing. Such zoning would reassert the "melting pot" dream of America.

Shared Housing

Shared housing offers a growing alternative for low- and moderate-income people. The National Housing Resource Center estimates that there were only 50 groups scattered throughout the United States involved in shared housing in 1980. Now there are more than 400 in 42 states, with some of the most active and successful programs in California.

Originally developed as alternatives to nursing homes for the elderly who did not require physical care, shared housing now includes help for younger generations; in particular, single parents unable to afford adequate housing on their own. The California Emergency Assistance Housing Program, for example, encourages people to make shared housing arrangements by offering higher housing payments for beneficiaries who choose shared living quarters.

Shared housing describes a wide variety of living situations. It can be as simple as two individuals or families sharing a single house, to congregate living facilities. Some arrangements evolve from voluntary agreements between two people to live together. Others in shared housing enter their arrangement after counseling and referral by social service agencies.

Shared housing auspices vary as well. They range from owner-occupied dwellings to facilities owned and managed by social service agencies. In between, there are many individuals who are buying older large homes, converting them as necessary to homes for sharing, and renting them.

The most prevalent reason for the rapid expansion of shared housing is the need to find a place to live on a low income. Home sharing also offers security, companionship and a support system for people, but this is only a secondary benefit of such an arrangement. Indeed, home sharing for many poses problems related to a lack of privacy and more general conflicts that people who live together experience.

On a policy level, shared housing offers a cost-effective way to have older people and younger people as well. The practice makes efficient use of the existing stock of older large houses in established neighborhoods across the country. It could also maintain the stability of older neighborhoods by keeping the houses occupied and therefore more immune to redevelopment, conversion or abandonment. As the practice of shared housing extends, it will become a major strategy for keeping people within the circle of housing.

Shared homes have been identified in a number of states. In California, there are at least 52 home-sharing projects. Ohio has appropriated $750,000 to develop shared living to house between six and 16 people. Georgia, Minnesota and Vermont are sponsoring housemate sharing programs.

Several problems may reduce the growth pattern and success of shared housing. Zoning laws that restrict the number of unrelated adults who can live under one roof pose the most serious threat. Some communities also resist the prospect of converting single-family housing to units that shelter larger groupings. Possible participants also fear that their benefits, particularly food stamps, will be reduced or eliminated if they share a home.

Despite these problems, the American Association of Retired Persons estimates that there are 670,000 unrelated people over 65 currently involved in shared housing, and single-parent families are increasingly turning to this option. A creative variation of shared housing brings single-parent families together with older people in shared living arrangements. This affords a chance to build extended families based upon the strengths and advantages of multigenerational living.[25]

Home sharing is not a panacea for the nation's affordable housing supply, but it does provide a sound option, among a series of choices, designed to keep people within the circle of housing when their income proves to be less than market rates for shelter.

Employer-assisted Housing

Large employers are not yet major suppliers of housing in the United States as they are in Western Europe and Japan, but this idea is emerging among public officials and business leaders. The shortage of affordable housing for workers in high-priced areas like Los Angeles, Boston, New York, San Francisco and San Diego, does not just hurt families and the homeless. It hurts business and job growth and threatens to undermine the economic stability of the entire region.

More than 50 large employers, including Hawaii Bell Telephone Company, Children's Hospital in Boston and Princeton University, have reported the adoption of employer-assisted housing programs or plans. The Colgate-Palmolive Company, for example, has adopted a mortgage-assistance plan that is open to any worker who has been employed for six months or longer. In this plan, Colgate subsidizes the mortgage-loan costs on owner-occupied one- and two-family units, condominiums, home improvements and refinancings. The University of Pennsylvania has been operating a successful program for the past decade in which any one of its permanent employees can receive free 100 percent insurance on mortgage loans that are made by Philadelphia lenders on homes in targeted neighborhoods around the campus. This mortgage guarantee lowers or eliminates down-payment requirements, fees and private mortgage insurance costs.

A coalition of private companies, including banks and manufacturers, has begun subsidizing 2,000 units of housing in the area for its employees. The high cost of housing there has made it so difficult to attract workers that the businesses are relinquishing their long-standing practice of letting their employees find their own houses and are actively moving into the housing field.

There are numerous reasons why business leaders should become involved in employer-assisted housing programs: Both management and workers are increasingly dissatisfied with high levels of redundant benefits (where overlapping spousal coverage means that firms pay for benefits that workers do not need); new housing-related employee benefit packages like mortgage insurance are likely to become available very soon; major labor unions have indicated an interest in bargaining for housing benefits; housing benefits can be targeted to improve or stabilize communities located near corporate facilities; housing benefits are consistent with many corporations' sense of social responsibility. Employer-assisted housing, already on the books of some companies, offers yet another positive direction for the provision of affordable housing.[26]

The Shift from Demonstrations to National Policies for Affordable Housing

The aforementioned approaches to affordable housing have yet to become policy on the large-scale level that is necessary to reverse the growing geographic and economic schism in cities throughout the nation. The public perception is still that affordable housing means "housing projects" in the worst sense of the word.

Most of the schemes described in this chapter are designed to prevent homelessness, thus responding to those people who are homeless-vulnerable. As indicated, this population has grown in dramatic proportions. Several of the welfare-based programs respond to the needs of those homeless people who are recently dislocated.

Homeless people are not just the latest social problem; they are harbingers of a portentous future, a warning of what awaits communities that do not house their people. Affordable housing must be produced now. Political leaders must dispel any fears of "projects" by pointing to examples of low- and moderate-income developments that have recently been built under new financial and management arrangements.

In a study of community attitudes to public facility location, Michael Dear and S.M. Taylor found that legitimate community fears could be allayed if efforts are made to minimize neighborhood disruption by using and rehabilitating existing buildings. They also noted that minor design concessions can increase and influence the degree of acceptance on the part of the community. Finally, Dear and Taylor's research showed that many community residents evidenced a low level of awareness of existing housing facilities for mentally ill people because they were planned in a non-obtrusive way.[27]

Other NIMBY reactions are being overcome in affluent communities that are experiencing a dearth of low-wage workers to provide essential services. Without low-income housing mixed into the higher end of housing, residents may be compelled to forgo basic services like baggers at supermarkets, public maintenance workers, health workers and schoolteachers.

A more positive and encouraging view regarding the future of affordable housing is that the universal need for this basic commodity has reached such a large dimension that resistance to mixed housing is dissipating in the face of such need.

Chapter 8

The Rental Market

For millions of Americans, the dream of affordable home owner-ship will never be a reality. A combination of low-wage jobs, in-adequate education and training, female-headed single-parent families, and many other factors that preclude people from ac-cumulating sufficient assets to make an initial down-payment on a first home indicate that the rental market will continue to provide a major housing resource. Those who are at risk of be-coming homeless, or are already homeless, tend to be more de-pendent on rental housing than home ownership.

Increasing financial barriers to home ownership have forced more people to compete for rental housing. The nation's rate of home ownership has declined from 65.6 percent of all households in 1981 to 63.8 percent of all households in 1986. These data rep-resent two million families who in the past would have been ex-pected to purchase a home.[1] At this rate, the high cost of buying houses will mean that only the wealthy will be able to own their homes. Lower-income people will be forced to live with other families, in their cars, or on the streets.

Overall, there are more apartments and houses on the market for rent now than at any other time in recent history. However, the vast majority of vacancies are at the high end of the market designed to meet the housing needs of less traditional families, families that move frequently because of their work, and high earners who remain either single or two-adult families and do not opt for the responsibilities of home ownership. Vacancies of low- and moderate-cost rentals in most parts of the country have become so scarce that a need exists for 350,000 new and rehabilitated housing units each year for the rest of the century. This estimate was produced in a Congressional Research Service study published in January 1987.[2]

Vacancy rates are only one guide to the availability of rental units. Family and unit sizes must be taken into account to include quality and standards of housing into considerations of what affordable housing exists. The Congressional Research Service study suggested that a minimum of $2.9 billion in additional rent certificates or vouchers would be needed annually just to rehouse the poor now living in inadequate rental units. The study defined "inadequate" as either overcrowded or structurally unsound, or both.

Both housing demand and housing losses have prompted this shortage.[3] More poor people are spending a greater share of their income on rent and are more frequently doubling up in overcrowded apartments. These data are presented in Chapter 6. On the supply side, federally subsidized rental housing absorbed 50 percent of all federal budget reductions occurring during the first two years of President Reagan's administration. By 1986, public housing had been cut by 69 percent, from a 1981 budget of $32 billion to $9.5 billion in 1983.[4] The Urban Institute described the impact of these cuts by estimating that one million fewer households were receiving housing assistance in 1985, and 300,000 were forced to reside in substandard dwellings.[5]

These data clearly indicate that the traditional homeless, the isolates and the outsiders are now being joined by recently dislocated low-income families forced out of apartments by rent increases, lower wages, urban renewal and reductions in federal support for housing. Contrary to popular images, not all of the people are receiving public welfare. Many are the working poor who live on the edge of poverty from paycheck to paycheck. One rent increase can push them into the street.

Unless something is done to reverse this trend of more poor people and fewer low-income rental housing units, more than 18 million Americans who are on the verge of becoming homeless will be without housing by the year 2003, according to a national study done by the Neighborhood Reinvestment Corporation. Specifically, the study predicted that from 1983 to 2003, the number of poor households in the United States will rise from 11.9 million to 17.2 million, while the number of low-income rental units will drop from 12.9 million to 9.4 million. This study defined low-income housing as that renting for $325 a month or less in 1987 prices.[6]

The most recent study of this problem, issued in June of 1988 in Los Angeles, reported that the mean 1987 rent in units that are not under rent control is $675 a month, including gas and electricity. The study also found that the number of households facing overcrowded conditions, defined as more than one person per room per unit, increased from 16 percent in 1984 to 21 percent in 1987. Finally, the study corroborated earlier findings that households earning less than $10,000 a year were paying 58 percent of their income in rent.[7]

Clearly, only long-term solution and prevention measures point to the creation of more low-income housing units in the rental market. The likelihood of this happening at the federal level alone is dim, even with the election of a new presidential administration. The deep cuts of nearly 70 percent in public housing funds have damaged that system so severely that it will take years to gear it up to produce the vast amount of low-cost housing now needed.

All may not be as dim as these data describe. State and local governments and community leaders have begun to pick up the slack in rental housing, as they have in making affordable home ownership available. The remainder of this chapter reviews these efforts as models for larger preventive measures.

State Models for the Production of Rental Housing

During the past 20 years, the states have entered the low-cost rental arena and have provided housing for tenants whose incomes are 40 to 80 percent of the area median by using tax incentives, public bonds and subsidies. In these 20 years, states have produced more than 635,000 rental units using tax-exempt bond authority. Most of these units were produced in coordination with federal Section 8, 236, or other programs. However, slightly under one-half the units were built without federal assistance.

States can have a more expansive role in rental housing production, particularly meeting the needs of those whose incomes are below the median.

Massachusetts and New Jersey have established sizeable programs that merit attention and replication by other states.

Massachusetts has bypassed the federal government in developing direct links with local public housing authorities. Through this arrangement the state and local authorities jointly manage and build rental units. Since 1983, the state-local partnership has built 10,000 public housing units.[8]

The state provides grants to local housing authorities for new construction, rehabilitation and for the purchase of units in private buildings. This model could abet any attempts to reinvigorate the federal role in public housing.

Massachusetts has also developed a program to stimulate the production of privately owned low-income rental housing, including those owned by non-profit corporations. SHARP, the State Housing Assistance for Rental Production, reduces the interest rate on Massachusetts Home Finance Agency mortgages to as low as five percent. In return for receiving this mortgage, developers must make available at least 25 percent of the units to tenants with incomes less than one-half the area's median.

In New Jersey, the New Jersey Housing Mortgage Finance Agency (HMFA) was created in 1984. This agency established a subsidiary corporation, the Housing Assistance Corporation, or HASCO.

The stated purpose of HASCO is to perform any task necessary to the production of low- and moderate-income housing projects for rental. Initially, HASCO offered technical assistance to private, public and non-profit developers. It has progressed to becoming the developer and owner of rental property, and can also act as co-developer with other entities.

The Home Mortgage Finance Agency issues the debt required for development. HASCO is not authorized to do so, but it can sell stocks in projects, or groups of projects, in capital markets. HASCO can also receive state and local donations of cash and land. The existence of HASCO means that every community in New Jersey has the capacity to develop public low-income rental housing.[9]

All states have some multi-family housing and development capacity. In addition to Massachusetts and New Jersey, New York and California have become major developers of non-federally assisted low- and moderate-income housing. No state, however, has sufficient fiscal capacity to meet the level of need.

Employer-Assisted Rental Housing

The negative history of "company towns" which acted as feudal benevolent dictators makes any consideration of employer-assisted rental housing a sensitive subject. Nevertheless, employers do have the resources to assist in the production of rental housing projects. In order to avoid the appearance and the mistakes of the earlier company towns, employer assistance arrangements need to be structured in ways that would insulate the employer-employee relationship from property maintenance and tenant management relationships.

Firms could donate, sell or lease surplus corporately owned land. They could also purchase land and then donate, sell or lease it at nominal costs for employee housing. To encourage firms to enter into rental housing, the federal tax code should specifically make such contributions of expenses tax-deductible.

Firms could also make short-term investments or loans to facilitate affordable housing construction. Short-term corporate borrowing is done in many other arenas, so that an investment in employee rental housing would not involve a major policy departure. Typically, such corporate borrowing is done at or near the prime interest rate — several points less than the long-term mortgage interest rates. Firms providing this borrowing power could save thousands of dollars on a typical housing project.

Any employer assistance plan for multi-family rental projects requires a supportive set of federal provisions. The most obvious and important would be a new set of tax laws permitting tax-deductible employer contributions to a housing program. Renting employees also need to receive the rental assistance as a tax-deductible benefit in order that the value of the benefit not be lost via additional tax liability.

Although there are no clear examples of such housing assistance, the concept is gaining increased prominence because it offers a new avenue for stimulating important and much-needed construction.

Urban Relocation

Urban planners and public authorities are now sensitive to the need to redirect the long history of urban renewal projects that destroyed housing and communities inhabited by low-income and frequently minority tenants. A combination of state relocation laws that require attention to relocation plans for displaced tenants and increased vigilance on the part of tenant organizations, public interest law firms, and more enlightened community redevelopment planners, are conscientiously formulating and implementing relocation plans for individuals, families and commercial establishments as key components of major development and expansion projects.

Los Angeles is demonstrating the efficacy of planned relocation in its widespread downtown redevelopment. Central to such planning is a commitment by the Community Redevelopment Agency that it will build a replacement home for every housing unit that it destroys. The agency is in the midst of completing almost 5,000 apartment units and houses throughout the city.

The Community Redevelopment Agency is in charge of acquiring properties for redevelopment, relocating residents, and demolition. Officials of the agency claim that they have informally adopted another requirement as their code of ethics: to make certain that the relocation proceeds with a minimum amount of hardship.

Under the Los Angeles plan, displaced residents have a choice of moving to a redevelopment agency housing project or choosing their own housing, and are eligible for several types of relocation benefits. The Community Redevelopment Agency will pay an allowance up to $500 for those wishing to move on their own. Several families have actually purchased their own homes using a down-payment assistance plan. Others have had an opportunity to move to larger, cheaper and newer housing.

Commercial tenants being relocated are entitled to moving expenses, storage costs and up to $500 toward finding new quarters. Other concessions include costs for packing, insurance, licenses and permits. For some, these benefits cannot cover all of the true costs, but the plan reflects a strong commitment to relocation with equity.[10]

One project alone — the expansion of the Convention Center — is responsible for the relocation of approximately 1,500 people and 60 businesses from a 40-acre site. The massive project has displaced more people than the Bunker Hill development of the 1960s.

This community relocation plan was formulated in response to a threatened suit by the Legal Aid Foundation of Los Angeles. Because state relocation laws do not consider the cost or the size of relocated housing, the threatened suit called for larger and less expensive housing for the displaced families.

Despite this adversarial history, the Convention Center relocation program has resulted in a smooth-running and well-informed operation. Housing specialists were hired to inform the residents of the proposed redevelopment plan well in advance of its groundbreaking. The Community Redevelopment Agency circulated leaflets and conducted a grass-roots campaign that included door-to-door contacts as well as public meetings. All communications were in English and Spanish. An office was opened on the project site to provide tenants access to agency staff.

Although no relocation plan can satisfy all displaced residents and business people, this project has become a clear model of how development and progress can occur without the loss of low-cost housing stock and with minimal anxiety to residents.

Battery Park City, the state-owned 92-acre project in New York City, provides a second example of how large development projects can relate to social need. As Battery Park moves into its next stage of development, Governor Mario Cuomo announced two important plans. He unveiled a blueprint for creating nearly $100 million worth of public parklands covering close to 30 acres, in an effort to make the development more than a high-rent residential and commercial area, but a recreational center for all New Yorkers.

He also promised an additional $600 million toward Mayor Koch's 10-year, $3.2-billion plan to rehabilitate or build nearly 250,000 units for people of low or moderate income in other parts of the city. This scheme does not specifically provide for relocation of residents displaced by the Battery Park project, but it does link housing and relocation for low- and moderate-income renters to major new development. The plan became viable after the Battery Park Authority submitted a cash flow analysis finding that the monies to back the plan were secured by income potential of four new buildings that are under construction. Again, this linking of social goals to commercial goals has proven to be financially sound, requiring no new commitment of state funds.[11]

Housing Rehabilitation

New York City offers another example of ambitious planning to rehabilitate hundreds of abandoned buildings in order to create new buildings. The New York rehabilitation plan is the largest in the nation: $3.2 billion to build or rehabilitate nearly 250,000 dwellings for people of low and moderate incomes. In a city where

28 percent of the renters have incomes below $10,000 a year, more than 57 percent of the city's 1.9 million renters report incomes less than $20,000 a year.[12] This rehabilitation plan reflects a major commitment to forestall the further erosion of affordable housing and prevent homelessness.

The plan relies largely on the creation of rehabilitated housing from the hundreds of abandoned buildings in New York City. Renovation of abandoned buildings has merit and warrants support. Unfortunately, few cities in the nation have such a large supply of abandoned housing. Most low-rental apartment buildings are owned by private individuals. This existing housing stock needs renovation as well as the abandoned housing.

It is commonly perceived that most low-rent landlords do not want to spend money for housing rehabilitation in poor neighborhoods. For some, this is undoubtedly true. But others would like to renovate their buildings and simply cannot afford to. To meet this need, the Community Preservation Corporation, a non-profit company, has been established by 31 New York banks to lend money for housing renovation in poor neighborhoods.

Sixty percent of New York City's housing is 60 years of age or older, with much of it deteriorating. The majority of the city's low- and moderate-income population live in these older dilapidated multi-family buildings, with the lowest-income tenants generally residing in the worst ones.

Landlords who complain that they cannot afford to renovate their properties cite the following cost analysis to support their contentions: The median rent for all apartments in the city in 1987 was $350 a month. Housing experts agree that owners of non-luxury buildings spend $250 to $400 a month per apartment just for basic operating and maintenance costs, depending on the condition of their buildings and the efficiency of their management. These basic costs do not include the paying of mortgage expenses, nor do they account for any profit.

This means that, particularly in older buildings, little money is left to pay for expensive renovations like new plumbing, roofs, windows, heating and electrical systems. Those most at risk are not the landlords, but the people who live in these buildings.

The Community Preservation Corporation, created in 1974 partially in response to the surge of abandoned buildings, has financed and helped supervise major renovations in privately owned buildings containing nearly 10,000 apartments. Such renovation has halted the trend toward abandonment in some neighborhoods. Of equal importance is the fact that it has helped prevent evictions and homelessness.

Unfortunately, several of the key government programs that the corporation packaged have become less effective in recent years and the problem of financing rehabilitation in privately owned buildings has again emerged as a threat to the supply of low-rent housing.

New York City still makes low-interest loans available for renovation, and provides tax abatements and exemptions. But the state agency that oversees rent control and rent stabilization takes at least 18 months to approve rent increases for certain renovation costs. Landlords claim that this delay discourages renovation. To complicate the problem, the federal government has stopped granting new rent subsidies to help low-income tenants who are unable to afford rent increases.

As this cycle continues its revolutions, tenant groups are challenging rent increases in the courts. They contend that landlords should be reimbursed only for the actual cost of renovations, rather than being allowed to earn a return on investment as well. Landlord representatives counter that if the tenants win they will not have sufficient financial incentive to undertake major rehabilitations in buildings where rents are low.

It is by now clear that if the federal, state and city governments do not spend more to subsidize the renovation of low-rent housing, both abandonment and homelessness are likely to accelerate.

Tenant leaders and housing advocates agree, but they contend that building owners should not be the ones to benefit. They have begun to argue for "social ownership" of buildings that house poor people, claiming that such housing should be removed from private hands if the owners cannot earn profits without government subsidies. The Association of Neighborhood and Housing Development, a non-profit coalition of local housing advocates, typically asserts that low-income housing would be less costly to operate if more of it were owned by the government and non-profit organizations.

The Community Redevelopment Corporation and landlord representatives counterclaim that 50,000 city-owned units are not managed as well as the best of privately owned buildings. What is clearly apparent is that the issue of ownership and rehabilitation has grown to unmanageable dimensions, and requires immediate attention. Resolution of this dilemma would seem to lie in maintaining a balance of public and private ownership. One method for striking such a balance could be the establishment of a financial formula which would limit the size of any public subsidy of private housing to a reasonably low percentage of the total cost of owning and maintaining the property. If the subsidy is insufficient, then the private property should become part of the public domain. Proponents of public ownership of all low-income housing ignore the real issue that there are not enough public resources to put all housing in the public domain.

The Tenant Management Movement for Rehabilitation and Ownership

The broad-based civil rights movement of the 1960s and 1970s spawned the tenants' rights movement. The basis of this movement was rooted in the efforts of tenants to preserve their apartment buildings from disrepair and abandonment. Of equal concern was protection against landlords who violated housing standards, charged excessive rents, or arbitrarily evicted tenants. Many buildings were stabilized and saved through these efforts, which were, for the most part, confined to single buildings or small communities.

Tenant management also emerged in public housing, originating with the first public housing rent strike in St. Louis in 1969. Tenants struck in response to an attempt on the part of the St. Louis Housing Authority to raise rents. The strike continued for several months and bankrupted the Housing Authority. In the course of the strike, tenants became managers and maintenance personnel by default. As a condition for settling the rent strike, HUD placed the Housing Authority in receivership and required that the tenants continue to play a significant role in managing the project. Today, the tenant management corporation operates 3,000 apartments and constitutes the most well-known experiment in tenant management in the United States.

Impressed with the success of the St. Louis project, HUD sponsored a tenant management demonstration program in 1976. The program turned the management of public housing projects over to tenants. The study concluded that low-income tenants could master the skills necessary to manage housing. It also demonstrated that tenant groups needed the money and subsidies to remain successful as housing mangers.

As tenants sought more money for management and major building repairs, they raised capital in many inventive ways. In St. Louis, the tenants converted their need for capital to social purposes. They established day-care centers and a catering business, and moved from management to ownership with plans to build 700 new housing units. From a community perspective, these tenant management groups became solidified and soon functioned as central leadership forces in their neighborhoods.

Tenant-managed housing has many positive aspects, whether in public or private housing. Tenants have more self-interest in maintaining building, grounds, and good behavior. They have overcome the waits and delays that typify maintenance schedules. As one would expect, tenant management fosters a sense of pride and peer pressure on the part of tenants. All of these factors have led the St. Louis Housing Authority to conclude that residents can do a better job of management than the Housing Authority.[13]

Tenant-managed housing has shifted in emphasis to tenant-owned-and-managed housing. Tenant ownership is more problematic. HUD's present move to encourage tenant ownership programs can emasculate public housing in the guise of tenant empowerment. No matter how well-priced conversion is, tenants will still need financial subsidies to maintain their property. Any proposal for conversion to ownership should include some provision with HUD for continuing operating subsidies. Because problems exist with the professional ability of some resident management or ownership groups, massive amounts of technical assistance are necessary to help residents make financial and technical decisions.

Of critical importance is the need for vigilance over tenant management and ownership projects so that they remain affordable to low-income residents. In New York City, for example, tenant advocates fear that the city is shifting its focus too far toward ownership by landlords and has become less willing to support tenant management arrangements, which take long to set up and require a great deal of organizational development. As real estate values in New York have increased, fewer buildings are being abandoned and taken over by the city. This is resulting in fewer opportunities for tenant-run buildings.

The history of tenant lease programs is one with an excellent record. Notwithstanding all problems, these programs have redeveloped people as well as buildings and communities. They have preserved a sizeable amount of low-income housing. The contemporary concern centers around new forces threatening the stability of such housing stock. Among these forces are the explicit government policies to abandon public housing by converting it to ownership. Another concern is continuing drives toward gentrification which inevitably result in a diminished stock of low-cost housing. Finally, tenant-managed housing can only succeed with financial and technical support from outside funding sources like the government or some arrangement with community non-profit corporations.[14]

Urban Homesteading

Poor people needing housing across the country have taken to "squatting" in abandoned properties and rehabilitating them with their own labor. This form of sweat equity has greatly expanded as federal government support for housing has declined. In many cases, homesteading has moved from squatting to renting to home ownership of a single property. The movement also offers another model of housing rehabilitation.

As early as 1974, the federal government responded to home-steading activities by authorizing the Federal Homesteading Demonstration Program, Section 810 of the Community and Redevelopment Act of 1974. Amended in 1983, the program targets participation to low-income families who live in substandard dwellings and pay more than 30 percent of their income for shelter. In 1986, the homesteading program spent $12.3 million to acquire 670 abandoned units and turn them over to low-income people. The homesteaders agree to bring the property up to code standards and occupy the building for at least five years. Homesteading can produce livable and affordable low-cost housing through a combination of sweat equity, subsidized rehabilitation loans, and low-interest mortgage loans to landlords and potential squatter-owners.

Organized homesteading campaigns have been launched in Atlanta, Chicago, Washington, D.C., Phoenix, Detroit, New York City and Wilmington. The most notable of them, ACORN, the Kensington Joint Action Council in Philadelphia, began its highly publicized squatting campaign in 1980 in an effort to force the city to turn over a number of its 26,000 abandoned housing units. The campaign led to a series of agreements with the city to provide low-cost housing. Typically, Philadelphia homesteaders received 50 houses and $200,000 of Community Development Block Grant money from the city, which they combined with sweat equity and bank loans based on Community Redevelopment Agency guarantees to provide houses at an average cost of $15,000. Some of these houses have been bought by owner-inhabitants. Others are purchased for lease. What is important is the fact that homesteading in ACORN has rehabilitated affordable housing for poor people.[15]

The other cities cited for homesteading programs have relied on the same combination of sweat equity and financial assistance to redevelop vacant, tax-delinquent housing for poor residents.

As in the case of tenant management, the success of sweat equity projects requires financial assistance in the form of subsidies and grants, as well as intensive technical assistance. Homesteaders need skills, money for building materials, and general training to build and maintain neglected properties.

Through the expansion of Section 810, community organizations like ACORN could acquire ownership interests in abandoned units, either as homeowners or cooperative lessees. This expansion would involve construction training and would designate contractors for technical rehabilitation. Of greatest significance, homesteading would provide an important source of low-interest loans for construction and redevelopment of lost affordable housing.[16]

Rent Control as a Protection for Low- and Moderate-Income Renters

Rent control, introduced in the United States during World War I, has generated intense legal and political controversy. In February 1987, the United States Supreme Court settled many of the contentious issues by ruling in a San Jose, California case that rent control is constitutional. In his majority opinion, Chief Justice William H. Rehnquist held that tenant welfare is a legitimate governmental goal, and rent control furthered that goal. The Chief Justice also noted that debates over social policy belong in the political arena and not in the courts.

The political debate is likely to continue as the popularity of rent control spreads. Currently, 200 American cities regulate residential rents, representing 12 percent of the nation's rental-housing stock. These numbers will increase because the conditions which make regulations necessary are not improving. Foremost among these conditions is the fact that more poor residents are spending a greater share of their income on rent, often doubling up into overcrowded apartments.[17]

The latest study of the effects of rent control, completed at the end of June 1988 for the city of Los Angeles, reported that the average gross monthly rent (including gas and electricity) for a controlled apartment was $525 in 1987, compared to $444 in 1984. In uncontrolled units, the average rent was $675 in 1987. Over the same time period, the average share of a renter's gross income devoted to housing rose from 28.5 percent to 29.2 percent. This is still below the federally defined affordability standard of more than 30 percent.

However, the report noted, 38 percent of all households living in rent-controlled units paid above the threshold, and one-quarter paid more than 40 percent of their income. As demonstrated in other studies, households earning less than $10,000 a year spend 58 percent of their income on rent in Los Angeles.

The report concluded that the city's rent control and rent stabilization regulations should remain intact without revisions; that they work well and largely achieve the goals set by the city council when it enacted the rent control law.[18]

Contradictory data, cited in Chapter 6, relate the shortage of low-income housing to rent control. These data, claim many housing analysts, bear out the reports that those with higher incomes are remaining in rent-controlled units and blocking people who most need them from low-rent vacancies.

The social policy framework of rent control is twofold. First, it seeks to preserve affordable housing for low- and moderate-income families. The second purpose of rent control is to prevent the hardship associated with losing one's home. Where alternative housing is unavailable, eviction can mean displacement from one's community. It can also mean homelessness. All Americans continue to share the goal of stable and secure housing. Yet for tenants, that goal can easily be shattered by rents that rise two or three times as fast as expected, or by displacement caused by eviction, demolition or conversion. As Justice Rehnquist noted in his opinion, this is not only a substantial hardship for affected tenants, but it drains the community of resources and imposes severe social costs.

Local government is generally more sensitive and responsive to the rental housing crisis than state or federal government. This is because the quality of neighborhood life has generally been a municipal concern. State and federal governments often note the severity of the problem, but leave it to cities to formulate solutions. However, a city's range of options is limited. Taxing and spending for social programs is not only out of vogue in the 1980s, it is often restricted or impossible because of property tax revolts like

Proposition 13 and the Gann Amendment in the state of California. Until these constraints on spending are removed, or the federal government reorders its priorities, cities will often turn to rent control. Similar mechanisms, such as condominium-conversion laws and protection from arbitrary eviction, like the Gottfried-Calandra Anti-lockout and Illegal Eviction Bill in New York City, also serve the goals of preserving rental housing and preventing tenant hardship.[19]

Opponents of rent control press two main points: that it unfairly singles out landlords to bear the brunt of social policy, and that it is counterproductive because it discourages investment in housing. These arguments, plus those relating low vacancy rates to rent control, cannot be dismissed summarily, but they must be placed in perspective. Landlords as a group have benefited from housing scarcity and other governmental policies such as zoning and favorable tax treatment; and most investors would prefer to be in rent-controlled Los Angeles or New York than in uncontrolled Houston. It is fair to target the causes of tenant hardship and displacement as rapidly rising rents and conversions.

Despite popular myth, little hard data have been produced linking rent control with housing deterioration. The Bronx, long viewed as a negative example of rent control, is now undergoing revitalization and economic redevelopment under rent control and stabilization regulations. Housing neglect does not occur in rent-controlled cities alone. It is the product of larger economic forces. Rent control can encourage investment by exempting new construction and providing rent increases for repairs and capital improvements.

In the final analysis, there are more apartments on the market for rent now than at any other time in recent history. But in the areas that are tight for low- and moderate-cost rentals, rent control, along with rent stabilization formulas, remains a justifiable strategy for preserving affordable housing.

Conversion of Welfare Hotels

Jonathan Kozol's expose of the Martinique Hotel in Manhattan dramatized the high cost and substandard conditions of welfare hotels, which have been a mainstay of local government housing for homeless individuals and families. For more than a year, a coalition of churches, synagogues and other housing advocates have been urging the Governor and Mayor of New York to provide rent subsidies that would enable homeless families to move out of New York City's welfare hotels. These hotels represent the worst of temporary living arrangements, and cities throughout the nation have similar versions of them.

In New York City, the proposed Homeless Accelerated Rehousing Program, or HARP, would place 3,515 families now in welfare hotels in permanent apartments at market rents around the city. The plan calls for rents above the welfare shelter allowance provided to a family of four, $312 a month.[20]

New York City has also announced plans to buy and shut down the midtown Holland Hotel, which has become a symbol of the plight of the homeless. Under the plan, the city will buy the hotel and immediately move families out of it. The city plans to renovate the hotel and turn it over to a non-profit group to run as a supervised residence for the elderly and mentally ill homeless. City officials have announced plans to offer permanent housing to the former Holland Hotel residents to the extent possible and where appropriate.

Although this is not a solid promise of rehousing, the move to close down a privately owned hotel that charged an average of more than $1,800 a month to house a family of four in a single room is an innovative and progressive initiative at the local level. It enables homeless families to live in private apartments instead of welfare hotels, while at the same time saving the government money. The HARP proposal represents a step to alleviate the plight of those who are presently homeless as well as those who are homeless-vulnerable.

The concept of substituting welfare hotels with permanent housing was supported in a New Jersey Supreme Court decision upholding the state's regulation that sets a five-month limit on financial aid to homeless families in welfare hotels and motels. This regulation and court decision have been accompanied by provisions barring immediate evictions of families whose time eligibility has lapsed.

The State Department of Human Services Commissioner has been highly critical of state and federal payments to welfare hotels for the homeless because the costs have increased from $9.1 million in 1987 to nearly $36 million in 1988, and because the money fails to provide permanent housing or to address the causes of homelessness.

Use of welfare hotels to temporarily house the homeless has yielded large profit windfalls to the hotel owners without putting any money into permanent solutions. Of all the solutions to the problem of housing the homeless, the welfare hotel is undoubtedly the worst. Although the decision to close down the welfare hotels or limit their use over time seems a callous eviction of homeless families, it does force consideration and responsibility for more permanent solutions and housing. The sight of a family living in a welfare hotel room offends even the most unsympathetic critics of homeless people. The spectacle of such a demeaning life at exorbitant cost to cities and states exacerbates the offensiveness of this spectacle.

Rental Housing and Homelessness

By now it is an accepted truth that a strong correlation exists between the lack of affordable rental housing and homelessness. This does not mean, however, that the core problem is lack of public housing. The great majority of people rent housing in the private market. As people in the United States come to rely more heavily on rental housing for their entire lives because of reduced wage structures and increased costs of home ownership, it will be incumbent on all housing providers, public and private, to develop new financial and organizational arrangements to produce and maintain affordable rental housing stock.

This chapter has identified a series of exemplary strategies that can cumulatively add to the supply of affordable rental housing. State and local government subsidies and tax incentives to developers and employer-assisted housing offer a new and sound direction toward this goal. Housing rehabilitation of abandoned or dilapidated buildings through subsidies and tax incentives, tenant management schemes and homesteading provide other contemporary examples of success in maintaining a rental supply for poor people. Any public effort to convert welfare hotels to permanent housing represents a substantial effort to add to the rental supply. Finally, rent control continues to be a matter of controversy, but data on vacancy rates and the costs of renting support rent control as a valid strategy for preserving affordable housing and preventing homelessness.

Secure and stable housing does not only mean home ownership. Vast numbers of Americans have traditionally relied upon rental housing for all or part of their lives. Indeed, many signs point to rental exceeding home ownership.

Chapter 9

Links Between Housing and Welfare

It is no accident that welfare reform and housing reform have reappeared on the nation's policy agenda. In attempting to address the needs of the nation's poor, housing and welfare unavoidably loom as key issues. However, no headway will be made in meeting either the housing or the income needs of the poor until housing and welfare are addressed as two parts of the same issue. As long as housing and welfare are addressed as separate items, people will experience housing problems that remain unsolved by receipt of a welfare check; and conversely, adequate housing accompanied by a low welfare check will keep people homeless-vulnerable.

Historically, the 1949 amendments to the Housing Act of 1937 authorized public housing, administered and built by the public sector, creating 135,000 units annually for six years. The Housing Act of 1937 provided the first federal subsidy for housing, but the program was concerned only with physical structure and construction of safe, sound housing that could be rented at low figures.[1] Despite the fact that the 1949 Housing Act articulated an expanded goal of a decent home and suitable living environment for every American family, the emphasis of all housing programs, whether public or subsidized, has been on physical construction and maintenance rather than on a suitable living environment. To implement the latter goal, a housing program needs to be integrated with a wide range of tenant services from recreation, vocational training and homemaking to social services in general, and public assistance specifically. The concept of "housing plus" must be put into practice as an effort to build a system of supports designed to keep people within the circle of housing.

By the end of the 1950s, it became apparent that housing policy was no longer a simple matter of building or stimulating construction, or maintaining standards and codes. Problems of poverty, class and discrimination required attention in the design of housing policy and programs.

Federal homebuilding programs provided no tenant services, despite the fact that the consequences of previous public housing programs led to the concentration of poor, usually public-assistance families in densely concentrated highrise buildings. This focused public attention on the multiple social problems confronting low-income families. The New York City Housing Authority became the first public housing authority to establish a division of community services intended to coordinate its efforts with other public and private social agencies.[2]

The proliferation of social programs in the 1960s further addressed the dual problems of housing and welfare in the Model Cities legislation of 1965. This legislation was originally intended to be a massive assault on the housing, environmental, social and welfare needs of cities. Established as a demonstration in 50 cities, the Model Cities bill was intended to display the effectiveness of a massive, comprehensive attempt to rebuild and restore inner-city blighted areas.

After reconciliation between the House of Representatives and the Senate, as well as the Administration, the total effect of the demonstration was reduced to a limited addition to the already existing conglomerate of diverse and largely ineffective social programs. It has been estimated that the Model Cities program received allocations and authorizations of approximately $390 million annually, or about 15 percent of the total of HUD's urban programs, about $2.6 billion.[3]

The Republican administration in 1968 dismantled the Model Cities program in stages as it began to experiment with "New Federalism," focused on local initiatives soon shifted the focus from poverty and low-income needs to more general needs in the population.

Despite the modesty of the Model Cities experience, as measured against its original goals of comprehensively coordinating physical and social services, the concept of the demonstration persisted and new programs were introduced attempting to coordinate housing and welfare services. Among these efforts was Title XX, amended to the Social Security Act in 1976.

Title XX Coordination of Personal Social Services

The Title XX amendments served two discrete objectives. Authorized by an administration determined to slow the rate of growth of federal spending for welfare programs, the amendments consolidated all categorical social service programs into special revenue-sharing block grants intended to give the states and local governments more flexibility in utilizing federal matching funds. At the same time, the federal government began to introduce savings in federal expenditures for welfare in the form of administrative budget cuts, operating under the assumption that the states and local government entities would handle more of the administration of services.

The second objective of Title XX was to maintain the federal presence in social services by requiring the states to develop coordinated service systems as a condition of receiving federal matching funds. The legislation did not specifically identify which services were to be included, leaving this up to the state. It did, however, articulate six major goals in the form of federal guidelines. These were: 1) achieving economic self-support or reducing dependency, 2) achieving or maintaining self-sufficiency, 3) preventing or remedying neglect, abuse or exploitation of children and adults unable to protect their own interests, or preserving, rehabilitating and reuniting families, 4) preventing or reducing inappropriate care by providing for community-based, home-based or other forms of less intensive care, 5) securing referral or admission for institutional care when other forms are not appropriate and providing services to individuals in institutions, and 6) case management to secure and assure the coordination of individual service and treatment plans.

Title XX did not designate the services required to achieve these goals, except that choices of service were to be based on the earlier Social Security Act categories of aid to the elderly, blind, disabled and children.

Housing and welfare did receive special attention, albeit in a negative sense. In an effort to reach beyond public assistance recipients, the law stated that one-half of the Title XX funds must be directed to public assistance or SSI or Medicaid recipients. The other half was to be directed to families not receiving cash payments but having an income not exceeding 115 percent of their state's median income for a family of like size.[4]

Housing, or room and board, was restricted to no more than six consecutive months. Such specific targeting against public welfare recipients and those in need of housing clearly restricted the meaning of coordinated services. Furthermore, because the amendments compromised the federal government's attempt to remain a presence in the policy arena of personal social services, they added to the troublesome ambiguity of the term "personal social services." How could any program of coordinated personal social services restrict the application of housing and public assistance as a strategy to reduce dependency? Rather than strengthening the links between the two essential services, Title XX exacerbated earlier policies that split the two.

Separation of Services and Income

Viewed from the perspective of developing linkages between welfare via cash payments and welfare services, the decades of the 1960s and 1970s were years of confusion about how to respond to dependency and growing welfare rolls. A major departure in federal policy was the separation of personal social services from income maintenance in the 1962 Social Service Amendments to the Social Security Act.

Prior to the passage of these amendments, services were provided in the course of determining eligibility and distributing welfare benefits. This system meant that public assistance recipients who were experiencing housing problems could receive help with their housing needs in the form of referral, advocacy and liaison with housing authority personnel, and emergency funds for heating and other utility needs.

By the mid-1970s, most public welfare offices were placed in separate quarters from eligibility and payment offices. Moreover, personnel declassification had been introduced to reduce public welfare expenditures so that trained social workers were no longer a regular feature of public welfare service or income programs.

Although the separation of services and income was viewed by its proponents, who came largely from the ranks of social welfare professionals and policy analysts, as a means of making the public assistance system less demeaning to beneficiaries, one of the unanticipated consequences of the new arrangement was that people needing tangible resources like housing went unattended in the new eligibility and payment arrangement.[5]

As originally conceived, the Social Service Amendments were intended to reduce the stigmatizing and demeaning character of determining eligibility for public assistance. Proponents of the amendments argued that people who were poor needed money, not services. To a large extent, this position was merited because many indignities were heaped on public assistance recipients in the guise of services. The infamous home visits and midnight raids to investigate the presence of a man in the house grew out of the linked system. Eligibility workers, authorized to counsel families and make home visits, frequently conducted themselves in the manner of earlier "friendly visitors" from the charity organization societies who were harsh and judgmental, rendering the public image of the social worker as a threatening and omnipotent welfare worker. Social workers under the earlier system possessed coercive powers which they could exercise as a condition of eligibility.

As is frequently the case with well-intended policies, unanticipated and negative consequences have emerged. The most troublesome consequence has been the diminution of social services often need by the poor. Tangible help with housing needs ranks high among services lost to cash assistance recipients.

A compromise position could involve placing social workers at intake positions where they could intervene under specific criteria of need. Several public assistance systems are now attempting to provide housing supports to homeless people and homeless-vulnerable people in this manner. The California Homeless Assistance Program and New York's Housing Alert are examples of linking housing and welfare.

Current Confusions Between Housing and Welfare Programs

Welfare recipients can now receive housing allowances through one of two programs. One allowance comes from HUD, and the other comes from the Aid to Families with Dependent Children Emergency Assistance Program. Under the HUD system, Section 8 housing subsidies cover the difference between the market rent and what the welfare recipient can afford, in addition to the basic housing allowance. Under the AFDC Emergency Assistance Program, women who cannot pay their full rent are evicted and then sent to a welfare hotel or motel where the public welfare program will pay the full bill.

No coordination presently exists between subsidies for low-income housing from HUD and shelter allowances under emergency-assistance welfare programs. The result is overlapping subsidies for some people and no subsidies for others who are equally needy. Moreover, welfare housing payments are not conditioned upon improvement in the housing quality. Determination of who receives HUD subsidies amounts to a lottery.

Under the welfare system, geography is the major determinant of the relative size of rent subsidy. Because there is no connection between the amount of the rent subsidy and housing quality, many communities spend relatively large amounts for their welfare populations with no tangible return.

Recipients of HUD assistance live in minimally decent housing, regardless of geography. Unfortunately, only a fraction of eligible low-income families receive such assistance. In 1983, for example, nearly three million renters on welfare did not receive housing assistance from HUD but had incomes as low as those who did qualify. HUD assistance is allocated on a first-come, first-served basis. It is a lottery, not an entitlement.[6]

In practice, this means that two single mothers, each living with two children in apartments costing $300 a month and relying on welfare for all of their income, both receive housing allowances of $250 a month, but one must take $50 from other expense items to pay the difference, while the other receives a $50 HUD subsidy. The mother who is forced to spend from her welfare allowance faces eviction, emergency assistance, and the infamous welfare hotels. She becomes a strong candidate for the isolate, or outsider type of homeless person, and hence deeply entrenched in homelessness.

Typically, when AFDC families find themselves unable to stretch their grant to cover food, rent, transportation and clothing costs, and are forced to seek emergency shelter, the connection between housing and welfare becomes obvious. Unless single-parent families receive other subsidies, such as housing, they cannot make ends meet.

With homelessness at crisis proportions in the United States, current welfare aid is simply not enough. Section 8 is adequate as far as it goes, but it does not cover enough people and is so bureaucratically cumbersome that it can take up to two years for an applicant to receive that subsidy. With the inability of the welfare system to keep up with rising costs, particularly in housing, it is small wonder that the fastest growing segment of the homeless population has become families, primarily single mothers and children.

Each system is unfair in its own way, but the combined effect is worse. The inequities and inefficiencies in the current system need to be addressed. Reducing or eliminating the regional disparities in welfare payments would be a step in the right direction, but would not by itself insure either equity or adequacy. Some low-income families would still receive welfare shelter grants and HUD subsidies. Some would receive neither. And many would receive welfare shelter assistance but live in substandard housing.

The crucial solution lies in a value system that espouses a societal and public commitment to provide minimally decent housing for all, along with the will to implement that commitment. To accomplish this goal as a key to inventing a non-homeless future, two actions are necessary. Housing and welfare policy objectives must be coordinated, and there must be effective links between housing support and housing quality.

Strong evidence, beginning with the Social Service Amendments separating income and services, suggests that merely providing unrestrained cash grants to the poor does not improve their housing conditions. This may argue for a two-tiered payment system. A full subsidy could be granted to households in units that meet program standards. A partial shelter allowance could be available to households that cannot find, or do not choose, a housing unit that meets program standards, with a clear understanding that the full allowance will be paid if standards are met.

Restructuring housing programs is difficult. Real coordination between two programs with different constituencies and vested interests is even more difficult. However, the case for both is compelling if we consider the requirements of preventing homelessness.

One clear direction for coordination would be authorization by the federal government allowing cities to use federal welfare funds to build low-cost housing for homeless people and those at risk of being homeless. By diverting some of the emergency assistance money now spent on providing temporary shelter in welfare hotels and using it to build permanent housing for low-income families, this plan would address the causes of homelessness and move the housing and welfare systems further along in the direction of prevention.

This concept contains a clear cost-effective benefit. In his November 1987 news conference, President Reagan asserted that he did not understand why New York City spends $37,000 a year to keep a family in a welfare hotel when it could build them a house for that amount of money. Since November, the Administration has adopted the reverse position, claiming that the Emergency Assistance Program was never intended to address the causes of homelessness, such as the shortage of low-cost housing. It was created only to respond quickly to a family crisis by providing temporary assistance. Additional grounds for opposing such a plan lie in the fact that it would put the Department of Health and Human Services into the housing construction and acquisition business.

It is precisely this rigid constructionist approach to government mandates that hampers efforts to address the housing needs of welfare recipients and other poor people. Fragmentation of bureaucracy in this way forces a policy and service bias that views clients and their problems narrowly as single issues. Even though a general level of consensus exists that relates homelessness to mental illness, economic conditions and the lack of affordable housing, no integrated service plan can be put in place that employs this broad-based understanding of homelessness under existing organizational domains. Instead, the different parts of the problem get parceled out. The Department of Mental Health gets the mental health part; the Department of Housing gets the housing part; and the Department of Welfare gets those clients whose homelessness could not be prevented. By viewing public welfare as a residual and categorical approach, departments of welfare serve people after all other resources have failed them. Homeless people, lost in other systems, thus require emergency assistance which is frequently more expensive than other help which does not fall into welfare categories of eligibility.

The absence of an integrated approach to services has set up a barrier to preventive planning and reinforces the belief that homelessness is a temporary problem. It also perpetuates flawed analyses revolving around the assumption that homelessness can be explained by a single cause.

A major example of such narrow single-cause thinking is the study "Chronic and Situational Dependency," derived from data collected at the Keener Shelter in October 1981 by the New York City Bureau of Management Systems. The study consisted of 128 interviews with men who had been residents of the Keener Shelter for more than two months. It combined these data with information about 45 men who had previously been interviewed by the State Office of Mental Health. In an interpretive schema that is said to be valid for two-thirds of the sample, the study explained homelessness by single causes. It listed the following causes and percentages:

Psychiatric only	34%
Alcoholic only	6%
Economic only	19%
Drug only	2%
Physical disability only	3%

This selection of categories reflects general public welfare departments' agenda about the psychiatric and employable populations that are homeless. Clearly, if one seeks single-cause explanations of homelessness, one can find single-cause explanations of homelessness.[7] By ascribing single causes to the problem, institutions can either claim responsibility for serving homeless people because they fall into the category of their service domain, or they can refuse to serve them on the grounds that other agencies are authorized to handle the specific problem causing an individual's homelessness. This bureaucratic client shuffle has clearly manifested itself between housing and welfare departments.

In the meanwhile, the need for low-income housing persists. By relying on the shelter system and the emergency assistance program, public welfare systems throughout the country have transformed shelters and welfare hotels, intended as temporary resources, into permanent homes.

Ultimately, human service institutions will need to adopt an expanded definition and understanding of homelessness and devise service plans that expand the scope of assistance available to those in need of secure housing to better serve the homeless and prevent homelessness. Arguing that the homeless need housing is the same as arguing that the poor need money. Both are true. The more difficult and challenging issue is what kind of housing, what conditions for providing income and what social services are needed. Answers to these questions can only be derived through service integration and policy analyses that promote multiple causality explanations of homelessness and comprehensive planning.

Homeless-prevention programs modeled on those described in Chapter 7 now operating in New Jersey, Pennsylvania, Maryland, California and Massachusetts, as well as those at the local level in St. Louis, Allegheny County and New York City, have moved in the right direction towards program coordination.

Because these programs function largely as temporary assistance of last resort to households facing eviction or imminent foreclosure for reasons that compel people to seek public welfare, they are actually coordinating welfare, in its broadest meaning, with housing.

The California Homeless Assistance Program is specifically targeted to recipients of Aid to Families with Dependent Children. It goes well beyond the provision of emergency assistance by paying move-in costs for permanent housing as well as temporary shelter. This program, still in the initial stages, merits national attention as a model of housing and welfare coordination. It also challenges the Reagan administration's position that emergency assistance cannot be used for permanent housing.

Special Housing and Welfare Needs of Women and Children

Recognition of the correlation between the lack of affordable housing and homelessness does not necessarily mean that the core problem is lack of public housing. In 1982, 22 percent of poverty-level renters lived in public or subsidized housing. In 1986, slightly more poverty renters (28 percent) lived in federally subsidized or public housing. These data underline the fact that the great majority of the poor do not live in public housing, but in private market housing.[8]

On the other hand, public housing authorities are the primary houser of poor women and their children. Women in public housing suffer more frequently than most from teenage pregnancy, domestic violence and abuse, divorce and desertion, and drug and alcohol addiction. These problems, coupled with increasing feminization of poverty, force attention to the need for expanded housing policies that combine shelter with social service programs focused on women's needs.

The current separation of housing and welfare systems fails to address any of the special needs of women who are at high risk of becoming homeless. The issue of affordable housing for women is at the point of crisis. This is why the nation's public housing program primarily houses single women and their children. The issue of adequate welfare and services is also at the crisis point; hence the passage of the Family Security Act.

Women in public housing units need day care, job counseling, transportation and financial planning that will enable them to leave the welfare rolls. They also need higher welfare payments pegged to an appropriate standard of need. The present lack of coordination at the federal level between HUD and Health and Human Services has resulted in higher welfare rolls and insufficient housing funds for new construction, rehabilitation, modernization and maintenance. Neither system is presently equipped to meet need.

Dolores Hayden alerts us to the idea that public housing is a crucial area for improvement in the combination of housing, jobs and services for its residents. The National Congress of Neighborhood Women in Brooklyn, New York has pioneered self-help efforts to build such services into public housing facilities. Other groups across the United States, like those organized in St. Louis, have begun self-help organizing around housing and services.[9]

Typically, these groups are organizing child care, job-training and job-placement services. In addition to incorporating services in public housing facilities, other multi-family housing sites need similar program infusions.

Housing policy must address the relationship between welfare and housing. Public housing programs are inadequate substitutes for an inadequate welfare system that does not provide realistic shelter expenses or the social supports necessary to give women the ability to become independent of public assistance. Unfortunately, nothing in the Family Security Act addresses this compelling need for the coordination of housing and welfare.

The more encouraging steps in the direction of coordination of the two systems are to be found at state and local levels in the homeless-prevention programs. With luck and careful planning, these programs can lead the federal government in their paths.

History has taught that concentration on physical housing does not necessarily improve either home or neighborhood environments. Provision of housing and changes in the physical environment positively alter the quality of the lives of the poor only when housing with reasonably good standards is made available, and when housing accompanies services. Such desirable services range from recreation and other amenities to counseling and cash payments. In the final analysis, the 1949 Housing Act, calling for shelter for every American family, has failed. Homes for everyone must be viewed as more than shelter. Neighborhoods must be made liveable, services provided, and facilities created to meet the needs of residents.[10]

Chapter 10

Government and Private Sector Roles
in Housing Policy

The combined effect of visible homelessness that evokes shame and guilt among the public and the real concern that the children and parents of middle-class Americans may not be able to afford housing has placed housing at the center of the nation's agenda once again. It is by now obvious to all that current housing policies cannot meet the demand and need for stable housing for a widely divergent group of people. Would-be homeowners must turn to the rental market for their housing. Renters are forced to pay disproportionately high shares of their income for shelter. For others, housing is either impossible or precarious at today's rents.

All of these factors compel the nation to formulate a national housing policy. For more than a century, the American government accepted responsibility for some affirmative role in helping to house people. In the 1980s, this responsibility diminished. Cuts in federal expenditures have been the dominant feature of national housing policies in the 1980s. Unless the federal government returns to a more active role in housing, the problems already under way will explode, creating a nation with more homeless and homeless-vulnerable people. Others will continue to live in substandard conditions or reduced housing standards.

National housing policy for the 1990s and beyond need not be based upon budget-breaking tax-and-spend programs, as suggested by many who confront the problem of homelessness and its prevention with despair. During the past three decades, new participants in social programs have successfully demonstrated their ability to contribute to human service arenas. In the housing sector, the states and local governments have achieved notable success through subsidizing construction, financing equity arrangements and providing grants for housing.

Many housing analysts view the innovations by governors and mayors, working with local non-profit housing developers, as the most encouraging activity on the horizon. Business has also moved into the housing arena. Other creative housing experts have concluded that the nation needs a social housing sector that would be specifically divorced from private market forces.

Few seek a return to housing policies of the past which resulted in the enrichment of private developers at greater rates than it supplied adequate and affordable housing. Even before the recent surge in homelessness, federal housing policies did not measure up to their stated goals and objectives. The 1960 census reported that 8.5 million families were living in substandard conditions, and an additional 6.1 million were living in overcrowded conditions. By 1970 there were at least 13 million poor households in the nation. Of this total, 6.9 million lived in physically inadequate units, and an additional 6.2 million were living in housing of excessive cost in relation to income and size. These data do not support returning to a replication of the earlier national policies, and they lend credibility to the criticisms of these early policies that inflated the coffers of developers at the expense of housing inhabitants.[1]

Even though the states, local governments, private business and the non-profit sector have evolved as key players in the housing market, they lack the resources necessary to convert their programs into larger-scale national efforts. Only the federal government has such resources. Any national agenda for housing should seek to forge partnerships between the federal government and more locally based housing efforts. Such housing partnerships should be welcomed and shaped by those who will implement it at the local level, including state and local governments, businesses, non-profit organizations and community groups.

The primary goal of any new national housing policy must be the provision of adequate and affordable housing. Housing policy must also be fair, offering housing to all Americans, rather than appealing to special interests and those who can afford to buy. It must be new rather than a replication or adaptation of earlier policies. It must respond to the diverse housing needs of contemporary American families who no longer resemble the traditional nuclear family. Finally, new housing policy must be responsive to political imperatives that will not sacrifice the electability of political leaders.

This chapter examines proposals and possibilities for national housing policy predicated upon relationships between the federal, state and local governments, business and industry, and non-profit organizations.

Federal Partnerships with State and Local Governments

State governments have invented and implemented initiatives that they have the ability to continue administering with an infusion of federal money. Among these innovations are down-payment assistance plans, reverse mortgage programs, homeless-prevention programs and direct subsidies. A federal matching grant program for states to continue these initiatives at increased levels would be a valuable strategy as an incentive for state spending at current and/or increased rates.

Encouraging the states to continue to expand their present activities warrants consideration on its own merits. However, national state matching grant programs have the potential to add standards for housing programs that ensure responsiveness to the diversity of needs and interest in the shelter industry. Foremost among these standards would be affirmative targets for contemporary American families, e.g., single people, single-parent families, the elderly, first-time homebuyers, minorities and generally smaller families.

Today's families, faced with barriers to buying, renting, converting, maintaining and improving their homes, need new forms of assistance. They need down-payment assistance loans to achieve home ownership, interest-rate buydowns if interest rates rise or recessions occur, housing for the frail elderly and single-parent families, emergency assistance and services for homeless-vulnerable people, as well as affordable housing for those facing eviction because they can no longer afford their rent or mortgage payments. New national housing policy must acknowledge that all of these measures to provide and maintain people in the circle of their housing are, indeed, homeless-prevention programs.

Restoration of budget cuts at the federal level, while essential, is no longer sufficient to meet the nation's housing needs. It is certainly no remedy for homelessness any more. Nor are state programs, with infusions of federal dollars, sufficient to meet need unless they include new building technologies and help overcome the many barriers which the real American families of today now confront.

Federal and state government leadership in housing directed to funding, building, maintenance and rehabilitation are important. To create housing policies that are relevant to the year 2000, financial and building arrangements must add social elements targeted to specific populations and their housing problems.

Schwartz et al. warn that any consideration of federal housing policy must presuppose that:

- State and local spending on housing will grow in the 1990s;

- A good portion of the administration of new federal housing programs will go to state and local governments, and community-based non-profit corporations;

- Much of the construction, financing and sale of new housing will continue to be done by the private housing market system.

These assumptions mean that the success of any federal housing policy will depend in large measure on the support and agreements of state and local officials, community activists and leaders, and shelter industry representatives. Without such support, implementation efforts will be doomed to failure or reinterpretation according to their special interests.[2]

For these reasons, federal housing policy related to the states should be largely derived from the state initiatives undertaken in the 1980s. These are proven efforts that benefit from existing support of governors, legislators, community leaders and shelter industry representatives. In most states, these initiatives have become sources of local pride that federal government policymakers can capitalize on in obtaining consensus for federal-state initiatives.

Federal-Local Partnerships

Most of today's homeless and homeless-vulnerable come from America's urban neighborhoods. The abandonment of federal policy has spelled disaster for these neighborhoods and their inhabitants. Because of the crisis proportions of the lack of decent and affordable housing in urban areas, some of the most innovative approaches to affordable housing have originated in local communities, stimulated by local government, business leadership and non-profit community-based organizations.

The hundreds of efforts to produce and maintain housing in local communities across the nation need financial bolstering that can only come from the federal government. Representative Joseph Kennedy has proposed a Community Housing Partnership Act designed to assist locally based non-profit housing groups. Through this proposed law, the federal government would provide matching funds in a three-to-one ratio to local non-profit housing organizations. The federal funds would match those raised from local government, business, private foundations, the United Way, churches, synagogues and other entities. Matching grants would help those communities that help themselves.[3] Sponsors of the legislation assert that it offers the best way to leverage federal money to get the most affordable housing for the taxpayer's dollar. The program appeals to the popularity of "self-help" that has become so well entrenched in American political theory.

Many housing advocates have called for a new National Housing Investment Corporation to function as a working, equity-sharing, and risk-sharing partner with local non-profit developers. This proposal is essentially the same as the Community Housing Partnership Act. Other variations proposed to stimulate and enhance the efforts of local communities include a national Old Buildings, New Communities Act that would co-venture the production of affordable apartments through the conversion and rehabilitation of empty buildings. This Act could provide local community organizations the funds and technical assistance they require to preserve needed housing, neighborhood stores and businesses. At present, no existing rehabilitation programs work in partnership with local community groups. Such a partnership between communities and the federal government could be a catalyst for rebuilding the nation's blighted urban areas. Two other major bills, both entitled "The Affordable Housing Act," have been introduced to Congress. One, sponsored by Representative Barney Frank, would authorize $15 billion for housing every year for the next year. A more expensive bill, sponsored by Representative Ron Dellums, calls for $45 billion in grants for housing and emphasizes social ownership.[4]

Whatever proposal becomes enacted, it is essential to acknowledge that hundreds of community-based organizations throughout the nation have built or renovated housing units. The non-profit sector could be a major low-cost housing provider in the future, if it gains support from federal resources.

Financial Resources for Federal/State/Local Partnerships

Financial resources for a new federal/local housing partnership could be facilitated by several methods. Modifications in the Community Development Block Grant (CDBG) program would be a first step. Financial intermediaries like the Local Initiatives Support Corporation (LISC), the Enterprise Foundation and the Neighborhood Reinvestment Corporation could continue to replace losses in federal funding. Linked development and inclusionary zoning can continue to be tools for the production of more low- and moderate-income housing.

The CDBG program, authorized by Congress in 1975, has been a primary method for federal intervention in local housing and community development. The Act gives local communities broad discretion in spending the largest remaining federal program funds targeted for the needs of low- and moderate-income families. The program suffered a 19 percent cut under the Reagan administration, but it still distributes approximately $3 billion a year, down from its peak of $3.8 billion in 1980. To merely catch up with inflation, CDBG funding should be increased to slightly more than $8 billion. The stated purpose of CDBGs is to improve communities by providing decent housing in a suitable living environment for persons of low and moderate income. However, increasing competition for these funds as resources become more restricted under the Gramm-Rudman-Hollings Act has directed much of this money away from use by poor people. Congress now requires that at least 51 percent of CDBG money be channeled to poor people. Even this requirement should be expanded to at least 75 percent to be consistent with the intent of the law and be a resource for low- and moderate-cost housing.[5]

LISC, the Enterprise Foundation and the Neighborhood Reinvestment Corporation have effectively filled the gaps left by the federal government in housing. They are not traditional grant-givers, even though they are sponsored by major foundations. LISCs receive funding from the Ford Foundation.

These financial intermediaries combined have successfully worked with over 1,000 community groups in nearly 200 cities to build thousands of new and rehabilitated low-priced housing units. LISC alone has raised $100 million from nearly 300 corporations to build or rehabilitate 10,000 units through loans to 400 community organizations in 120 cities.[6] As national funding intermediaries, these organizations identify and analyze projects and coordinate the social investment plans of corporations. They generally provide below-market or higher-risk loans to non-profit community development corporations like the Chicago Equity Fund, the Boston Housing Partnership and the Nehemiah Plan in New York.

Cities with sophisticated non-profit housing corporations, including Boston, Baltimore, New York, Cleveland, Chicago and San Francisco, have extended their fundraising beyond the corporate sector to include support from local governments, private foundations, financial institutions, religious organizations and unions. These growing networks of community housing corporations have developed improved productivity and efficiency, economies of scale, and expanded the scope of development in the low-cost housing arena. Federal partnership with these financial intermediaries is the essence of the proposal for a Community Housing Partnership Act.

The aforementioned co-venture program proposed under the National Housing Investment Corporation would be another important revenue source. So would the Federal Housing Trust Fund, as a revenue source for major new matching grant programs for local governments and non-profit organizations. Schwartz et al. advocate that federal matching grant programs set conditions that provide incentives for local government to more fully use their taxing, zoning and partnership-making powers to provide more affordable housing.

There are numerous methods for federal-state partnerships that do not require massive new spending or taxes. Many of these methods are self-financing because they contain revenue growth generated by new housing with modest taxes and new appropriations.

By far the largest source of revenue can be derived from the recapture of tax revenue from federal and state partnerships that stimulate housing construction. The implementation of a national affordable housing program could generate hundreds of millions of dollars from federal wage taxes alone. Corporate income taxes would add to this revenue pool. Housing analysts estimate that the construction of 540,000 units of moderate-income housing units annually would pay for itself in tax recaptures.[7]

The successes of state housing trust funds in at least 17 states, including Florida, California and New Jersey, can form the model for creating a federal housing trust fund that is both responsive and supportive of state efforts. The value of trust funds has been established in the Social Security program. Trust funds accomplish several desirable ends. They designate a specific problem or need that they address. They create a sense of permanence that resources will remain constant, and they emphasize a "pay-as-you-go" financial policy. All of these elements are popular in contemporary American political circles, as well as with the general populace. None of them carries the burden of uncontrollable tax-and-spend policies.

A federal housing trust fund, set up to support state trust funds, could target affirmative goals and objectives for housing specific groups as a way of assuring that federal monies go to areas of greatest need.

Another central feature of trust funds is that they create a connection between the use of the revenue and the entity being taxed. A federal housing trust fund could accomplish this by adding a single new revenue source in the form of a one-percent tax on mortgage-backed securities. In 1986, mortgage-security issuers, including the Federal National Mortgage Association, the Federal Home Loan Mortgage Corporation and private mortgage-security issuers sold or traded approximately $200 million in mortgage-backed securities. A simple one-percent tax on these securities would generate more than $2 billion annually. This sum, along with the required state and non-profit matches, would add up to more than $4 billion annually, enough to subsidize 300,000 units.

An activist national housing policy needs also to be based upon a supportive tax policy. Supportive tax policies are needed to encourage employer-assisted housing and to prohibit tax liabilities for either employer or employee. The acute need for affordable housing has become so critical that tax policies specifically directed to stimulating employers to enter the housing arena in their best interests could greatly expand the supply of affordable housing. The Tax Reform Act of 1986 affirmed the position that employee benefits for housing are tax-exempt. Further tax revisions need to be made to encourage the nation's employers to invest in housing.

A supportive tax policy could also benefit the expansion of lease-purchase housing arrangements. Such a tax policy would allow private builders to secure tax-exempt financing for the development of lease-purchase housing.

Under the Tax Reform Act of 1986, the Congress limited state mortgage revenue bond programs by establishing a cap on private activity revenue bonds of $75 per capita, reduced to $50 per capita in 1986, and prohibiting the states from issuing mortgage revenue bonds for single-family home-ownership programs. State revenue bond programs have been the largest of the state housing programs in terms of dollars spent and units developed. In the interest of deficit reduction, elimination of tax exemption from these programs offered significant revenue replacement.

As discussed earlier, housing construction and maintenance is labor-intensive and, therefore, produces jobs, wages and taxes. The elimination of state authority to issue tax-exempt mortgage bonds is thus counterproductive. It is also inconsistent with the national goal of a suitable home in a decent environment for every American family. This goal was cited when the Congress chose to retain the mortgage interest rate deduction for primary and secondary residences. The Tax Reform Act of 1986 has effectively precluded support for the construction of new and affordable housing and, simultaneously, protected existing homeowners from taxes. A tax code that favors the haves, and blocks the have-nots from housing violates the intent of progressive tax policy and contradicts the stated tax reform agenda of revenue neutrality. There is, in fact, no acceptable or valid reason for this tax treatment. The federal government should act quickly to restore the states' unlimited authority to sell housing revenue bonds as a part of national housing policy.

The one effort of the federal government to support housing through the tax code is the creation of the "Tax Credit for Low Income Rental Housing" section of the Tax Reform Act of 1986. This new tax credit is targeted to a defined low-income population of people whose income is 50 or 60 percent of the area median. Previous tax incentives for low-income housing defined "low income" as 80 percent of the area median. The program, as it was passed, authorized $10 billion for low-income housing assistance, including rehabilitation, for more than 300,000 units over a three-year period.[8]

From its inception, the tax-credit program has been greeted with skepticism regarding its feasibility. Schwartz, et al. recommend a series of minor adjustments that Congress could make to increase investor confidence in the program at little cost to the Treasury. Among these adjustments are: extension of the program beyond 1989 to allow investors more time to become familiar with the program; easing of the amount of passive loss that can be taken by low-income housing tax-credit investors to offset risks for investors in low-income housing; and indexing of the tax credit to fluctuating mortgage rates. This would increase the value of the tax credit and encourage additional investing in low-income housing even in times of high interest rates. It would also preserve construction industry jobs through negative business cycles.

Federal tax credits and exemptions on mortgage bonds will not provide a foundation for a solid national housing policy directed to reversing the demise of affordable housing in the nation, but it does offer one direction for stimulating investment in housing.

America's housing trends and housing policies have negatively covaried together for more than a decade. Nothing so clearly demonstrates the need for a a new national housing policy than the mass crisis of homelessness that is decaying our cities, suburbs and rural areas and making a mockery of our claim to be a decent, humane and prosperous nation.

Building upon state and local initiatives, national housing policy should address an array of items that affect the life of communities, such as schools, recreation, jobs and taxes. The Model Cities legislation of the Great Society was dismantled in the Congress and HUD before it was implemented. Its goals remain viable as the foundation of a housing policy that would keep people within their circle of housing with all of the necessary social supports and amenities. The major thrust of this chapter has been an argument that national housing policy is essential, but need not be predicated on massive new tax and spending programs. Application and coordination of state, local and non-profit initiatives with federal stimuli and incentives can address most of the housing needs of contemporary Americans. The impact of state and local initiatives will diminish without national financial and technical resources that are attainable without a major overhaul of the federal budget.

None of the above discussion of national housing policy should be misconstrued as support for the idea that public housing should disappear. For millions of Americans, home ownership will never be possible. Simple and affordable rental housing remains the only option for many of the elderly, disabled, minorities, working poor and single-parent families. Public housing is the housing of last resort for those who would otherwise have no shelter. Its residents have grown poorer than the rest of society.

Congress must take immediate steps to guarantee that Section 8 housing vouchers will be renewed when they expire. However, these vouchers must be set at market rates along with tax and mortgage refinancing policies that encourage private owners to continue their participation in the program. Similarly, steps must be taken to retain Section 236 housing units for low-rent tenants.

Finally, the federal government must return to producing public housing units. This program, a central component of any national housing policy, was dismantled in the Reagan decade. In 1986 fewer than 4,000 units were built, and no units were scheduled for fiscal year 1988. Housing analysts estimate that 40,000 new public housing units need to be produced annually. Rebuilding the public housing program can provide opportunities to control costs by simplifying HUD review proceedings and the bureaucratic delays that drive up the costs of construction. The existing public housing stock also requires modernization and repairs to remain at standard and retain their value.[9]

Even under the most generous system of entitlements, the poor continue to be among us. Poverty need not mean homelessness. The critical function of public housing is to keep people within their circle of shelter by providing last-resort housing.

Social Ownership of Housing

Some of the most creative thinking about national housing policy reform in the United States derives from a socialist theoretical framework. Even though the need for housing reform is so pervasive, the socialist view has not been publicized recently because of the current preference for conservatism.

At the center of the socialist structural analysis of American housing policy is an assertion that both the current conservative and liberal perspectives on housing are inadequate because they rely upon solutions that accept the market-based housing economy. This analysis leads to the development of more far-reaching alternatives for change that reject market-based strategies.

One proposed alternative for change is the social ownership of housing. This alternative would reinforce the concept of treating housing and land as a socially owned resource. This approach, proposed by Chester Hartman, would create a social sector of housing units that could never be resold for profit. Government would pay for the construction cost with a one-time capital grant. These units would not be like public housing, however. They would be built, owned and managed by diverse local groups. Hartman calculates a $50,000-per-unit construction cost, meaning that 100,000 units of social housing would require a one-time government subsidy of $5 billion. Unlike Section 8, which requires continuous payments, Hartman's social housing model would never require the government to make up the gap between an escalating market value and affordable yearly rent.

The Neighborhood Reinvestment Corporation offers another

example of social housing modeled on West Germany's successful system of mutual housing associations. Since World War II, mutual housing associations have produced 15 million dwelling units in West Germany. This model uses a mix of renting and owning in which the resident is nominally a part owner, but forgoes the right to speculate on the market value of the dwelling in exchange for secure housing tenure at a below-market rate. The government subsidizes initial construction and reinvests profits in the construction of additional units. Mutual housing analysts support the proposed Community Housing Partnership Act as a politically legitimate approach to mutual housing because it supports community non-profit sponsors. Mutual housing can take the form of collective tenant ownership, low-equity cooperatives and ownership by community-based non-profit organizations.

Under any scheme rejecting the nation's privatized housing system, the federal government would become more involved in providing direct financing for tenants, cooperatives, and non-profit community-based organizations that would both own and manage housing. Experiences with social ownership and mutual housing associations in Britain, Austria, West Germany, Sweden and Cuba serve as models for how the public sector in the United States could more effectively help low-income people with their housing needs.

Social ownership of housing, as well as mutual housing, form the main focus of the socialist agenda for American policy. This agenda includes more than concerns for physical shelter. It stresses equality, social and collective ownership, and self-help on the part of disadvantaged people.[10]

A third approach, proposed by the Mayor of Charleston, South Carolina, Joseph Riley, would retarget some of the $34-billion tax subsidy that now goes to home ownership. This subsidy is regressive, with an estimated 67 percent going to households earning more than $50,000 a year, according to the Congressional Joint Tax Committee. Roughly five million households with earnings over $75,000 a year get higher tax subsidies than the poorest five million households get in direct subsidy for theirs. Under this scheme, the housing tax subsidy on mortgage interest would be viewed as a partial loan, requiring the homeowner to repay it out of eventual capital gains. The proceeds from repayment would subsidize affordable housing for poorer households. This idea offers an equitable use of subsidy dollars and targets them to socially useful and necessary spending. The Joint Tax Committee deleted Riley's plan from its final report. It remains an option for housing policymakers and the Congress to consider.[11] The government currently subsidizes middle- and upper-class housing at about four times the rate that it subsidizes housing for the poor. This amount includes only the mortgage interest reduction. The rate is far higher when one adds the tax subsidy a homeowner receives from not having to pay tax on the rental value capital asset in which he lives, and higher still, counting the tax avoidance of a steadily appreciating capital asset.

As the search for new ideas to move the nation closer to the ideal of housing the poor grows, new actors have joined the effort. Key among these is the American Institute of Architects and the American Institute of Architecture Students, which are working with the Neighborhood Reinvestment Corporation on a special project intended to advance the national dialogue on housing low-income populations. This project, Search for Shelter, plans to identify practical, workable approaches to housing homeless people and keeping them in low-cost housing by applying architects' skills and experience to the problem, marshaling the resources of students and educators and by linking the profession to the community at large. Search for Shelter does not address the causes of homelessness; it is aimed at proposing solutions.

Search for Shelter plans to create a network of models, project evaluations, and case studies of successful small and large housing cooperatives to assist in persuading the federal government to accept responsibility for securing low-cost housing. New housing structures are high on Search for Shelter's agenda, housing that is capable of expansion and regeneration, owned by those interested in providing a decent quality of life and who accept the need for good design in housing — well-functioning, enriching, simple places to live that give dignity to their residents.[12]

European Housing Models

Search for Shelter, Chester Hartman and the Massachusets Institute of Technology-Harvard Joint Center for Housing Studies are all examining prior models of housing cooperatives and mutual housing that have been implemented in Europe for nearly a century, as well as communal and nomadic structuring of communities. Although homelessness is not confined to the United States, the earlier housing systems of key European countries have served to prevent the massive burst of homelessness. European nations, equally affected by economic restructuring, poverty and mental hospital deinstitutionalization, have dealt with homeless people more successfully than the United States because their national housing policies have maintained many welfare-dependent people in housing. This section presents some of the major European housing exemplars as strategies for inventing a non-homeless American future.

Britain

Britain has intervened more directly in the housing market than most capitalist countries. British political leaders from the right to the left agree that the provision of decent housing is a right for which the state must take responsibility. There is also a clear acceptance of government responsibility for the homeless.

Although public housing has been cut back sharply in the last decade, Britain maintains a much larger publicly rented housing stock than the rest of Western Europe — six million units, or almost one-third of the nation's total housing stock. In the past, this resulted in the use of public housing by broader segments of the nation than the poor. Recent attempts to privatize the best of Britain's council housing have reduced the scale of social differentiation in housing and "creamed" the best 10 to 20 percent of housing units from the public sector. This has narrowed the social base of public housing dwellers for the first time, relegating council housing to the poor and near-poor and reducing support for expanding public housing.

The British experience suggests that, rather than try to completely stanch the private housing market, a program of selective takeover by the private sector could satisfy market interests and imperatives and simultaneously provide public housing. An even larger lesson from British housing is that the degree of public support for the principal of state intervention for those in need has limited political attempts to privatize housing. The reality of a public housing sector as large as Britain's cannot be easily reversed. Even in a time of conservative retrenchment, this in itself is an important asset.

Even under the conservative Thatcher government, Britain acknowledged the right to housing for all families and elderly persons who were homeless. The Homeless Persons Act, passed in 1977, stated that local housing authorities have an obligation to "secure that accommodation was available" only for households in priority need. These households were defined as families with dependent children, those over retirement age, pregnant women, and those vulnerable because of serious physical or mental illness or disability. Since the Act came into force, about 500,000 households have been helped. About 20 percent of local authority rentals are to homeless families who are presenting themselves at the rate of 90,000 per year.

Although the Homeless Persons Act excludes single people and couples without children, who make up the largest demand for new housing, it has enabled far more homeless people to secure permanent housing than any system in the United States. Internal problems related to strict limitations and boundaries between local authorities have weakened the Act, forcing families to wait for months in cheap hotels paid for by local authorities until they can be accommodated in public housing. Nonetheless, the Homeless Persons Act guarantees entitlement to housing, and not just shelter.[13]

Sweden

Sweden, with a mixed socialist-capitalist economy, has gone further than any country in the world in insuring that its residents are decently housed. A central element of Sweden's housing

policy has been a tradition of democratically controlled cooperative housing that employs national-level financing at attractive
terms and technical assistance to local tenant-owner associations
created by the national housing cooperative organization.

Sweden's approach is particularly applicable to the United
States in that national policy attempted to develop non-market
housing alternatives along with traditional market approaches.
However, these private business efforts are highly regulated. In
attempting to offer inducements for socialized housing, Sweden
employed strategies that feature interest subsidies, land-use planning and controls on rents and prices. Some of the results of this
mixed approach, based upon a strong national commitment to the
housing sector, have been a virtually slumless society, subsidized
housing that is affordable for all, high-quality housing standards,
an impressive array of planned high-density new suburban communities, and democratic control of housing.

Like Americans, Swedish people retain the ideal of home ownership, so that the socialist housing alternative must be balanced
with individual agendas and interests. Recently, however, as in
England, the move towards privatization and home ownership
has accelerated, but no one in Swedish public life seriously questions the general housing approach that has proven so successful.

For American housing, the time has come to adopt some of the
Swedish approaches because housing conditions can only get
much worse under the present inequitable and wasteful housing
system characterized by high interest rates, speculation and inequitable tax policies. As growing numbers of Americans are ill-
served by the private marketplace, alternatives are essential.

Lessons from the Swedish housing system include the following recommendations:

- A third stream of non-profit housing must be developed to
  end speculation and assure long-term affordability. This
  stream would coexist with private homes and private rentals and would consist of equity-controlled cooperatives
  and community-owned public housing. To reduce construction costs, financing should be made available to local

governments, allowing them to hold the land as a protection against speculation. Management of this housing should be democratically run and administered.

- Housing production financing should be overhauled to reduce production costs and curb speculation. Such financing could take the form of reduced interest subsidies, as in Sweden, or selective credit controls where private lenders subsidize targeted housing by charging higher rates on other loans.

- Tax policy should be revised to steer housing investment productively. Tax shelters used to encourage investment result in speculation. Other financial inducements that discourage speculation would stabilize the production of affordable housing. Similarly, the regressive homeowner deduction could be replaced with a system of tax credits for both renters and homeowners, subject to a ceiling to insure against overconsumption and tax-sheltering.[14]

No recommendation for American adaptation of Swedish welfare models can go a by the caveat that Sweden is a homogeneous society that more readily accepts collective planning strategies. Nevertheless, Swedes aspire individualistically to high achievement goals, and private home ownership features centrally among these values. This strong similarity between the two nations supports the likelihood that Swedish housing policy could work in the United States. At the very least, Sweden's policy can point to a lack of homelessness as a rationale for exhorting several of its key housing policies.

Cuba

Cuba's housing record stands in sharp contrast to the rest of Latin America, where one-third to one-half of the urban population subsists in slums and shantytowns, and the rural population is even more poorly housed. Homelessness and street life in Latin American countries remain a paramount image. But Cuban families enjoy secure housing at low costs in racially integrated neighborhoods. Residents participate in management, construction and maintenance in a national housing system that is socialized and removed from privatism. Housing is produced to meet social needs, not for profit.

The Cuban socialist revolution made housing an important aspect of its central agenda. The 1960 Urban Reform Law was particularly significant because it outlawed private investment in housing for profit and established the goal of free housing as a public service rather than a commodity.

Early measures implementing this goal included halting evictions, reducing rents, ending land speculation and initiating self-help and government construction of housing. New measures were introduced as Cuba's general policies evolved. For housing, this process culminated in the comprehensive 1984 Housing Law promoting home ownership and greater community participation in building and maintaining housing.

Cuba presents an important case study of how housing can be provided to owners and renters in a country where profit has been eliminated as a driving force. Any direct implications for the United States are limited by the fact that Cuba is an underdeveloped country with a strong socialist commitment. Nevertheless, Cuba's government housing output nearly doubled in the first half of the 1980s, in direct contrast to the shrinkage of American public housing. Overall production reached eight units per 1,000 population, which favorably compares with levels in Western Europe. This occurred because Cuba gave housing the highest priority among nonproductive investments, with proportionately fewer resources invested in health and education.

Older urban areas, dilapidated and near decay, were placed under historic preserve, thereby halting indiscriminate demolition and stimulating rehabilitation of main streets and squares. The United Nations, through UNESCO, granted Old Havana "world cultural heritage" status in 1982, rendering it a major international preservation site.

Cuban lessons for America and other capitalist countries are mixed. Housing advocates who lay claim to socialist housing goals in capitalist countries overlook the Cuban lesson that housing problems of undersupply and allocation to targeted groups do not disappear under socialism. They are only handled differently. Conditions of scarcity predominate in Cuba and make justice, equity and fairness in housing complicated. Perhaps the most compelling lesson from the Cuban experience lies in the outcome of housing policy when profit is not the driving force in the economy or the housing sector. The commodity nature of housing and other apparently capitalist forms, such as home ownership, interest and differential land pricing, continue under socialism, but the general context in which they function is different. This leads to a reexamination of whether the issue in capitalist countries is the commodity nature of housing or whether the presence of profit is the prime mover in the economy and the housing market.

The final Cuban lesson is that transition to socialism does not occur neatly and in a linear fashion. The struggles of transition mean that housing policies intersect with broader economic strategies and shares with the rest of the economy both insufficient resources to meet social needs and the experience of uneven development of resources, institutions and public consciousness. Given these limits, the degree to which Cuba has managed its housing problems is an inspiration to other developing countries and a challenge to capitalist industrialized countries to make better and more equitable use of their resources for housing.[15]

The Relationship Between Housing and Homelessness

A decisive issue is whether homelessness should be explained as a situation confined to problem populations, or as a manifestation of broader systemic difficulties in the nation. Homelessness on the scale that we confront today clearly reveals several deficiencies in the structures available to meet people's basic needs. Prominent among these is the present inability of the United States to provide affordable and decent housing. Although housing is not the only contributor to homelessness, it ranks high along with economic restructuring, poverty and an under-resourced mental health system.

To underscore the prominence of housing as an antecedent of homelessness, one has only to look back to the postwar period when there was little or no homelessness as we now know it. What did exist was confined to the smaller Skid Rows. But during that postwar period, poverty and hunger were more prevalent and welfare benefits were lower than today. Ex-mental patients presented no problems because they could be housed. Unemployment was high, but could be contained within job-training and other manpower programs. Rising welfare rolls were considered manageable through welfare reform, while welfare recipients could still find housing and pay their rent. Once the supply of affordable low-cost housing became depleted, unemployment, poverty, inadequate public assistance and deinstitutionalization consigned people to homelessness. This suggests that housing is the critical issue for preventing homelessness. The solution is not that simple. Homelessness has multiple causes. In the absence of housing, marginal living circumstances that were once palatable become desperate. The final demise of America's reluctant welfare system is manifested in the inability to secure housing.[16]

PART III

THE MENTAL HEALTH SYSTEM

Chapter 11

Mental Illness and the Homeless

A review of surveys conducted across the nation indicates that approximately one-third of homeless people in most communities are mentally ill.[1] This figure does not diminish the serious plight of the mentally disabled homeless who are the most vulnerable and pitiful homeless people. But it does caution those who address the problem of homelessness against assuming that homelessness is essentially a mental health problem. If we were to house all mentally ill homeless people, two-thirds of the homeless would remain in the streets and shelters.

It is important to note that the United States is the only nation in the world that attributes homelessness to mental illness. All other countries view homelessness as the inevitable result of a reduced housing supply and restructured economy. As homelessness has grown in England, particularly among Pakistani and West Indian immigrants, the British have added an explanation of recent homelessness, domestic violence and abuse. This has resulted in increased service for battered women, but even these services are in the form of shelters rather than mental health services.

The popular notion that the deinstitutionalization movement of the 1960s was a well-intended social policy failure that resulted in homelessness does not entirely hold up under the scrutiny of research, history or anecdotal evidence. The majority of today's chronic mentally ill population are too young to have been placed in the former state mental hospitals, so they never experienced deinstitutionalization. One can claim, on the other hand, that they would be in institutions if they were available today.

Jim Baumohl and Steven Segal have noted that today's generation of chronic mentally ill is comprised of people who are less accepting of institutional care, and who would exercise their strong patients' rights protections against commitment. The chronic mentally ill people of the 1980s have grown up in a era of strong patients' rights, protections against involuntary commitment and psychoactive medication.[2] These factors have stimulated a greater sense of independence and demand for rights, as well as longer periods of stability under medication. This assertiveness of much of the contemporary mentally ill homeless population indicates that they would tend to resist institutionalization.

Most of today's chronic mental patients live with their families or in sheltered living facilities, such as board-and-care homes. Some live in SROs or other hotels. Others move in and out of psychiatric hospitals and some are homeless continuously. While a minority of the chronic mentally disabled are actually homeless at any one time, their numbers are large and growing, and they do represent a tragic social problem.[3] Nevertheless, deinstitutionalization is only a proximate antecedent of homelessness, and it clearly is not synonymous with homelessness.

The more precise link between homelessness and deinstitutionalization is one whereby mentally ill people who are vulnerable and unstable lose their housing through one crisis or another. Rather than go directly to an institution, they find themselves on the streets and are less able to cope with their problems than people with greater emotional and financial resources. The lack of institutions, along with other needed facilities and services, places them at risk and justifies a consideration of deinstitutionalization as a proximate antecedent of homelessness.[4]

A second important explanation of the links between mental illness and homelessness lies in the condition of homelessness itself. Life in the streets, shelters, SROs and board-and-care homes is precarious, ominous and frequently dangerous. Healthy people become mentally disabled because of their homeless condition. Compelled to search for food, shelter, menial jobs and even enough money to use a telephone, people lose their time orientation, reality perception, and their family or social connections. Any one of these conditions, or any combination, can lead to severe mental deterioration.

Critics who link deinstitutionalization to homelessness must not overlook the fact that many mentally disabled people lost their most stable resource when they were declared ineligible for Social Security Disability Insurance benefits. This program, a mainstay in the support system of mentally ill people, represented as serious a loss as deinstitutionalization 20 years earlier. For many, the loss of disability benefits made the difference in their ability to pay for housing and reduced them to street life.

Far more important in its impact on the homeless population has been the failure to implement the goals of the community mental health movement and legislation. Intended to establish 2,000 community mental health facilities throughout the United States, implementation of the Community Mental Health Centers Act of 1963 resulted in a mere 750 community facilities. This has meant inadequate and, more frequently, inaccessible care for those who were initially let out of state hospitals, as well as today's generation of mentally ill people.[5]

In the absence of institutions, community care facilities, housing and money, it is not surprising that many mentally disabled people end up in the streets, or in shelters. Nor is it surprising that shelters are poorly equipped to solve even the basic problems of the homeless mentally ill. This is no indictment of the shelter system because shelters are not designed for mentally ill people. They offer what they claim: food, clothing and a bed — "three hots and a cot." But the presence of the mentally ill in shelters further attests to the inappropriateness of shelter as a response to homelessness.

Ellen Bassuk claims that shelters are appropriate solutions for people who are temporarily unemployed, or victims of natural disasters. The mentally disabled homeless need a range of supports to reintegrate them into society. For many homeless mentally ill, the goal of reintegration is unattainable because they will never be able to live independently. Prevention of homelessness for these people requires continuing support and supervised living facilities.[6]

It is also notable that most shelters turn away mentally ill homeless people because they may be unmanageable in environments that are characteristically volatile without having mentally ill residents to aggravate the situation. As shelters have become increasingly overcrowded with the proliferation of homelessness, they have been forced to turn away people seeking their services. In an atmosphere of scarcity, it is small wonder that the mentally ill would be the first to be rejected.

To be sure, recognition of the problems of the homeless mentally disabled has become quite evident. Model small-scale demonstration programs and larger comprehensive public systems abound. Some homeless advocates have publicly complained that disproportionate resources have been allocated to the mentally ill homeless population at the expense of those who are more able-bodied, thus following the "poor law" tradition of punishing the able-bodied and serving the disabled, or truly needy, in the social policy context of the 1980s.

While this represents an extreme position, it exemplifies the complexity of homelessness and the need to address the multiple problems of the heterogeneous population living in this condition. In a political and economic environment of scarcity, homeless advocates and service providers find themselves too frequently politically divisive in their search for resources. They are also compelled to compete for limited resources to treat symptoms when they would prefer to focus on the underlying causes or antecedents of homelessness.

The Problems and Needs of
the Homeless Mentally Disabled

A federally supported research project was conducted in 1983-84 by: the New York State Psychiatric Institute, the Ohio Department of Mental Health, the New York City Office of Human Development, the Massachusetts Department of Mental Health, the Los Angeles County Department of Mental Health, the Wisconsin Office of Mental Health, the Michigan Department of Mental Health, St. Elizabeth's Hospital in Washington, D.C., and the Massachusetts Association for Mental Health. The purpose of this broad-based program was to identify the service needs of the homeless mentally ill and analyze barriers to their care.

Study participants were in agreement about the following items concerning the homeless mentally disabled:

- Within the clusters of the homeless across the country, substantial numbers exhibit psychopathology.

- The homeless mentally ill population has been increasing, with a heavy concentration of young adults who are at risk of chronic mental illness. Some of this problem results from the failure of the mental health system to adequately meet the needs of the chronic mentally ill.

- No known characteristic can be applied to the homeless mentally ill, except for their homelessness. This means that descriptions of the homeless mentally ill should be expressed in central tendencies and ranges.

- Most notable of the diagnostic groups in which the homeless mentally fall are schizophrenia, affective disorders, personality disorders and substance abuse. The latter prevails more as a secondary diagnosis or a complicating condition.

- Many homeless mentally disabled people have no histories of hospitalization, or any contact with the mental health system.

- Substantial numbers exhibit degrees of mobility and transiency, but they frequently travel along established routes.

- Many homeless mentally ill people experience a set of conditions that warrant special attention. Included among these are poverty, stressed social networks, revolving-door utilization of mental health services, revolving-door involvement in the criminal justice system, high prevalence of physical illness, and a high degree of resistance to traditional treatment.

- The diversity of this population indicates the need for a wide variety of service interventions.

- A substantial number of the homeless mentally ill who could benefit from existing services experience geographic, psychological, economic and regulatory barriers to such care.

- Homeless individuals, including those who are mentally ill, often share subcultures that are unknown to mental health workers and researchers. These differences demand special attention and sensitivity.

- Effective personnel who work with the homeless share certain personal and professional characteristics. They are knowledgeable about the population, are non-judgmental, empathic and optimistic, and capable of adapting to the special circumstances of the homeless mentally ill.[7]

The most recent data about this population are more precise in terms of numbers and specific diagnostic categories. The Rand Corporation just completed an evaluation of the state of California's Homeless Mentally Disabled Program. This program operates in 58 counties, offering a wide range of services from basic needs to reintegration. The state has allocated $20 million annually to the program under California's Mental Health Services Act of 1985. This is one of the first statewide programs directed specifically to the needs of this population. It emphasizes outreach to the homeless mentally disordered (HMD) and to those at risk of becoming HMD, and coordination of care among community service agencies.

The Rand study, intended to determine the accountability of the funds and to assess the effectiveness of the program, identified the following demographic and mental disorder characteristics of persons served: Approximately 30 percent of the homeless population studied have severe mental disorders, e.g., schizophrenia, bipolar affective disorder, and major depression. A range of 54 to 93 percent of the homeless with severe mental disorder also have a history of alcohol or drug abuse and addiction. Substance abuse rates are the same for the non-mentally ill homeless population. Both the mentally disabled homeless and all other homeless people are predominantly male, unmarried and under 45, and about one in five has served in the armed forces. Both groups share similar subsistence patterns. They sleep mostly in shelters or outdoors, and they get their food from soup kitchens.

Among the differences between the two homeless groups, the most prominent is that severely mentally disordered homeless people are likely to be women. They tend to be functionally disabled and to have greater difficulty getting enough to eat and accomplishing even the simplest of tasks. They perceive themselves as being in poorer health and are less likely to be married or working.

More mentally disabled homeless people are likely to be receiving benefits and using mental health services than other homeless, but they are nevertheless underserved. One in ten receives Social Security Disability Insurance; fewer than one in four receive Medi-Cal or Medicare. Only one in three uses outpatient services or medications for mental health or substance abuse problems. Over half had received help from a program or a clinic in the last month of the study. This help was typically limited to shelter, food and clothing.[8]

Leona Bachrach cautions that there is an implicit risk in relying upon most research on the homeless because it is conducted in an atmosphere of urgency, and findings may be interpreted uncritically. Several conceptual issues remain unresolved in research projects focused on the homeless mentally ill. Foremost among these is the absence of a universally accepted definition or understanding of homeless mentally ill people. This population is generally viewed as people who are both severely mentally disabled and homeless. However, each of these terms is controversial and ambiguous.

Although there has been some effort to standardize a definition of chronic mental illness referring to persons with major mental disorders whose illnesses are severe, persistent, and prevent social and vocational functioning, precise clarity is still lacking. For research and program design purposes the precise indicators are the severity and persistence of illness and dysfunction.[9]

This definitional question is further complicated by differing and contrasting approaches to understanding the homeless mentally ill. One approach views the prevalence, or correlates, of mental illness among the homeless, while another regards the incidence of homelessness among the mentally ill. This is not merely a matter of semantics. There are contrasting approaches that spell the difference in the kinds of research questions raised and investigated, case-finding, research protocols and, ultimately, in determining service priorities. For example, policymaking that emanates from determination of mental illness among the homeless will be concerned with strategies for engaging the mentally ill in the mental health service delivery system. In contrast, planning derived from determination of homelessness among people who are chronically mentally ill would be more likely to focus on cracks, or gaps, in the mental health system through which the mentally ill fall, e.g., perfunctory discharge planning or incomplete compliance planning and case management.

One final caution against stereotyping is essential for understanding the mentally ill homeless population and its service needs. These people remain highly mobile and diverse, so that the findings and descriptions of the homeless mentally ill in one community or one research project are not easily generalizable to other settings. Each community, or catchment area, must specifically study its own population and formulate strategies and interventions accordingly. Model programs from elsewhere may be useful, but they will most likely need to be adjusted to different circumstances. National policies also require a basis in local conditions. This is not a major problem at the present time because the structure of the mental health delivery system is highly decentralized from central to local government.

The Needs of the Homeless Mentally Ill

Despite the plethora of programs recently developed to serve the homeless mentally ill, few of them meet the needs of the entire population. Some also serve the mentally ill who are not homeless, thus compounding the plight of all mentally ill people. The national average state expenditure for mental health is $52 per person annually, meaning that all are underserved by the mental health system. This apparent reluctance to serve the mentally ill in general, contributes to homelessness among the mentally ill who only have shelters as a last resort when the mental health system either fails them or is inaccessible.[10]

A central concern of this book is with prevention of homelessness among the chronically mentally disabled. Separate areas of inquiry in research and literature deal with concepts of mental illness prevention. The claims and evidence that support the principles of preventive psychiatry have great merit and constitute an important direction for mental health service delivery. However, explorations in this direction would both obscure and digress from this book's principle focus on prevention of homelessness.[11]

Ball and Havassy conducted one of the few surveys of self-identified homeless recidivists in their effort to better understand the underuse of community mental health services and repeated use of hospital-based psychiatric services. The survey was conducted in 1983-84 in San Francisco. Respondents were asked to identify the most important issues they faced or problems they had.

The data show that the respondents were primarily concerned with a lack of material resources, opportunities for employment, privacy, and personal and physical protection. Concerns about social, medical or psychological care were secondary. The data clearly point to a mismatch between the kinds of services that community mental health agencies typically provide and the kinds of services the homeless population studied felt they needed. In addition, many respondents identified barriers to using relevant available services. Even those with stronger adaptive capacities cited barriers that include the high level of organization and tenacity needed to navigate through the geographically dispersed sources of food, shelter and government assistance, citing long lines, crowds fighting for shelter beds, and sitting through mandatory sermons before gaining entry to mission shelters.

The most keenly and frequently expressed need of the mental health consumers in this survey was housing. This supports those who assert and believe that permanent and affordable housing and linkage with financial resources or other income sources are as high among the homeless mentally ill as they are among the general homeless population.[12]

Ball and Havassy's data support the important principle that interventions must begin with the patient/client's perception of his or her situation and immediate needs. This implies that meeting the basic survival needs of the homeless mentally ill would increase the likelihood that they would use continuing care in the community. Such basic bottom-line assistance might also help overcome the resistance and skepticism with which homeless people regard public and private service agencies.

The importance of housing for the chronically ill homeless is corroborated by a one-year study, completed in 1987, of 49 homeless chronic mentally ill patients. One group of patients was placed in an experimental residential treatment program following discharge, and the other group received standard post-discharge care.

The study demonstrated that it is feasible to place discharged hospital patients in a residential setting. All who were offered this option accepted it initially and, at the end of one year, 69 percent of the subjects were still permanently housed. The study also clearly showed that residential care can improve the quality of a patient's life. Compared with the control group, the subjects in the residential facility spent more nights in adequate shelter, fewer nights in hospitals or homeless, and were generally satisfied with their living arrangements.[13]

The implications of this important, although small and exploratory, study are that mental health services must be secure, dignified and humane, and that patients must percieve them as responsive to their needs. For mentally ill homeless people who are, at best, fragile individuals, a decent residential facility offers a substantial improvement over a shelter which is often overcrowded and where residents frequently prey upon each other.

The Rand Corporation study of California's homeless mentally disordered programs identified a series of needs of the HMD population and suggested that the program is not fully meeting the needs of all HMD.

More than one in three respondents reported that they do not get enough to eat. Over half must sleep outdoors at least once a month. More than two out of three have a history of drug and alcohol abuse. Nearly half rated themselves as in poor or fair physical condition. Fewer than two out of five eligible recipients received Supplemental Security Income or state welfare income. Only one out of five participated in the state Medi-Cal or Medicare program. Only one out of three had outpatient visits for mental health or substance-abuse reasons during the one-year study.

Rand researchers call attention to the problem that these needs are unmet in spite of the fact that the state program is operating at full capacity. One major flaw in the HMD program is that it concentrates primarily on those who are currently homeless, rather than the at-risk, or homeless-vulnerable population.

A majority of the HMD are also substance abusers, referred to as dual-diagnosed clients. HMD staff reported that they are unable to effectively treat this population of dual-diagnosed clients because of their inexperience in dealing with the program and the lack of access to substance-abuse treatment programs. The severely mentally disabled who also use drugs or alcohol are, therefore, extremely difficult to treat.

A further complication in treating dual-diagnosed homeless clients lies in the HMD legislation which prohibits using funds for serving substance abusers unless it is a secondary diagnosis, and provides no funds for actually treating substance abuse. Relationships between county mental health facilities and substance-abuse treatment centers are weakened by general capacity limitations and uncooperative institutional relationships. The net result is that neither mental health treatment programs nor substance-abuse treatment programs are presently equipped to treat dual-diagnosed clients. A preventive approach to inventing a non-homeless world for mentally ill people must address this wide gap in the service delivery system.

The underserved group who are at risk of homelessness, those living in board-and-care homes who may be on the verge of eviction, or those living independently but vulnerable to recertification requirements for entitlement benefits, require monitoring through regular contact with these people or those who live around them. This is a difficult procedure, and is frequently an impossible one. New information technologies offer a partial solution. With appropriate procedures to protect privacy and confidentiality, on-line information exchanges about clients' service needs, medications, resources and living arrangements could enable a case manager to track clients and intervene if circumstances warrant.[14] A simple marker on an individual's welfare or Social Security file could indicate that he or she is mentally disabled. If that person failed to appear for recertification, case managers in the homeless program could be notified to intervene.

Case management has proven to be an indispensable approach to work with chronic mentally ill patients, homeless or not. However, for too many planners and practitioners, it is the current panacea that is expected to accomplish the entire job.[15] Because many case managers are frequently uncertain of their roles and the organizational supports for their activities, agencies must agree upon a common definition of the case management function. For purposes associated with homeless and mentally ill people, case management must be broadly defined as "the coordination of services to ensure that clients' needs are met as effectively as possible, given the available resources. Steps in case management include assessment of needs, development of service plans, and the monitoring and evaluation of service delivery." [16] Case management uses and maximizes the complex roles that arise from actions designed to coordinate services.

Intrinsic to this definition of case management is the necessity to employ case advocacy measures, because homelessness among the mentally ill frequently means helplessness. Case advocacy implies that direct service workers advocate on behalf of their clients and intervene in the procurement of services.

Case management is most appropriate in work with chronically ill homeless people who present the most unwieldy problems to practitioners. They tend to be the most isolated of homeless people, and may no longer be capable of independent living.

The Chicago Coalition for the Homeless identified the following problems as the most serious among homeless individuals:[17]

Table 1 - Biggest Problem

Financial	23%	No problems	4%
Emotional	20	General (Everything, etc.)	3
Shelter/Food/Clothing	15	Weather	3
Other street people	10	Showers	3
Police	7	Substance abuse	2
Crime/ No security	5	Other	5

Data from the Homeless Youth Project in Los Angeles indicated a similarly wide range of needs, but the data are instructive because they document the categories of services provided, as well as requested and identified. This project operated for two years, from 1983 to 1985. (See Table 2)

This multiplicity of problems and needed services strongly supports the conclusion that case managers are indispensable to the proper functioning of efforts to support homeless people. Without proper service coordination and aggressive case advocacy as basic as standing in the seemingly endless lines at the general welfare office with people who fear service agencies or are ignorant about their rules, even the most innovative program will falter.

In addition to case management services to coordinate a continuum of care, nearly every homeless person experiences situational problems that are crises. No program can effectively function unless it includes provision for crisis intervention. Many people who are not mentally ill or substance abusers come to agencies needing immediate help to overcome situational emotional distress. For these people, time-limited crisis therapy and intervention may be all that is needed. Others who are mentally disabled require crisis intervention before any longer-term planning for care takes place. Careful diagnosis, consultation, screening and referral are critical tasks in crisis intervention. They must form the core activity of crisis intervention and planning for long-term treatment of mentally disabled homeless people.

Table 2 - Initial Data Summary[18]

WHAT SERVICES DID CLIENTS INITIALLY REQUEST?

Shelter	102	50%	Need I.D.	73	36%
Medical Care	44	22	Drug/ Alcohol Problem	6	3
Job Training/ Placement	174	86	Food	64	32
School	98	48	Clothing	54	27
Family Counseling	10	5	Questions About Sex	7	3
Individual Counseling	38	19	Legal Help	11	5
			Protection From Danger	6	3

SERVICES PROVIDED

Shelter:		**Type of Counseling:**	
Shelter Days at YMCA	834	Mostly Task-Oriented	71
Number of Shelter Clients	34	Mixed	29
Average Stay	25 days	Mostly Psychodynamic	15
Job Assistance:		Foster Family Placements	4
Job Counseling	440 Sessions	Total Placement Days	118
# of Clients Counseled	155	**Independent**	
Placements Made	41	**Living Assistance:**	
Counseling - Individual:		# of Sessions	113
# of Sessions	647	**Concrete Services:**	
# of Clients	118	Birth Certificates	17
Average # of Sessions	5.5	Bus Coupons	55
Counseling - Family:		Clothing	55
# of Sessions	52	Food	85
# of Clients	18	Household Items	30
Average # of Sessions	3	I.D.	15
		Transportation	47
		Financial Assistance	32
		Court Appearances	6

Those who work with the HMD report a high rate of non-compliance with established treatment plans. Initial resistance to seeking help explains much of such non-compliance. George Wolkon conducted a variety of studies in the past five years that sought an explanation for the high rate of non-compliance in mental health continuous-care plans. His studies showed that the clients who tend to continue with care possess the high motivation level for improvement and change characterized by the YAVIS (young, attractive, verbal, intelligent, successful) client. Most homeless mentally ill patients do not fit this description.[19]

Wolkon suggests that attempts to enhance compliance and attract resistant psychiatric patients utilize patient-linking techniques; in particular, assertive outreach. The outreach model of care identifies people who appear to need assistance and introduces and connects them to appropriate resources. Such a program is typically structured around community systems in which the social agency responsible for outreach efforts negotiates the system for the client, develops and cultivates a service network, and informs outreach workers of existing services, as well as any changes in services. Most outreach programs employ teams of workers that frequently include social workers and paraprofessionals. The social worker's knowledge of diagnosis, engaging people and assessing their needs, combined with a broad knowledge of community resources is vital to outreach efforts.[20]

A small but growing group of self-help and consumer-run programs are emerging to serve the homeless mentally ill population. Based upon the general principles of mutual aid and self-help, these mental patients' groups have demonstrated an ability to attract people who have refused treatment in the past. The principle feature of mental patients' groups is that they perceive their responsibility as the protector of patients' rights. They emphasize that people who refuse treatment will not be forced to accept it, and they rely upon peer support instead of forced treatment.

A final and compelling crisis in the system of care for all mentally ill people, and homeless mentally ill in particular, is the lack of hospital beds for emergency and long-term care. Cities and counties are reporting that hospital emergency rooms are overburdened, with some patients waiting for seemingly endless periods to be admitted after sleeping on chairs, being strapped to stretchers, or, in the case of prisoners, being handcuffed to wheelchairs. Patients brought into hospital emergency wards on 24-hour involuntary holds for diagnosis and stabilization frequently cannot be seen for more than 24 hours.

Overcrowding in all mental health facilities results in backups throughout the system. This poses the most serious problem for the homeless mentally ill population, who are regarded as the most difficult clients to work with. Dr. Harold Searles, Administrator of Mental Health for Philadelphia, best described the problems of these people by asserting the following:

> They refuse ordinary services; they've been hospitalized and medicated against their will, suffered all sorts of physical abuse, they dread shelters — they are the people the traditional mental health system has failed.[21]

Many mental health workers familiar with the long-term care facilities available for mental patients claim that, although there is a wide range of facilities, they are not yet able to provide the kind of care and handle the numbers that are needed for the homeless mentally ill. Some mental health practitioners estimate that at least 60 percent of the homeless mentally ill need long-term care.

Recommendations for
Mental Health Intervention for the HMD

Mental health intervention, designed to solve the problems and meet the needs of the homeless mentally disabled, could be most effectively organized in three basic phases:

The first phase, the emergency phase, demands that help be given under acute circumstances to the homeless mentally ill through mental health professionals working in shelter programs and other homeless organizations on a daily urgent-care basis.

The second intervention phase provides some type of short-term stabilization for the homeless mentally ill individual. This would require the establishment of a number of stabilization centers offering a combined multiphasic approach, stabilizing the individual's mental and physical health problems and needed social services. These stabilization centers would offer specialized housing to the homeless mentally ill individual for a one- to three-week period working in tandem with other agencies for an established plan of long-term care. In the third intervention phase, the key task is the provision of long-range assistance. It is essential to plan for long-range assistance, not only for treatment of chronic mental illness, but also for community and social supports. Homeless mentally ill people also need long-range housing and a feeling of belonging in a safe and caring community. Finally, they need vocational rehabilitation as an essential component of stabilization.[22]

This paradigm of continuous care can only succeed if it incorporates the significant treatment approaches of case management, advocacy, outreach and self-help.

The following chapters in this section focus on comprehensive and preventive care program models for the mentally ill in general, and the homeless in particular, including case management, outreach programs and consumer-run programs. Chapter 16 reviews current proposals to change the involuntary commitment laws that are based on the assumption that relaxed commitment laws will offer a viable strategy for treating those homeless mentally ill individuals who either refuse care or do not comply with treatment plans.

One final note of caution must be sounded before attempting to demonstrate that any approaches to care and practice are acceptable paradigms of treatment for chronic mentally ill people. Although crisis intervention, case management, advocacy, outreach, and appropriate facilities provide models for practice with chronic mentally ill people, the best mental health practitioners must be in a position to call upon their personal adroitness and energy. The overwhelming lack of resources, coupled with the magnitude of problems experienced by all homeless people, requires workers to coax food and clothing from voluntary and religious organizations. Young people, students and more experienced volunteers, social workers, nurses, and doctors must be encouraged to work in clinics that treat the mentally disabled.

These workers also need to be experienced and determined to negotiate the complex maze of public welfare offices, ongoing ordinances, police emergency units, and the mental health system.

Mental health practice remains a combination of art and science in spite of the burgeoning theoretical knowledge about practice. People who work with the chronic and potentially homeless mentally ill population may be forced to rely equally on art as well as science in the application of ingenuity to meet the many needs of a growing population where resources are few. As noted earlier, personnel who work effectively with the chronic and homeless mentally ill are skilled in adapting their professional expertise to the special circumstances of this special population.[23]

Chapter 12

Programming for the Homeless Mentally Ill

By now most states and local governments have established some form of comprehensive mental health system for the homeless mentally ill. Not all are as large and well-funded as the Homeless Mentally Disabled program in California, but they all feature certain common elements. In addition to these programs, the National Institute of Mental Health Community Support Program and the Program for the Homeless Mentally Ill have set up service systems, research and demonstration projects around the United States. This cluster of programs, services and research data provides the basis for formulating a paradigm of a preventive community-based comprehensive mental health service system for the homeless mentally ill population.

This preventive paradigm is also based upon a vision of a mental health service system that is centered around the stated needs and preferences of primary consumers, and that promotes empowerment through involvement by primary consumers in all aspects of planning and providing services.

In defining and implementing the ideal system, states and local communities would use varying service system configurations and organizing structures, depending upon geographic, political, socio-economic, racial and ethnic minority factors. In rural areas, for example, it may not be financially possible to develop a comprehensive system in each locality, and alternatives such as shared services and transportation arrangements may need to be considered.

Central to all current policy strategies directed at improving the care of chronically mentally ill people is the goal of better service coordination and integration, in the belief that the flaw in existing services is their lack of organization as a coherent system that addresses patients' needs in an effective and efficient manner. This translates into a model of care referred to by such terms as "case management," "continuous care teams" or "comprehensive case management teams."

Four new policy strategies for promoting better services for the chronic mentally ill have emerged and are being tested in different parts of the country: 1) continuous care teams, 2) integrated entitlement programs, 3) local mental health authorities, and 4) capitation payment systems. All four share the common vision of promoting optimal coordination and integration of services for patients, but differ on their levels of intervention for achieving this goal. The success of any of these interventions depends not only upon a system's capacity to regulate services, but to ensure that presumed incentives to deliver cost-effective services filter down to well-trained and motivated front-line staff.

No matter how states and communities organize service systems, the services and opportunities described in this chapter should be accessible, available, and acceptable to all adults with severe disabling mental illness in accordance with the principles enumerated below.

Service System Principles

The following are guiding principles for the provision of comprehensive services with severe disabling mental illness. These principles apply to the general population of severely impaired people as well as to the homeless mentally ill. They are based upon a concept of care that would provide needed services for mentally ill people and, in so doing, would prevent them from becoming homeless.

Services should be consumer-centered. They should be based upon the needs of the client rather than the needs of the system or the needs of providers. For example, highly structured environments or services provided only at a program site may be easier for providers to manage and control, but may be less effective in meeting client need. This is particularly important to acknowledge in designing services for homeless consumers.

Services should empower clients. They should incorporate consumer self-help approaches and be provided in a manner that promotes clients' retaining the fullest possible control over their lives. At the treatment level, to the extent possible, clients should set their own goals and decide what services they will receive. At the services level, clients should be active in planning and policy-making decisions and be included on all relevant committees, boards and councils.

Services should be racially and culturally appropriate. Services for members of racial and ethnic minority groups, women, gay men and lesbian women, children and youth, and the elderly should be available, accessible and acceptable. Strategies to assure provision of such appropriate services include use of culturally appropriate needs-assessment tools, relevant quality-assurance indicators, alternative service-delivery models, neighborhood systems, adequate representation on boards and committees, cross-cultural training for staff, and use of indigenous workers and bilingual staff with cultural sensitivities.

Services should be flexible. They should be available whenever and for as long as needed and should be provided in a variety of ways, with individuals able to choose services and to move in and out of the system as needs vary. Most individuals with severe disabling mental illness do not progress in a linear fashion, and many will not wish to attend the same kind of program.

Services should focus on strengths. Services should be built on the assets and strengths of clients to help them maintain a sense of identity, dignity and self-esteem. This will discourage clients from adopting a sick role, and service systems from developing an environment organized around permanent illness with lowered expectations and the need for separateness and specialized facilities.

Services should be normalized and incorporate natural supports. They should be offered in the least restrictive, most natural setting possible. Clients should be encouraged to use the natural supports in the community and integrate, to the greatest extent possible, into the normal living, working, learning and leisuretime activities in the community.

Services should meet special needs. Services should be adapted to meet the special needs of sub-groups of the severely mentally ill, such as elderly individuals in the community or institutions, mentally ill people with hearing impairments, mental retardation or substance-abuse problems, and individuals who are homeless or reside inappropriately in the correctional system.

Systems should be accountable. Service systems should be accountable to the users of the services and monitored by the state to assure quality of care and continued relevance to the service area and client needs. Primary consumers and families should be involved in planning, implementing and evaluating programs.

Services should be coordinated. In order to develop systems of care, services should be coordinated through mandates or written agreements that require ongoing communication and linkages between levels of government and agencies. In order to be effective, coordination should occur at the community, program and state levels. According to Public Law 99-660, the State Comprehensive Mental Health Plan Act of 1986, state mental health plans must describe how services will be coordinated within the state.[1] Exhibit 1 provides additional detail on the general characteristics of coordinated systems.

Exhibit 1. Characteristics of Coordinated Systems

Characteristics at the program level include:

- A single point of contact which is usually a manager or, to the extent possible, a team of individuals who work with the client immediately upon entering the system and are available to assist the client regardless of the services or settings involved.

- Client needs assessments conducted in a comprehensive manner to develop one integrated, individualized service plan for each client, with one set of rehabilitation goals.

- A written discharge plan for each person prior to discharge from inpatient care, which is developed in conjunction with the community case manager, client, and with the family, where authorized by the client.

- Discharge arrangements, such as for housing and other supportive services in the community, begun early in an individual's stay, so that community services are available when the person is ready for discharge.

Characteristics at the community level include:

- A single core service entity with a broad perspective and legitimacy to convene other agencies (most appropriately a public agency or local unit of government with multi-jurisdictional public authority) that is responsible for assuring the delivery and coordination of all services and opportunities for all clients in a geographically or politically defined area.

- Coordination among the various community agencies providing services to individuals with severe disabling mental illness, including hospitals, community programs, substance-abuse agencies, Social Security offices, housing authorities, vocational rehabilitation agencies, the educational system, social service departments, the Veterans Administration and the correctional system. Coordination is formalized through legislative mandates or written agreements.

- Linkages with natural support systems and informal helping networks, such as churches, businesses and park recreation activities, to promote use of these normalizing settings.

Characteristics at the state level include:

- Leadership and advocacy to assure that each state plan (e.g., Medicaid, housing, vocational rehabilitation, SSI) addresses the comprehensive needs of the population.

Exhibit 1. Characteristics of Coordinated Systems (Continued)

- The existence of a unit or individual(s) responsible for coordinating issues involving the population, identifying barriers to the provision of services, and engaging in interagency collaboration.

- Collaboration with other state-level human service agencies to sensitize them to the needs of the population, to clarify roles and responsibilities, and to develop interagency agreements that will facilitate cooperation at sub-state levels.

- Mechanisms for monitoring the performance of sub-state authorities in order to identify barriers that require state-level interventions.

- Ongoing communication between the executive and the legislative branches

- Contractual agreements between mental health and other state agencies such as Medicaid, vocational rehabilitation, and housing or joint funding, to maximize mainstream resources available for services for the priority population, planning and monitoring services, and other regulatory activities.

Although many of these principles clearly do not apply to those who are homeless and mentally ill, it is essential to bear in mind the fact that most people who are homeless originally came from homes. If the principles stated above were incorporated in all comprehensive mental health systems, many mentally ill people could remain in their homes. This is the quintessential meaning of a paradigm of prevention.

Service System Components

A comprehensive system provides the full range of outreach housing, treatment, life- and social-support rehabilitation, crisis response, protection, and advocacy services needed by adults with severe disabling mental illness. Most of the services can be provided or arranged for in a variety of ways such as through natural supports, mental health agencies, general hospitals, family members, consumer self-help approaches, or through the use of recovering consumers as paid or volunteer staff.

Comprehensive services are organized into a system of care

through case management at the program level and a coordinating agency at the community level. The coordinating agency could be any of the agencies providing services, such as a community mental health center, a local government unit or authority, or a super-agency that has only coordinating and oversight responsibilities. Exhibit 2 is a graphic representation of a client-centered, comprehensive coordinated mental health system that includes the following service components:

Client identification and outreach - Because many individuals with severe disabling mental illness will not seek help, there should be a mechanism to locate clients, regardless of where they live, and to inform them of available services. There should also be individualized outreach programs provided to persons who decline to attend a formal program or treatment center, or who are unable to do so; e.g., elderly people in board-and-care homes, homeless people or individuals in foster family care homes.

Included in client identification and outreach services, there should be plans for crisis stabilization, medication checks, assistance in meeting basic needs, skills training, and referrals to appropriate health or welfare agencies. In addition, particularly in rural areas, services should include transportation assistance to help individuals access needed care.

Effective outreach is particularly critical for persons who are mentally ill and homeless. These individuals are among the least able to find agencies, programs or resources. Outreach should occur in non-traditional in-vivo settings, such as soup kitchens or shelters, drop-in centers or on the streets, and must be done in non-threatening ways for extended periods of time.

Mental health treatment - Mental health treatment and clinical services should be available that include diagnostic evaluation by medical personnel; supportive counseling and psychotherapeutic treatment; medication and management services, including prescriptions, assurances that needed medications are available and are carefully monitored to assure maximal therapeutic effectiveness, minimal dosage and adverse side effects, and client and family education on the nature of the side effects; and programs that accept and provide services for persons with mental illness and substance-abuse problems, including services provided to the general population of severely mentally ill adults, but also detoxification and other drug and alcohol abuse treatments.

Crisis response services - Ongoing support and contact with the system, along with client, family and staff education and training, can prevent the onset of many crises. Because of the episodic nature of the illness, however, there will be instances that require acute care and quick-response crisis-stabilization services. These should enable the client, family members and others to cope with the emergency while maintaining the client's status as a functioning community member to the greatest extent possible.

The services should be available on a 24-hour basis and be known to providers, families, clients and the community. Immediate psychiatric consultation should be available for rapid evaluation, diagnosis and chemotherapeutic interventions as indicated. They should include: a 24-hour hotline; walk-in crisis and triage services to identify clients most in need of immediate treatment; mobile outreach approaches for dealing with in-home crises; community crisis residential beds for temporary respite care outside the normal residential environment when needed; and a small number of inpatient beds in a protective environment for crises that cannot be handled in other community support services, which could be in a psychiatric unit of a general or community hospital, or in a nearby state hospital.

Health and dental care - Because severely mentally ill people have significantly higher rates of physical illness, they should have access to general health care and to dental services.

Housing - There should be permanent affordable, acceptable housing available for the majority of clients in the normal housing arrangements typically used in the community. These could be in houses, apartments, or in foster family care settings. To the extent possible, the individual should exercise choice and control over his/her living environment. The skills training, supports and services needed to enable clients to reside successfully in their own homes in normal community settings should be available and accessible regardless of where the individuals are living. There should also be a small number of supervised, structured settings for extremely dysfunctional individuals.

Aside from permanent housing, homeless individuals who are mentally ill require special living situations with varying degrees of supervision and structure. These include emergency shelters to provide alternatives to the streets and transitional housing to allow time for homeless mentally ill people to receive treatment and assistance in making the physical and emotional transition from a shelter to long-term housing.

Income support and entitlements - There should be assistance available to help clients obtain income supports and other entitlements which they may need in order to live in the community.

Peer support for clients - There should be consumer self-help groups and consumer-operated services in every locality, and they should be self-defined and consumer-controlled. They should also be voluntary and based on choice, shared power, and people's needs for survival, friendship, and a sense of useful participation. This plan would generally supplement services of the formal mental health system and meet a variety of social- and life-support needs through: peer-support groups that meet regularly to share ideas and information and provide mutual support; drop-in centers or social clubs for individuals to socialize and build support in the neighborhood; independent living programs that provide services such as assisting individuals to obtain financial benefits, housing, counseling and employment; consumer-run housing, businesses, respite care or crisis-assistance services; and public education on mental illness and the potential of individuals with mental illness to lead productive, satisfying lives and to contribute to the communities in which they live.

Family and community support - Because many persons with severe disabling mental illness reside with their families, there should be assistance to families that provides education on the nature of mental illness, consultation and supportive counseling on handling daily problems and intermittent crisis situations, appropriate involvement in the treatment planning process, respite care, and referrals to family support groups and advocacy organizations such as the state and local affiliates of the National Alliance for the Mentally Ill and the national or local mental health associations.

In addition, in order to facilitate community integration and acceptance, backup support should be available to landlords, employers, friends, community agencies, and others who come in frequent contact with individuals with severe disabling mental illness. Strategies could include media campaigns, use of volunteers, and presentations to civic organizations, schools and the community.

Rehabilitation services - Social and vocational rehabilitation services are critical for most individuals living in the community. These should be coordinated with or linked to treatment services.

In order to help the individual gain or regain practical skills needed to live in and socialize in the community, social rehabilitation services should be available that teach clients how to cope with their disabilities and assist them in developing social skills, interests, and leisure-time activities that provide a sense of participation and personal worth. These would include opportunities for age-appropriate, culturally appropriate daytime and evening activities, and tasks that teach daily and community living skills such as diet, personal hygiene, cooking, shopping, budgeting and money management, housekeeping, and use of transportation and other community resources. To the fullest extent possible, these activities should occur in the natural setting where the client lives, works, learns and socializes.

Vocational/rehabilitation services should consist of a wide range of vocational training and employment opportunities available to assist clients to prepare for, obtain, and maintain employment. These could include vocational assessment and counseling, pre-vocational job readiness, career development, on-the-job training, job sharing, transitional employment, supported employment, competitive employment, job development with local employers, and innovative approaches to using recovering consumers as mental health workers.

Protection and advocacy - There should be grievance procedures and mechanisms to protect client rights, both in and outside of mental health and residential facilities, and ways to inform each client and family of their legal rights and resources. These procedures and mechanisms are an inherent responsibility of the service facilities. Protection and advocacy services and the investigation of grievances against the system are handled through various state and local agencies and voluntary organizations.[2]

Public Law 99-319, the Protection and Advocacy for Mentally Ill Individuals Act of 1986, established protection and advocacy (P&A) systems in each state. The intention of the Act is to ensure that the rights of individuals who are mentally ill are protected while they are patients or residents in facilities providing care or treatment for 90 days following discharge. The P&A systems are authorized to protect and advocate for the rights of persons with mental illness in conformance with constitutional, federal and state mandates, and to investigate incidents of abuse and neglect when they are reported to the system, or if there is probable cause to believe that the incidents have occurred. States should also assure that their laws reflect the Bill of Rights for Mental Health Patients, which is appended to Public Law 99-319.[3]

Case management services - There should be case management (sometimes called resource management) services available for all clients who need them and, according to Public Law 99-660, who receive substantial amounts of services supported through public funds. This involves having a single person or, to the extent possible, a team of persons responsible for maintaining a long-term supportive relationship with the client, regardless of where the client is and regardless of the number of agencies involved. The case manager is a helper, service broker and advocate for the client, and functions in a manner that is client-directed and client-empowering.

Among the specific case management functions performed are: 1) identifying clients who need and desire case management services, 2) working with the client to develop a comprehensive service plan based on the client's needs and goals, 3) providing information to help the client make an informed choice about opportunities and services, 4) assisting the client, as requested, to obtain needed services, supports and entitlements, 5) being available and accessible during and after regular working hours, 6) advocating at the systems level for needed improvements.

For homeless mentally ill individuals, effective case management must be intensive, ongoing, and take place in the shelters or on the streets. There should also be an aggressive outreach function to build trust and engagement and prepare clients to receive needed services. All of the above elements of a comprehensive and coordinated mental health system are displayed in Exhibit 2.

Models of Comprehensive Services for Mentally Ill Homeless People

Although the preceding section outlined normative standards and principles for a client-centered comprehensive and coor-

Exhibit 2.[4]
A Client-Centered
Comprehensive Mental Health System

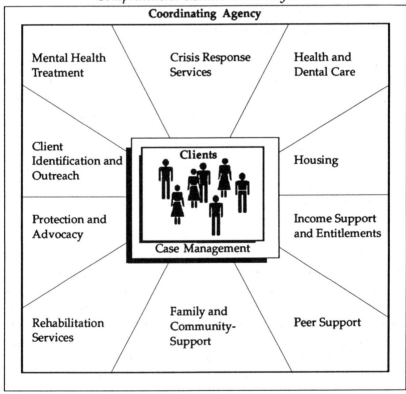

dinated mental health system for all mentally ill people, including those who are homeless, the argument for constructing a paradigm of preventive care requires further development through an exploration of exemplary, or model, services that have been developed to serve this fragile population. The existence of such models indicates that the norms articulated above are attainable.

The drama of thousands of homeless people has compelled a growing number of public and private agencies to carefully develop integrated multi-service systems designed to meet a wide range of mental health needs.

Among these are the Skid Row Mental Health Service, sponsored by the Los Angeles County Department of Mental Health, the Pine Street Inn in Boston, the Downtown Women's Center in Los Angeles, and the Saint Francis Residences in New York City. Finally, the Commonwealth of Massachusetts established one of the first state comprehensive systems of coordinated care for the homeless. These programs are described and analyzed because of their efficacy as models of service to the mentally ill homeless population. All of the programs incorporate prevention and treatment components.

Skid Row Mental Health Service -   This program operates in the Skid Row section of Los Angeles under funding from the Los Angeles County Department of Mental Health state-funded program. It includes case management, counseling, therapy, referral, outreach and community organization.

Staff offer the full range of traditional outpatient services for the population, including medication, individual supportive therapy and case management, groups, and psychological testing. For those who are chronically mentally ill, the emphasis of treatment is to reduce psychotic symptoms and behavior and to assist patients to meet their basic needs. Each patient sees a psychiatrist and is assigned to a case manager who retains client responsibility until the case is completed. Completion means that a patient leaves the Skid Row area with a plan, and that continuing case responsibility is transferred. Outpatient activity is limited in scope, and the program does not generally offer insight-oriented long-term psychotherapy. Because many chronic mentally ill people walk into agencies, the Skid Row Mental Health Service maintains a staff member on full duty every day to assess all walk-ins and referrals regardless of their presenting problems. This person bears responsibility for disposition to the appropriate facility and any necessary follow-up. People who are not mentally ill receive support and referrals to the appropriate giving facility, substance-abuse program or other needed service. For those with situational emotional distress, time-limited crisis therapy is offered. Patients who are within the target population but not yet compliant with treatment can be seen as needed until they are ready to have a formal chart opened. A great deal of the direct clinical treatment is done as consultation, screening and referral.

Outreach forms an important component of the program. Staff spend up to half of their time at service agencies and in the streets in or near Skid Row. They have continuous collaborative relationships with every agency, shelter, soup kitchen, drug and alcohol program, shop, hotel and movie house in the area. They work with the staff, and managers of these agencies and businesses providing personnel support, in-service education, programming for activities, consultation on individual patients, and individual or group direct service to patients. The goals of this activity are to meet the mental health needs of each facility in an integrated way, to enhance the ability of personnel in all Skid Row facilities to work effectively with the target population, and to bring the mentally ill into ongoing outpatient treatment.

Most of the Skid Row population are eligible for Supplemental Security Income (SSI) if they are mentally ill, or general assistance if they are not disabled. However, many have been unable to obtain these entitlements because of difficulties in negotiating the application process. The Skid Row Mental Health Project has developed a unique collaborative structure among several agencies in an effort to eliminate the barriers that patients encounter in applying for SSI and general welfare. Program staff provide overall case management, psychiatric evaluation, a mailing address, and representation or advocacy during the initial stages of the application process. Clinical social workers at the Department of Public Social Services (DPSS) screen and refer General Relief recipients who have been certified as disabled. DPSS Adult Protective Services staff accompany patients from one facility to another. The Social Security Administration sends staff to the Skid Row Mental Health Service to take applications. The Disability Evaluation Division of the State Department of Social Services works with staff to develop case files. The Asian Rehabilitation Service prepares vocational assessments for the case files, and the Mental Health Advocacy and Patient's Rights Division of the County Department of Mental Health provide representation for cases that go to the hearing stage.

The program is located near the bus terminal, which is the arrival point for many homeless people who go to Los Angeles. Staff make extensive efforts to retain linkages with Traveler's Aid Society, the missions, soup kitchens, and other agencies that have initial contact with travelers, to identify these patients and intervene as quickly as possible. This population often is extremely compliant and agreeable to a return trip home or placement. Without rapid intervention these patients would decompensate and require hospitalization, or would become victims of crimes on the streets of Skid Row.

The Skid Row project is addressing the needs of the dual-diagnosed patient through parallel treatment programs in collaboration with residential or outpatient substance-abuse programs. This requires extensive open communication among the Skid Row project, the substance-abuse programs, and the patients.

Staff work closely with the County Department of Mental Health Psychiatric Emergency Team by screening emergency calls in Skid Row. Staff are authorized to hospitalize patients involuntarily, but make every effort to resolve these calls with voluntary alternatives.

To sustain their resource network, staff participate fully in community organizations concerned with homelessness and chronic mental illness. These organizations bring needed public attention and increased services of all types to the homeless.

The Skid Row Mental Health Service has also opened a day program designed to be non-threatening, with low expectations, and informal. It emphasizes socialization and such task-oriented group activities as money management training. The Service also arranges for three- to five-day beds for mental patients pending placement in residential facilities, as well as a 60- to 90-day residential program for alcoholic and drug-addicted mentally ill people.

This program incorporates the principle of a continuum of services. Potentially it meets the needs of all people on Skid Row, because it is fully integrated with the countywide mental health system and with all of the service providers on Skid Row.[5]

Of special note is the fact that the service discourages agencies outside of the Skid Row area from referring people to Skid Row. The atmosphere within this area is so threatening and hostile that newcomers could rapidly decompensate. The program design, however, need not be restricted to Skid Rows. It bears equal relevance for more stable communities which include large mentally ill populations.

Despite the integrated program design of the Los Angeles Skid Row Mental Health Services Project, its major limitation remains the lack of adequate emergency shelter and low-income housing. For the most part, large public emergency shelters or church-sponsored mission shelters and soup kitchens dominate the services available to homeless mentally ill people. These offer little or no social services and are the least preferred by homeless people. Nevertheless, an encouraging number of modestly successful organizations have begun to effectively use whatever truncated services are available.

Pine Street Inn - The Pine Street Inn in Boston has a long history of providing shelter which is safe, comfortable, dignified and comprehensive. Pine Street serves approximately 300 men and 50 women on a first-come, first-served basis each day. The philosophy which guides the program is simple: "acceptance and respect for every individual." A total of 140 employees work at Pine Street, which is an impressive 1 to 3 ratio of staff to guests. It also employs three full-time nurses who assist in psychiatric referrals and basic medical services. In addition, counselors are on hand to provide support and follow-up services which may include referrals and transportation to federal and state benefit programs, hospitals, detoxification and rehabilitation programs and/or the Department of Mental Health. Pine Street also provides food and clothing.

Management of the Pine Street Inn claims that it serves the homeless at a cost far below that of government organizations. It derives its income from the Commonwealth of Massachusetts and donations, as well as in-kind services. Pine Street Inn serves as a model of decent and humane emergency shelter which is well integrated with the range of services needed by homeless people and which operates on a cost-effective basis.[6]

The Downtown Women's Center and Saint Francis Residences - The Downtown Women's Center in Los Angeles and the Saint Francis Residences on Manhattan's East Side and West Side are repeatedly cited as examples of decent transitional or long-term inexpensive care for chronically homeless people. The Saint Francis Residences were former single-room-occupancy hotels that were renovated through donations to Francis of Assisi Friends of the Poor. The Downtown Women's Center began as a day center for homeless women in a renovated warehouse on Skid Row. The Center receives funds from private foundations, individuals and corporations. It intentionally refuses all government funds because it wishes to retain control over its policies. The Center built a single-room-occupancy hotel next door so that it can offer a full range of services to its population of approximately 50 chronic mentally ill women. The Franciscan programs and the Downtown Women's Center attempt to demonstrate that there are alternatives to warehousing the chronic mentally ill homeless in large public shelters and missions. Staff demand respect for the dignity and privacy of each resident. The Franciscan residences guarantee tenants a room of their own for which they pay less than in commercially run hotels. Tenants pay for their rooms and meals out of their Social Security, Supplementary Security Income, Disability Income, or General Welfare allotments. Some have jobs and they pay out of their salaries.

Residents receive individual and group counseling, but therapists report that they use highly pragmatic approaches and frequently violate notions of what constitutes good practice. They apply insight-oriented therapy only in a limited number of cases. Occasionally one of the men or women requires hospitalization, in which case their room remains available upon their return. Most clients respond to this respectful and personalized environment. Many consider these settings their homes and view other residents as family. This clearly reflects the intentions of the organizers and staff.[7]

People who are both homeless and sick face a multitude of problems that mitigate against their receiving adequate medical treatment. Frequently the hospital emergency room is their primary entry point into a social service system. A survey of the homeless in shelters in Baltimore, Maryland, found high rates of hospital and outpatient medical use both in the missions and shelters; half of the sample had been in a hospital in the last ten years, and more than half had used outpatient medical services. The high inpatient rates, in part, reflect the fact that many poor people can only receive certain treatment on an inpatient basis. Those who can pay receive such services as outpatients.[8]

The lives of homeless mentally ill people are so crowded with survival, alcohol and drugs that it is extremely unlikely that they will seek care. Even when they receive medication, their living conditions seriously hamper compliance with treatment plans. For example, essential coatings to pills become destroyed by moisture from the weather. Insulin is another dramatic example of a storage problem for homeless people. How can they keep their insulin in a refrigerator without a home?

Some of these problems have been alleviated through a $25 million grant from two charitable foundations which will provide free health care to the nation's homeless. The Pew Memorial Trust and the Robert Wood Johnson Foundation selected community organizations in 18 American cities to supervise health clinics that are to be placed in shelters and soup kitchens this year.

Under the program, private non-profit organizations in each city have received two-year grants and are eligible for two additional years of support. All of the projects have large outreach components, as well as case management, crisis intervention and referral arrangements. They include referrals to local public health agencies for communicable diseases and drug problems, and coordination with state, local and private services to provide housing arrangements, jobs and welfare assistance. Staff are required to aggressively reach out to people in the streets, and they report that such streetwork comprises their most crucial task. The strength of the program lies in the fact that it provides a mechanism to address a wide range of physical and social needs of homeless and/or mentally ill people by focusing on health as the presenting problem.[9]

Trends in Community Mental Health

A 1987 survey conducted by the National Council of Community Mental Health Centers tracked key trends shaping community mental health today. Results of this survey disclose some positive direction in the provision of services for the chronic mentally ill, but persistent problems of resources remain a serious concern.

The results of the survey identified the scarcity of funds, leading to service cutbacks and more competition for dollars as the dominant trend shaping community mental health today. The second, and more positive trend, is the emphasis and priority on programs for the chronic mentally ill. Although mental health professionals generally deride this emphasis because it precludes important primary and secondary care for people with less severe emotional problems, there is common agreement that this priority prevents mental health agencies and practitioners from "skimming" the easier-to-treat, more motivated clients. In the earlier years of the community mental health movement, such skimming was not only pervasive, but also occurred at the expense of chronic patients.[10] The current priority attempts to redress this imbalance in treatment.

If the earlier promises of the Community Mental Health Centers Act had been fulfilled, chronic mentally ill patients would not have experienced the lack of care associated with deinstitutionalization. Clearly, a comprehensive mental health system should incorporate elements of care for the severely disabled and those who experience mild disorders and temporary adjustment problems.

Competition for resources should not divide those with emotional and mental problems in this manner. Nevertheless, the current needs of the mentally ill among the homeless can be more adequately met under present regulations favoring treatment of the chronically ill.

Another disturbing trend included the increasing difficulty in recruiting and retaining clinical staff. Given the need for well-trained personnel who possess special personal qualities as well as a sound knowledge base of practice and theory in working with mentally ill people who are homeless, the scarcity of good clinical staff in most community mental health centers must be addressed as a priority measure in preventing mentally ill people from becoming homeless.

There is no mental health system in the United States that adequately serves all of the needs of all of the people who experience mental and emotional disorders. Community mental health centers receive only about five percent of the funds expended on mental health in the nation. State hospitals, general hospitals and nursing homes spend about 70 percent of total mental health expenditures. George Albee presents alarming data that dramatize the lack of resources for the mentally ill. He claims that "If every therapist in the country saw 34 clients each week for one 50-minute hour, this would mean that one million therapists would be required to provide this amount of therapy." [11] There are currently about 45,000 mental health professionals in the United States, or less than half the number needed to treat each person one time a year.

The escalating demand for treatment, coupled with diminishing resources, continuously threatens disaster for all people with mental problems. The poor, who are largely served by public mental health services, suffer the most under scarce resources, and this means that chronic mentally ill people who are at risk of homelessness are further imperiled by underservice.

One solution for the short term would be to treat only the 15 percent of the population who comprise the 32-36 million "hard-core mentally ill." [12] A longer-term solution would be to actually reallocate resources and build the 2,000 community mental health centers that have yet to be built under the promise of the Community Mental Health Act.

Chapter 13

Outreach Efforts
to Prevent Homelessness

The persistence of scarce resources for treatment of the mentally ill too frequently translates into an inability of the present service network, through its categorically organized and nonintegrated systems, to respond to the most socially isolated people who cannot manage to negotiate, or even request, services without considerable support and guidance. These problems, along with a sense of powerlessness and victimization experienced by many mentally ill people, produce hard-to-reach and hard-to-work-with clients who all too frequently are missed or avoided by agencies lacking sufficient resources to meet existing service demand.

This group of socially isolated and disaffiliated people, homeless or not, are the target of assertive outreach programs that meet people on their own grounds and persuade them to voluntarily accept help. Outreach programs began in 1979 in Manhattan in an attempt to provide services to the chronic mentally ill people living in the community. It soon broadened its focus to people who appeared to be adrift in the streets and were either homeless or homeless-vulnerable. By now, most cities and counties have incorporated outreach programs modeled on the New York Project Reachout in their mental health systems. Smaller privately operated social agencies also feature outreach services. The consistent application of this service strategy has become a strong and positive force in preventing homelessness and rehabilitating those who have become homeless. This commitment to outreach services is particularly welcome in light of the fact that most programs operate at capacity and are stretched for resources. Despite this, outreach has evolved into a basic service strategy for the severely mentally disabled, thus indicating willingness to maximize service utilization on the part of agencies.

The outreach plan of service seeks to identify men, women and children who appear to need assistance and to introduce and connect those individuals to appropriate community resources. To be effective, outreach programs must be structured around community systems in which the social agency responsible for outreach programming negotiates the system, develops and cultivates a service network, informs outreach workers of services and any changes or additions.

Most outreach programs employ teams of workers who act together and collaboratively. Typically, the teams include trained social workers, paraprofessionals and any other professional whose discipline relates to the services provided, such as nurses when outreach focuses on health care. The social workers use their knowledge of diagnosis, engaging people and assessing their needs, and they rely upon the broader understanding of the community resources possessed by the paraprofessionals in Project Reachout.

Outreach Program Models

Much outreach work demands the courage to be street-wise. This is particularly so in attempting to work with children and adolescents who have become "street kids" whether they have a home or not. Preventive work, starting with aggressive outreach, has spelled the difference between rehabilitation and destruction for many young street people.

A project named Streetwork exemplifies the basic elements of street-wise outreach work. Streetwork is an experimental program that was set up in 1984, with $78,000 of federal money, to reach teenagers in the Times Square area of New York City. Most of these young people have become so deeply involved in a life of sexual exploitation that they would not come into any agency to seek help. Instead, Streetwork staff go into the nooks and crannies of Times Square — the video-game parlors, pizza joints, dance halls and parks. They offer counseling, medical care and a place to sleep if young people have no home, or are temporarily away from home.

Though the director of the project possesses minimal social work training, her most powerful credential is experience: several years as a prostitute. In one year, her "I've been there" approach won over about 300 regular clients. In several instances, she found it possible to convince runaway youth to return home after one encounter. More frequently, it takes several weeks of conversations to build trust before she can successfully work with the young people. Not all cases end happily, either. Some youngsters seemingly respond well and then turn up in the hospital as victims of drug overdoses or brutality. Some simply disappear. Unfortunately, this occurs in all programs for mentally ill people, but mental health workers and other social service personnel expect to encounter these losses in any setting with any population.[1] Hard-to-reach and hard-to-work-with clients are clearly more prone to slip away from even the best of programs and the most caring and skillful workers.

Outreach to at-risk youth is considered so critical as a preventive measure that the Robert Wood Johnson Foundation sponsored a nationwide High Risk Youth Project based upon outreach. The foundation is the nation's largest private resource for health-care funding. It sponsored a series of programs that operated collaboratively between large city hospitals and community-based agencies. Using the community agencies to reach out to young people, offering them anything from Coke and pizza to clothes, or helping them to find jobs, the program identified runaway youth, street children, drug addicts and adolescents who came from unstable homes where parents were either unwilling or unable to care for them. The hospitals followed up on the tangible assistance of the community agencies with careful psychiatric and medical diagnosis, and planning for any long-term care.

As is customary with foundation grants, programs operate as demonstrations. If successful, it is expected that sponsoring institutions will continue to support and operate the programs at the completion of the initial demonstration phase. The High Risk Youth program has been adopted by all of its original sponsors, and forms a successful core of preventive services for young people that starts with outreach.

Project Reachout has been replicated in Philadelphia, Boston and Los Angeles. It has proven so effective that the original team has been expanded to three teams, all equipped with vans and radios. It is operated by the Goddard-Riverside Community Center, a non-profit settlement house on the upper West Side of Manhattan, and receives $600,000 a year in New York State mental health money channeled through the city. The project serves 3,000 street people a year and has started a day program so that clients will have a safe place to go.[2]

Initially, the funding for Project Reachout could only be used for the homeless who met specific criteria of previous psychiatric hospitalization. Later, it was agreed that all mentally ill people were at risk of homelessness and that all homeless people were sufficiently at risk of mental illness so that the project now serves homeless and non-homeless mentally ill people.

Project Reachout staff approach people on foot, identifying the program and its services, offering food, beverages and clothing. They also inform people where they can get a hot meal and a bed, and offer to escort individuals to any referral source. Once someone is persuaded to accept a bed or a hotel room, the next steps are to get financial aid and teach them how to do laundry and buy food, and generally reintegrate them in permanent living.

Outreach is, in effect, the bait and is the beginning of a helping relationship. Once the outreach has been established, workers move systematically through three states of care leading to maximal support and permanent residence. In the first stage, the worker offers access to emergency medical and psychiatric needs, temporary shelter and socialization services. The focus of the second stage is on connecting individuals with appropriate service systems like general relief, SSI and other benefits. The third stage aims to establish a permanent residence and maximum use of community support and aftercare services. The team remains with the case until the client is able to manage independently or moves into another community service agency that takes on the responsibility for continuing case management. This continuum of care serves to rehabilitate and prevent further deterioration and long-term homelessness because it seeks out people who are not seeking help on their own. The underlying principle in this strategy is to begin working with people by giving them what they want, rather than what agencies are mandated to provide.

When San Francisco began to organize a service delivery system for its homeless in 1982, Mayor Diane Feinstein appointed a task force to advise her on issues of the homeless. A working group of service providers, The Shelter Providers Coalition, grew out of the Mayor's task force. The coalition, like many of those organized in cities across the United States, consisted of a broad membership including representatives from the Social Security Administration, veterans and welfare rights groups, all city shelters, San Francisco Community Mental Health Services, and so on. One immediate result of this coalition was the development of an outreach program that operated in eight sites and provided temporary residence for approximately 500 homeless individuals at any one time.

Two multidisciplinary teams worked on four sites and were composed of a part-time physician, a nurse-practitioner, a social worker, a psychiatric technician and two social work interns. The teams rotated throughout all eight sites and provided a wide range of services. Initially, the program was only designed to provide minimal direct treatment and social intervention. Clients were to be referred to other mental health agencies for more intensive or longer-term care. Because existing services were so overloaded, they excluded homeless people. Mental health programs preferred to serve only those who made and kept appointments and refused to see any clients who even smelled of alcohol. Substance-abuse programs served only those who were able to remain abstinent and did not serve people who used psychotropic medications. This was not a matter of agency bias or preference, but a legal requirement. People without proper identification could not apply for SSI or other financial benefits.

All of these problems forced the outreach program staff to focus on the development of networks with agencies that would serve their clients. Outreach staff spent a major part of their time advocating on behalf of clients, educating other program staff about the needs of the homeless, and encouraging them to better serve homeless people.[3]

The San Francisco outreach program is clearly not an example of homeless prevention. It serves more as an example of the importance of outreach as a service to the homeless mentally ill because traditional service approaches and agencies are not sufficiently equipped to meet the many needs of homeless mentally ill people.

Effective outreach programs cannot end with the provision of temporary shelter. They have the potential to be highly instrumental in long-term housing placement of mentally ill people. In Orange County, California, for example, outreach staff placed 50 people in board-and-care facilities, nine in room-and-board hotels, and 96 in mixed settings, including families and hospitals. All of this was accomplished in five months between July and November of 1987. During this period, the outreach program team served 422 people, with a total of 155 placed in housing.[4]

An important strategy of the Orange County team is that it works in settings that attract homeless-vulnerable people such as the general relief office, the police station, mental health clinics, medical clinics and soup kitchens. The team would like to expand this site location to include the Social Security Administration, unemployment office, and food stamp outlets.

A Conceptual Framework for Outreach Programs

Outreach as a service strategy has always been considered key to serving people who need care but do not seek it. The early history of the organized social work profession stressed reaching out to people in need through the Charity Organization Societies that introduced the practice of friendly visiting and the settlement houses that actively recruited individuals and families in their surrounding neighborhoods.[5] The early social reform impulses of many social workers during the progressive era (1890-1920) manifested themselves in aggressive case-finding that is now referred to as "outreach."

The end of the progressive era marked the emergence of the modern social agency that adopted a more formal pattern of office-based practice that precluded home and neighborhood visiting or outreach. The next social reform era in the human services occurred during the 1960s, and this period marked significant changes in traditional social agency practice. Most notable of these changes was the establishment of neighborhood-based services like storefront service centers, the hiring of indigenous "new career" paraprofessional workers who could relate to the needs of communities, and a reliance on crisis and outreach programs. Mobilization for Youth in New York City served as the model for many social agencies that sought to broaden their roles by working more aggressively in the community.[6]

In the mental health arena, the Community Mental Health Centers Act of 1963 mandated Consultation and Education services as one of the five core functions. Although the precise meaning of the term "consultation and education" remained ambiguous, common agreement did exist that outreach was clearly a critical function under this part of the law. The Act focused on primary prevention and outreach services quickly became a prominent approach to prevention.[7]

With the demise of the Community Mental Health Centers Act and its replacement, the Mental Health, Alcohol Abuse and Drug Abuse block grant, outreach services have remained a priority in mental health care. The current emphasis on serving the acute and chronic mentally ill cannot be carried out in the absence of out-reach programs.

Under the block grant legislation, community mental health centers and private contracting agencies are expected to provide comprehensive mental health services for the chronic mentally ill, the severely ill elderly, and identifiable underserved popula-tions.[8] All of these populations characteristically resist or only minimally comply with mental health treatment, so that outreach intended to induce this hard-to-serve and hard-to-reach clientele logically plays a key role in contemporary mental health practice.

Any consideration of preventing homelessness among the men-tally ill must focus on the critical role that outreach can play in at-tracting high-risk people on an individual basis similar to Project Reachout, or through other community agencies that have regular contact with acute and chronic mentally ill people such as law en-forcement, public assistance offices and community care facilities.

Unfortunately, too many of the current outreach programs that are receiving both public attention and public funding have been set up to function after the fact, when people actually become homeless. One vivid example of such shortsighted planning is a national program for homeless veterans.

This program, operating at 20 sites nationwide, has a $15 mil-lion budget to provide medical and psychological treatment for homeless veterans, who are estimated to make up between 18 and 30 percent of the homeless in the United States. Set up after the U.S. Congress reviewed surveys showing that a large number of veterans are living on the streets and need help but are either un-aware of the benefits available or unable to seek help because of physical or mental problems, the program sends Veterans Ad-ministration social workers to search for veterans. Program per-sonnel boast that they go out and look for veterans, rather than wait for them to come to the hospital door seeking help.

After eight months of operation, the program has not returned any homeless clients to permanent and stable living, but this may occur in time. The real point of this case description of the VA Homeless Veterans Program is that the outreach efforts should have begun at the point of discharge from military service.

Veterans Administration personnel, veterans' advocacy groups, and the general public have been aware of the special problems of veterans who fought in Vietnam and were victims of the defoliant agent orange, as well as substance abusers, that case-finding and outreach should have occurred before they became homeless.

A separate preventive measure related to homeless veterans involves the conduct of Veterans Administration hospitals. Many of these hospitals are overcrowded and present barriers of medical bureaucracy to physically and mentally frail veterans who either have given up trying to use them or have been carelessly treated. Participants in the Homeless Veterans Program report being sent back to the streets with serious medical conditions and to the missions for food.

The conceptual irrationality of spending $15 million in new money to enable the Veterans Administration to carry out its mandate to care for and rehabilitate veterans underscores the importance of prevention as more cost-effective and more humane. There is simply no justifiable reason why the vast network of Veterans Administration hospitals and other service centers cannot serve veterans at risk of homelessness before the fact.

The above criticism of belated outreach programs to high-risk groups is not confined to the Homeless Veterans Program. The outreach model has become a central feature of the new shelter system. While the outreach model was initially developed to extend services to the disaffiliated and isolated at-risk populations, it soon became apparent that it was an important strategy for bringing homeless people into some form of care. As outreach programs for the homeless spread, along with the proliferation of homelessness, outreach programs for non-homeless at-risk people decreased in the competition for scarce resources.

Ideally, each social agency should have an outreach program to serve people who might otherwise go unnoticed and unserved until they need more intensive treatment or become homeless.

A final note of caution about outreach programs concerns the capacity of the mental health system to provide the follow-up services to people who are attracted through this strategy. Given the strain on mental health systems that are stretched beyond capacity and overburdened, outreach programs can add more strain to the system. From the perspective of patients, outreach that welcomes frail people into a service system that cannot meet their needs ends up as just one more frustrating encounter with human service agencies that have failed and disappointed them in the past. If outreach means only a sandwich, cup of coffee, clean clothes and a bed for the night, it represents another broken promise to alienated people.

One reason that community care never materialized was political. Towns and unions dependent on the big institutions limited the transfer of funds to cities where most of the mentally ill went to live. In recent years, state legislatures and mental health departments have spread mental health services to more communities. However, most money for community mental health has gone to established programs and agencies. While many offer excellent services, they require that patients come to them. The most desperate patients, wandering the streets and occasionally showing up at shelters, revolving in and out of hospital wards, are not likely to enroll.

Outreach for these patients is the only means to attract them to existing services. Recognizing this need, the State of New York Commissioner of Mental Health has designed a comprehensive outreach system that could move the state ahead in the provision of care for the mentally ill and the prevention of homelessness. The new program would create a corps of case managers to seek out seriously mentally ill people. Each mental health worker would be assigned no more than 10 patients and would follow them on the streets if necessary. Case managers would try persuading their clients to come in for treatment, make sure they take medication, and provide continuing support.

This plan recognizes that community mental health care depends as much on the availability of services as on such outreach. Each case manager, therefore, could draw upon $4,000 per year in state funds for each client. This would permit expansion of programs tailored to actual needs. In theory, at least, it could allow fewer people to fall through the cracks and into the streets.

The proposed program would begin with 500 case managers dealing with 5,000 patients in New York State at a cost of $35 million annually.[9] It is a creative and humane idea based upon systematizing outreach connected to coordinated care directed by case managers.

Chapter 14

Consumer-Run Programs for the Mentally Ill

It has been shown that mentally ill persons have multiple and diverse needs, yet they often experience difficulties in obtaining services, entitlement benefits and other resources. Mentally ill people, in particular those who are likely to become homeless, may also reject traditional mental health services because they fear rehospitalization, medication, stigmatization and bureaucratic behavior.

For these reasons, it appears that formerly homeless persons, or persons with a history of mental illness, can be effective in reaching out to mentally ill people and engaging them in services. Drawing upon past experience, a former mentally ill homeless person can be extremely helpful in practical problem-solving and in assessing a client's needs. Former consumers of mental health services also tend to be far less threatening than clinicians because they share a common experience and identity.

The National Institute of Mental Health (NIMH) has begun to explore the potential of consumer-run self-help groups to provide a wide range of services for both severely mentally ill and homeless mentally ill people. NIMH has awarded two grants to study this matter: the first was given to the Mental Health Association of Southeastern Pennsylvania for a consumer-run services demonstration project (Outreach, Advocacy and Training Services, or OATS); the second grant was to conduct a review of published and unpublished literature on self-help programs for mentally ill persons along with a series of site visits to exemplary programs across the United States.[1]

Much of the material in this chapter is based upon the reports of these two projects.

Background of Consumer-Run Self-Help Programs

Many former mental patients have made important contributions to the field of mental health. Foremost among these was Clifford Beers who founded the National Committee on Mental Hygiene (now the National Mental Health Association) in 1909. He used his experience as a mental patient[2] to work toward more humane conditions for those committed to psychiatric hospitals. In the 1930s, Anton Boison developed clinical pastoral training that uses mental patients to train chaplains and other clergy in clinical skills.[3] Both men drew heavily upon their experiences as mental patients, but they did not use a self-help model of organization. Nevertheless, they demonstrated that former mental patients could play a significant role in building mental health services. This led to the concept that former patients could also staff and run programs.

Many former mental patients refuse to use their experiences to help others and view that period in their lives as a closed, and frequently embarrassing, chapter. Others have chosen to use their experience to help others and, in the helping process, gain insight to their own situations. These people have laid the foundation of the self-help process in mental health.

Claude DuTeil, founder and director of the Institute for Human Services in Honolulu, Hawaii, exemplifies this attitude applied to working with homeless mentally ill people. DuTeil has run a "peanut butter ministry" for ten years. Having started in a tiny room in Honolulu's Chinatown, his program fed its clients on peanut butter when money ran low. Now in larger quarters, the program provides shelter, food, clothing, counseling, activities and showers. DuTeil conveys his past experience as an alcoholic and mental patient in his work to empathize with his clients, but he also uses his experience to keep them from taking advantage of their disabilities or failing to achieve their potential. This dual focus is common among former patients in helping roles.

In addition to the use of personal experience, self-help groups add a group process to design and provide services for current and former mental patients.

Prototypes of mental health self-help communities are Recovery, Inc. and Alcoholics Anonymous. Recovery, Inc. is, as far as known, the first mental health self-help group. Organized by psychiatrist Abraham Low in 1933 in Chicago, Recovery groups now number nearly one thousand across the United States.

Meetings of Recovery begin with readings from Low's writings. Members discuss their current behavior and how Low's principles of emotional balance, bearing discomfort, being average and accepting setbacks apply. Members are encouraged to praise each other, and they are discouraged from being in contact with each other outside of the setting, or from being clinical in the group. Many members are also in the care of professionals, and the group supports this relationship. Leadership is carried out by experienced members who have been appointed by the central Recovery organization, and who attend continuing training workshops.[4]

Alcoholics Anonymous (AA) began at about the same time as Recovery. It has influenced many other self-help groups by demonstrating that those who experienced a problem could help others who suffered from the same problem, and that they could do this without professional leadership. The first Alcoholics Anonymous was set up by two alcoholics in 1935. Using the guiding principle of the Twelve Steps and Twelve Traditions, AA self-help groups have been successful in an area where professionals had a poor record of success.[5]

AA members are required to carry out several tasks that have become the basis of practice for some mental health self-help groups that developed later. One such task is the admission of one's mental illness history in a public meeting. A second is the open discussion of one's behavior in a closed meeting, while offering support to others who have a similar problem. A third task is the sponsoring of a newer AA member to provide orientation and to respond to his or her crises. A fourth is by personal testimony to carry the message of self-help to all alcoholics.

Some of the AA prohibitions — against public controversy, accepting contributions from outsiders, revealing the identities of leaders and members — have not been adopted by the mental health self-help groups. A significant difference also lies in the fact that AA focuses on behaviors supporting a central task: abstinence from alcohol.

The effectiveness of AA led to the development of many similar programs that rely upon the principle of the wounded as helpers. The proliferation of Twelve Step programs to deal with compulsive behavior like overeating, gambling, debt and drug dependency has become a matter of common knowledge among the lay and professional worlds.

A third form of self-help group emerged in the 1960s, the anti-psychiatry self-help groups. The ideology of these groups was usually expressed as hostility to the practices of hospitalization and medication. In some cases, the groups organized alternatives to professional treatment. They responded to the concern that mental patients lacked a sense of control over their lives because of the professional control imposed upon them while they were under treatment.

Consciousness-raising is also another significant issue in anti-psychiatry self-help groups. This reflects the need to restore people's self esteem and confidence and to counteract the low expectations placed upon them in the mental health system and in society at large.

The Ruby Rogers Advocacy and Drop-In Center is based upon these principles. The center is named for the plaintiff in a lawsuit that established the right of mental patients in Massachusetts to refuse medication. The Center began with state funding in 1985. It provides a safe, non-threatening, comfortable place where members offer mutual support and advocacy for each other. Leaderless support groups focused on different topics follow members' interests.

The group has three part-time staff members, including the coordinator. All staff are called "paid members" in keeping with the group's egalitarian style to remind them that they are members like everybody else. Workers receive training through feedback from other members, including a hiring committee that was established to supervise the mutual work. Not all members are capable of being "paid members," especially those who are too needy themselves to think of the needs of others. All decisions are made weekly at a general membership meeting.

Other self-help groups, such as On Our Own in Baltimore, are critical of some aspects of the mental health system but consider themselves as essentially a part of it.

On Our Own began in 1981 and opened an evening and weekend drop-in center in 1983, funded by the National Institute of Mental Health. An early interest of the group was to inform mental patients of their rights within the mental health system. The group held a conference of current and former mental patients in 1982, and one outcome was a law suit against the state to provide adequate legal services within psychiatric institutions. The plaintiff won the suit. On Our Own publishes a regular legal rights pamphlet and a newspaper.

The mental health self-help movement is now divided between two wings: an anti-psychiatry wing, organized as the National Alliance of Mental Patients, and a wing that considers itself an essential part of the mental health system to which it contributes a patient-centered point of view, represented by the National Mental Health Consumers' Association. The basic difference between the two wings lies in their attitudes toward psychiatric treatment. NAMP affiliates tend to oppose the use of psychotropic medication and forced commitment to psychiatric facilities because of the harm that these treatments are perceived to do. NMHCA affiliates tend to believe that medication and commitment are necessary under certain circumstances, and they confine their criticism of mental health systems to the lack of resources for successful life in the community, as well as criticism of treatment that is not sensitive to the human needs of mental patients. Both groups attempt to work together on issues on which they agree.

One possible explanation for the shift among some mental health self-help groups from an anti-psychiatry position is that the professionally led mental health treatment system has changed, in some respects, to be more sensitive to the needs and rights of patients. Developments such as therapeutic communities, Fairweather Lodges, Fountain House and other psychosocial rehabilitation innovations that recognize more of the capabilities of mental patients than did older programs may have changed the way some former patients respond to the system.

The therapeutic community concept is an attempt to engage mental patients in taking responsibility for what happens while they are in treatment. At first restricted to hospitals, the concept has expanded to outpatient programs. Its main premises are that communication within the treatment system should be two-way, that everyone in the system, including patients, should be able to contribute to the decision-making process, and that there should be constant examination of roles and feedback at all levels of the community. This approach diminishes the traditional differences between staff and patients regarding status, autonomy, authority and responsibility.

The therapeutic community developed from ego psychology behavioral theory. A great deal of day-to-day decision-making is delegated to lower-level staff members and patients. This is viewed as strengthening the patients' ability to manage their own affairs once they leave the hospital or treatment program.

Fairweather Lodge and Fountain House also rely on a high level of participation in the operation of the program by members, as clients are called. The more capable members act like junior partners to staff members. This introduces members to a work routine in a supportive environment. An important advantage of this system is that the work done is real while in the facility, and as members progress they work for outside employers.[6]

Fairweather Lodge's approach places clients in a group while they are in the psychiatric institution. Upon discharge, they go with their group into a living and working situation that they must manage, with some staff consultation. Patients must join this system voluntarily because the formation of the group and its training require a longer period of hospitalization than is now usually the case. Once released from the hospital, the group is established in a house or apartment and provided with work contracts, often for office cleaning. The group is self-governing, monitoring member activity and medication, making decisions about taking on team responsibilities and work tasks and distributing money. The group may even decide to refer a member for hospitalization, if the member's behavior seems to warrant it. Both the Fairweather approach and the Fountain House approach have contributed to the idea that former mental patients have the ability to manage their own lives and to care for others.

Over the past 25 years, self-help groups comprised of former mental patients have proliferated across the United States. The National Mental Health Consumers' Association identified 368 formal groups in a recent survey.[7] These groups vary in size, ideology, mission, structure and sponsorship. They also use different terms to describe themselves. But they all share certain characteristics and activities as groups bound together by a similar experience. In general, these activities and characteristics focus on mutual self-help, fighting the stigma of mental illness, advocacy for individuals or groups, or some combination of all three.

Mutual self-help is based upon the "helper" theory of Frank Riessman whereby a helper not only enjoys enhanced status while playing the helping role, but also assimilates the group's approved ideology and behavior into his or her thinking while persuading someone else of its validity. The group member, whose usual role is dependent and stigmatized, has the opportunity to take on a supportive and approved role, and to belong to a network of peers. The assigned group role places the member in an active participatory mode, rather than the more usual inactive and passive role.[8]

Self-help groups focus on different issues than professionally directed therapy groups. Perhaps the different values in the group's process (member control and passing the helping role around) are as important as the content of the interaction.

People who have or have had a mental illness are the victims of discrimination in social relations, employment, housing and other important areas. Many people whose lives have been disrupted by mental illness try their best to hide their experience. Belonging to a self-help group is an act of courage for many because it represents at least a semi-public challenge to the stigma attached to mental illness. Bolder statements by self-help groups include protests when the media portray mentally ill patients in a negative manner, public pronouncements challenging stigmatizing statements, and public education programs to show the harm and unreasonableness of prejudice and discrimination.

Advocacy has become a singularly important role for self-help groups. Many individuals who have, or have had, difficulty in obtaining services, or are being treated inappropriately, are often represented by assigned individuals or groups. Self-help groups form alliances with related groups, sometimes service providers, sometimes parents of people with mental illness, to lobby for resources or for changes in laws.

The passage of the Protection and Advocacy for Mentally Ill Individuals Act of 1986 authorized the monitoring of the performance of mental health and retardation institutions by outside groups.[9] Several states, including Maine and California, have made Protection and Advocacy funds available to mental health self-help groups so that they can act as advocates within psychiatric hospitals. Representatives of self-help groups meet with patients, and subsequently with staff, to investigate complaints.

The significance of self-help among former mental patients may be underestimated without an understanding of the very limited potential expected of mental patients by mental health treatment systems in the past. Some systems continue to have these attitudes today. The work of self-help groups has demonstrated that many current and former mental patients could not only perform at a much higher level than had been expected, but that they could be helpful to others.

The various functions of self-help groups have become an important resource for expanding the opportunities and self-expectation of severely mentally ill people. They have prevented some people from repeating self-destructive behavior, encouraged others to monitor their behavior and remain on medications, stimulated some to accept responsible positions in the work force, overcome stigma, and prevented many from remaining in a cycle of illness, despair and street life. Because of their achievements, the Federal Community Support Program of the National Institute of Mental Health decided to make self-help programs one of its priorities in 1983.

Types of Self-Help Groups for Homeless Mentally Ill People

The extension of self-help programs for homeless mentally ill people is relatively new, but they have achieved successful outcomes leading to permanent living and stabilization. Nearly all of the consumer-run self-help programs for the homeless mentally ill began within the past three years. More may develop with funding from Public Law 100-77, the Stewart B. McKinney Homeless Assistance Act of 1987.

Six types of programs have been identified as consumer-run self-help programs for the homeless mentally ill. These are described in this section. They are a food program, a drop-in center, a transitional residence, an entitlement advocacy, an outreach and advocacy program, and a combination consumer-run center and outreach program. No mental health consumer-run shelters have been identified so far, although two programs carry on some of their work in shelters run by others. The lack of shelters among the consumer-run programs may be related to a lack of money, but most people working in the programs attribute it to a philosophical position that housing, even transitional housing, is far more preferable than shelters.

Program Descriptions

Friends of the Homeless, Bronx Psychiatric Center, Bronx, New York. (Food distribution program)

This program is different from the others described here in that it is run by patients who live in a psychiatric hospital. A recreation therapist began the process that led to the formation of the group when a patient engaged him in conversation about the amount of food that was left over each day at the hospital cafeteria. The conversation led to the delivery of excess food to homeless people in the Bowery area of Manhattan.

Gradually, more patients became involved, and the food began to be gathered from bakeries, supermarkets and fast-food stores. The network of distribution widened, spreading to soup kitchens in the Bronx, to parks in Manhattan and to the major New York bus and train terminals.

This project is virtually entirely run by its members. They contact the suppliers, they decide on the delivery routes, they carry out the work involved in getting the food and transporting it on the subway or bus to its destination. If they are distributing the food themselves in a park or a transportation terminal, they approach the homeless people there in a natural manner. "They just walk up and start talking with them," reports the director. He believes that their ease in doing this is based on their identification with the homeless mentally ill. "Helping others is something that clients thrive on, once they are past the acute phase of their illness," says a ward psychiatrist at the Bronx Psychiatric Center.

Those who want to work with the group are either recommended by the director or by the group itself. Group members look for a person on the ward who seems to be a hard worker, and who would not get the program in trouble by acting irresponsibly. If a person is not working out, the group requests that he or she be reassigned. Some group members who are discharged from the hospital continue working with the group. New members are only taken from within the ward, because that makes communication much easier for everyone.

The group assigns members to tasks in pairs according to experience (new with old) and strength (strong with weaker). The members meet regularly to plan and to discuss policy.

Participants were not paid during the first two years the project was in operation, but then began to be paid through the Client Worker Program. Workers start with a limited number of hours at $.95 per hour and can progress to full-time work at $3.50 per hour. Attendance is high compared to other rehabilitation programs (95% as compared to 55-75%).

Several members of the group have been homeless, and their experience has influenced the work of the group. One church that had been helpful to one member when she was homeless, for example, was added to the recipient list as of October 1987.

Berkeley Drop-In Center, Berkeley, California. (Drop-in center) Based in three rooms located in a former school, this program provides peer support, advocacy, a hot lunch, telephones for personal business and a safe place to be for people who are homeless or precariously housed. Bus tickets are available for transportation to job interviews and other important appointments.

The Center opened in April 1985, serving a primarily white population that had been identified as having a mental illness. It now serves approximately 200 different individuals each month, in comparison to a total of only 530 last year. The majority served are black and homeless or at severe risk of becoming homeless. It is open three and one-half days per week, with other activities — a women's group, a psychiatric issues group, and special events — scheduled in addition. The staff is composed of a coordinator and three facilitators, all of whom are former patients. The facilitators are formerly homeless people. Volunteers assist with some of the other important tasks. All participants must have been clients or be potential clients of the mental health system. The Center's philosophy opposes forced psychiatric treatment.

Initial funding for the Center came from private fundraising. In its first year, it received a modest amount of funding through a federal Community Services Block Grant. In its second year, the program was enhanced by an infusion of state Bronzan funds, a special appropriation for services for people who are homeless and mentally ill.

Local Emergency Assistance Bronzan funds recipient agencies are required to meet together regularly, and the Drop-in Center's coordinator reports that the program has been accepted as one of Berkeley's established agencies.

Decisions are made at meetings of the whole drop-in center community that convene weekly to address all major issues. There is a steering committee that handles operating matters. Participants are elected to this committee through a complicated process that reflects the various constituencies of the Center.

Problems that arise frequently are lack of a place to live or be sheltered, finding sources of food, difficulties with entitlement funds, badly run board-and-care homes, and designated payees who do not dispense the disability funds they are holding according to the needs and wishes of the member.

Because it was drawing such a large number of participants, the Center attempted to move from its formerly too-small facility at its present location to a storefront on a major avenue of the city. Residents near the storefront mounted a stormy campaign to oppose the move. While the controversy was at its height, the Center was able to rent more space at its current location, and now has adequate space. Surviving the controversy about location was important to the Center's image. "Now people know that we're here, and that we're sticking around," reports the director.

A major accomplishment that the Center has worked toward is making its staff and membership reflective of the racially and ethnically mixed character of Berkeley. The Center was intentionally located in a predominantly black neighborhood, and has seen the majority of its participants at all levels become reflective of the neighborhood's composition.

Another issue that has arisen has been behavior within the Center. The membership reluctantly set up a Rules Committee to enforce behavioral standards, and now appreciates the contribution this Committee makes to the quality of life at the Center. The Committee has the authority to bar anyone for breaking the rules, and if the infraction is serious or repeated, the banned person must meet with the Committee to discuss what should be done about this behavior in the future.

Family House Project, Dorchester, Massachusetts. (Transitional residence) Family House Project began as a program of the Phillips Brooks House Association of Harvard University, an organization that finds service roles for Harvard students. In 1983, a shelter was set up at a church in Cambridge, to be administered by students. In 1984, at the end of the shelter "season," it was closed by the church. The residents and student staff, by then a closely knit group, set up a tent on Boston Common to attract attention to the need for housing. Negotiations with the city and state led to the group's receiving a rundown house in Dorchester. In September 1984, the group, somewhat transformed by a summer on the streets, moved in and began to renovate the house.

There are 18 beds, 17 for clients, in the house. Applicants referred to the house by various mental health agencies are allowed a two-week trial period when a vacancy occurs. The other residents then vote on whether the person may become a probationary resident. The probation period lasts thirty days, governed by a preliminary contract related to the person's goals. The contract specifies the chores a person must carry out, how much the person will contribute to the expenses of the house (based on ability to pay), and self-development activities agreed to by the probationer. If this period works out, the person can become a regular resident, with a longer-term contract.

Residents vote on rules, admission or dismissal of residents and other important matters at a weekly meeting. Interim decision-making is vested in a six-member board composed of three residents, two staff members and a representative of the sponsoring organization. If a resident violates the rules of the house, the board may recommend to the resident community that the person be suspended or dismissed. The community then votes on the decision.

The activities in the house include peer counseling, carrying out nearly all the chores involved in running the house, and various educational projects. Residents cook the meals and clean up according to an agreed-upon schedule. Regular social activities are held. Students and other volunteers provide a variety of educational, recreational and social activities.

The staff of the house began as a wholly student staff, but now the assistant manager has been hired from the resident population.

The role of the house is as a transitional residence, helping guests move on to more independent living for those for whom this is possible. Some, however, will continue to live there indefinitely. There is no fixed term. A number of the residents are working, some at night as security guards.

Family House Project has subsisted up to the present time on private grants and contributions from residents and others. The houses were given by the City government. Family House Project is working toward financial independence from its sponsoring organization.

A recent graduate of the Harvard Divinity School, the director lives in the house. He finds that it is a struggle to get residents to take control of the house and to exercise their prerogatives of governance. Residents do not like to deal with rule-breaking and to make decisions. "Let the staff do it," seems to be the attitude. He is working to overcome this attitude.

Oakland Independence Support Center, Oakland, California. (Community center) The Oakland Independence Support Center was created when the Alameda County Network of Mental Health Clients was able to obtain funding from the Alameda County Department of Mental Health to provide services for homeless people with a mental illness. The Network of Mental Health Clients, begun in 1982, had grown out of Mental Health Consumers Speak Conferences, a process for developing consumer leadership and networking that began in 1982.

The Department of Mental Health gave the new program a three-year demonstration grant using federal, state and county funds. The program's features were designed by people who were or had been homeless. These programs include a community center, a mailing address, bathroom and shower facilities, referral to shelter and other services, advocacy for benefits, peer counseling and money-management assistance. The Center occasionally supplies food and clothing when they are available.

By coincidence, the staff person who has most recently been homeless has been the one in charge of getting shelter beds. This arrangement has worked well because that person has the most recent memory of what it was like to be without shelter. A shelter, a separate agency, is located on the second floor of the building that the Center occupies. A transitional residence, also separately run, is located on the third floor. The Center also uses other shelter facilities in the community.

The Center has a housing program that includes providing housing referrals, teaching independent living skills, teaching how to get housing, and providing legal information when people are discriminated against. The housing specialist has good relationships with landlords, and she promises to intervene if a landlord has a problem with a tenant. The original director of the Center reported that after more than a year of its housing operation, the Center has had only three clients evicted.

Staff members are all people who have been clients of the mental health system and who are or have been homeless. Participants usually qualify to be staff members by working as volunteers within the program. However, full-time staff positions are open to everyone, so that the program may be able to hire the most qualified person. On two occasions, persons from outside the Center have been hired. There has been a concern to have the staff reflect the racial, ethnic and gender characteristics of the client community; goals in this area have been met.

Weekly client-staff community meetings make recommendations about the program to the Center board, which makes decisions for the program. The board's membership must be at least 60% clients; other members include staff and community leaders.

The Center has become closely allied with the local branch of the Union of the Homeless.

Portland Coalition of the Psychiatrically Labeled, Portland, Maine. (Drop-in center and Advocacy program) The Portland Coalition was founded in 1979, and met in members' homes and churches until it rented office space in 1983. Rental of that space was financed by the proceeds from a stigma-fighting slide presentation that the Coalition had produced and shown to community groups. Buoyed by the recognition that a regular office provided, the Coalition applied for and received funds from the Campaign for Human Development that allowed it to deliver services on a more organized basis.

The Bridge, a shelter for homeless people with a mental illness, had been opened next to the first office, and a natural relationship developed between it and the Coalition. One of the Coalition's board members is a board member at The Bridge, and continues to work in the shelter, even though the Coalition's drop-in center has now moved. The new drop-in center is in an office building downtown in order to be accessible to homeless and physically handicapped people. Because public transportation is limited, the downtown location makes it easy for mental health consumers to drop in. Because local shelters turn people out early in the morning, a drop-in center is very useful.

The Portland Coalition has been the consumer Protection and Advocacy agent for the local state psychiatric hospital. Until recently, members of the Coalition visited patients at the hospital, and followed up on complaints. Meetings were held with the ward staff about individual cases, and with the hospital administration about conditions in general. The Coalition received federal Protection and Advocacy funds as a major source of funding, but recently dropped this contract because of disputes over money and delays in payment.

The Coalition has a strong tradition of public education and advocacy. *Stigma*, the slide show illustrating the dangers of stigma, is of professional quality. The Coalition has produced a videotape for training law-enforcement officers on how to respond to people with a mental illness. Representatives of the organization serve on boards of directors and public advisory bodies to present a mental health consumer's point of view.

When the Coalition first had money to hire staff, it hired members to carry out the various functions. This led to problems, in that some members were not fully qualified to carry out some functions. The Coalition's director points out that many people have their first episode of mental illness at about the time they would begin their first work experience. Thus they may lack certain job-related skills.

The Coalition is now developing an "Associates" program that would allow non-patients with needed competencies to assist the Coalition in its work, while leaving control in the hands of former patients.

Project Bacup (Benefits Assistance Clients Urban Project), Los Angeles, California. (Entitlements advocacy program) Project Bacup provides assistance in the process of applying for entitlement benefits. This program, consumer-staffed and consumer-run, has operated in Los Angeles since May 1986.

Qualifying for disability benefits and other entitlements involves both producing documents that may not be easy to obtain and enduring a long and complex application process. Homeless people with a mental illness may have great difficulty doing both of these things.

Staff members, who have been trained by the Social Security Administration to fill out applications, assist clients in doing so as accurately as possible, because any fault in the form is grounds for delay in receiving benefits. Staff members also go to appeal hearings when benefits are denied, since administrative law courts allow applicants to be accompanied by non-attorneys. If the applicant does not succeed in the hearing, the case is referred to Mental Health Advocacy Services, where attorneys are available to make further appeals, when this is justified. Staff members must understand the diverse problems of homeless people, ranging from Vietnam veterans suffering flashbacks to people with bipolar disorders. They must also be familiar with a bewildering variety of benefits systems.

All of the staff members have had a mental illness, and all have had to qualify for benefits. There are two full-time and eight part-time staff members who work at the main office or at a satellite walk-in center on Skid Row.

The organization stresses the need for skill on the part of staff members, because ineffective performance means that clients are denied benefits they are entitled to. "We have an obligation to the client community first," the director says, "to provide an accurate, reliable service."

"We are also trying to give valuable job experience," he says. Regular training sessions are scheduled on benefits procedures and other related subjects. He has decided not to hold support group meetings for the staff, but to focus primarily on the work at hand, while being attentive to the personal needs of staff members.

Funding has been provided from state funds administered through Special Services for Groups, a United Way agency in Los Angeles. The Los Angeles Network of Mental Health Clients proposed the program to the funding source and participates on the program's advisory board. Because of a funding problem, salaries and hours were recently cut. Hopefully, the new budget year will find the funding restored to its previous level.

A critical frustration is that even when clients do receive benefits, they do not have enough money to pay market-rate rents in Los Angeles. Project Bacup keeps in touch with clients who have gotten benefits and refers them to appropriate services. A solution to the lack of affordable housing is not in view, however.

Outreach, Advocacy and Training Services for the Mentally Ill Homeless (OATS), Philadelphia, Pennsylvania. (Outreach and advocacy program) OATS, sponsored by Project SHARE, a network of consumer-run programs sponsored by the Mental Health Association of Southeastern Pennsylvania (MHASP), has been operating since April 1987. It is based on the philosophy that people who have been homeless and have experienced mental illness are especially able to relate to people who are currently homeless and mentally ill. Such workers not only empathize with clients' difficulties, but also know the mental health system from a consumer perspective. They are able to speak knowledgeably about what it means to take medication, for example, to a person who is fearful.

OATS staff members also provide consultant services to shelters and other programs on how to relate to homeless people with a mental illness.

They are especially interested in those potential clients who have rejected traditional services in the past. After helping the clients to connect with services they want, staff engage them in self-help activities, including advocacy activities. Consumer-run self-help groups are being organized within shelters and specialized residences. Meeting space in central Philadelphia is planned for self-help activities for those who live on the street or who were formerly homeless, and who prefer not to attend meetings in shelters. Among the self-help activities have been speak-outs and forums to encourage clients to express their opinions about their needs, as well as educational meetings on self-advocacy. Feedback from the speak-outs and forums has helped to inform official task forces on homelessness. One example of a result of this process will be the opening of an evening drop-in center that will employ consumers as staff members.

In coalition with other consumer self-help and advocacy programs, OATS staff participated in a "sleep-out" that was staged to influence mental health officials to provide special housing for the mentally ill homeless. The ensuing agreement envisions six to eight residences that will provide 150 beds, with consumers and formerly homeless people employed as staff members.

Among the funds to support OATS have been a Community Support Program demonstration grant from the National Institute of Mental Health through the State Department of Welfare and MHASP. OATS has applied for a grant from the County Office of Mental Health to train current and former homeless people with a mental illness in areas of self-advocacy, social services and case management. The five full-time staff members have all experienced homelessness and mental illness or substance abuse. A stipend program has been developed to hire other current and former homeless mental health consumers. The director of OATS describes the program as a way to enable people without recent or extensive work experience to begin to enter the work force.

OATS has gradually won acceptance among professional providers. For example, OATS staff members now accompany city mental health outreach teams on their rounds in order to add their expertise as consumers to the thinking of the team. Following a unanimous vote of the Mayor's Task Force on Homelessness that a formerly homeless person be named co-chair, OATS' director was elected to that post.

Justice in Mental Health (JIMHO): Project Stay and Project Doors, Lansing, Michigan. (Information, referral and advocacy center; Drop-in centers) Project Stay is an information, referral and advocacy center established by Justice In Mental Health, a mental health consumer-run self-help organization. Project Stay is located in Lansing above a street-level drop-in center operated by JIMHO. Visitors to the drop-in center are referred upstairs to take care of problems with housing, entitlements, legal assistance, or any other problem. Project Stay has a single paid staff member, who is assisted by volunteers: all are mental health consumers.

When people come to Project Stay, they are often in frustrated, angry or anxious moods. Enabling them to calm down may include sitting and letting them express their feelings, or taking a walk with them. It may also involve letting them spend some time in the "quiet room," or helping them to differentiate at whom they are angry. Once they are calm, staff members help them to identify their needs, and then to make a plan to meet these needs. Staff members accompany clients to the appropriate agencies, and try to help them find decent housing. A very important principle is that no one makes a decision for anyone else. If a decision affects someone, that person must be a part of the decision-making process.

Housing is a serious problem in Lansing, because only dilapidated and unsafe housing can be afforded by people who are living on entitlement incomes. Project Stay was not established just to meet the needs of the homeless, but that problem has become a major priority, given the needs of the client population.

Funding for Project Stay has been provided by grants from the Michigan Department of Mental Health and Lansing's Department of Human Services. Unfortunately, these grants only support the salary of one person, which is not sufficient to meet clients' needs. Volunteers supplement the work of the staff person. Project Stay served 800 different clients in 1987.

Project Doors is a six-city replication of the drop-in center that occupies the floor beneath Project Stay. Justice in Mental Health has been funded through a grant from the state legislature to establish six drop-in centers throughout the state. In Benton Harbor, Grand Rapids, Hamtramck, Kalamazoo, Muskegon and Pontiac, local mental health consumers were contacted and formed into a board for each center. They were then given technical assistance to set up a drop-in center. A one-time grant of $25,000 was provided to each board to fund start-up costs. Local mental health clinics are expected to pick up the programs in their next year. All seven drop-in centers are in operation and drawing clients. JIMHO expects to open more drop-in centers in other parts of the state.

Consumer Self-Help Center, Sacramento, California. (Drop-in center and Outreach program) Sponsored by the Mental Health Association/Sacramento Chapter, this program reaches out to draw homeless, or those at risk of becoming homeless, people with a mental illness into participation at the newly opened Consumer Self-Help Center. The outreach program, begun several years ago, originally formed self-help groups that met in the local emergency shelter, in a day center for homeless people, in transitional residences and at the State Capitol (a magnet for homeless people). The groups at the shelter and the Capitol continue, and the program now includes a daily group at the local Community Mental Health Center.

The advantage of using self-help in these settings is that the mutual aid groups give participants immediate access to social support, raising self-esteem and providing peer assistance to deal with problems.

The sponsoring organization was active in helping to set up the Consumers Speak conferences that played an important role in enhancing the consumer movement in California, and it continues to operate a wide range of self-help activities, including the training of self-help leaders.

A typical outreach meeting focuses on a theme prepared by the Center's director, who is a mental health consumer and experienced group leader. Those present would include homeless people and a variety of volunteers. The group leader might have brought along a resource person who would be able to offer information or other assistance about a particular problem that had been raised at an earlier meeting. Each person would speak voluntarily, or would be gently called on. Brainstorming is frequently used to enhance group interaction. Participants may make suggestions to each other based on their own experience. The group leader models a supportive interaction style that encourages participation and values each member's contribution, however modest.

Among the subjects discussed at these meetings: meeting personal goals, helping oneself by helping others, courage, organizing one's time, friendly relationships, and similar subjects.

In late May of 1988, a long-sought objective was achieved: the Consumer Self-Help Center was opened. This drop-in center, whose staff is wholly composed of consumers, provides structured activity. Classes, groups and clubs are featured, with the formation of clubs available to any two members who agree to work together. The Center's space includes extensive grounds for a garden, so the garden club is an important activity.

The Center's internal operations are controlled by the Center Committee, composed of members, who decide about Center rules, program, decoration and disputes, if any. The director continues his outreach activity. Some of his former outreach groups are now included in the activities of the Center.

Other programs based upon these models are getting under way as the evidence mounts of the efficacy of consumer-run self-help groups for the mentally ill who may or may not be homeless.

The programs described above share key similarities and differences. They have the following common characteristics:

- They are either led by former mental patients or have substantial leadership from current or former patients, many of whom have been homeless.

- Clients, residents or members, whichever they are called in each group, have considerable weight in making decisions, such as admission to the program, hiring and setting program priorities.

- At least some of the clients, or members, are paid to carry out the work of the program, and others have the opportunity to become employed. As they have evolved, the programs have become able to select applicants based upon their ability to function in a program role, rather than primarily on the basis of group membership or past psychiatric experience.

- The programs have attracted outside funding, either public or private. In most cases they require this funding in order to continue operating.

- All of the programs are intended to be transitional, rather than lifelong, for many participants.

- The programs have become linked in some way with the traditional mental health treatment approaches. For example, most are required to account to funding resources for the number and type of contacts they make with clients.

- Nearly all of the programs have a strong advocacy orientation. In some cases this is a primary function of the group, and in some other cases it is a by-product of problem-solving or public education.

The differences between the programs are equally important:

- Some of the programs concentrate on serving clients who will not become members of the organization, serving "others" rather than "ourselves," as would be true of a self-help group.

- The programs differ in their attitudes toward the mental health treatment system, with some holding that medication and any kind of forced treatment are harmful, and others led by people who have found that medication or another type of treatment has made a productive life possible for them. All support the principle that a person should have treatment, but opinions about requiring people to get it vary widely.

- The programs differ in the amount of their variation from the traditional peer-governed model toward a hierarchical model of operation. Some shift in this direction seems to occur as programs become accountable to funding sources. In some cases, these differences reflect the different histories of the programs, e.g., whether or not they grew out of, and are still responsible to, an existing self-help group.[10]

Challenges Faced by Consumer-Run Self-Help Groups

Alan Gartner and Frank Reissman have pointed out the potential of self-help to overcome some of the problems of the professional service system such as excessive credentialism, an overly intellectualized orientation, and limited ability to reach various hard-to-serve populations.

However, Gartner and Reissman also point out some of the potential limitations of self-help. These include: 1) substituting for professional services, rather than complementing them, 2) potential for conflict between professional and self-help services, 3) victim-blaming, e.g., "He's not ready for our help," 4) letting the system off the hook for not providing services, 5) escaping into privatism, 6) leaving the poor unserved, 7) doing poor imitations of professionals, 8) fostering life-long dependence, 9) being authoritarian and rigidly orthodox, 10) lacking accountability, 11) having an anti-professional bias, and 12) fragmenting social change by focusing too narrowly.[11]

Consumer-run self-help groups for mentally ill homeless people have addressed many of these issues. For example, rather than competing with professionals, they are reaching out to a population that the professionals have largely left alone. In many cases, they are working collaboratively with professionals, and are funded by the mental health system. Instead of letting the mental health system "off the hook" for not providing adequate services, many of these programs are involved in advocacy efforts to make the system more responsive. Their target is the poorest of the poor, so they are not leaving the poor underserved, as feared by Gartner and Reissman. Because many are publicly funded, they must account for their activities. These programs are special types of self-help, and some of the larger and more general concerns about self-help programs do not apply to them.

These new programs face different and serious challenges. Foremost among these is a dearth of resources for mentally ill persons in general, and homeless mentally ill persons in particular. The most needed resource is housing, and this is the most difficult to provide. Even when a client has an income, there is little or no housing that can be afforded in most communities at the income levels provided either by entitlements or low-paying jobs.

All programs face the challenge of obtaining adequate and secure funding. Most programs described above are temporarily funded on a demonstration basis, or staff earn below subsistence salaries, with other parts of operating budgets run on a shoestring. The heaviest burden is placed upon consumer workers.

Neighborhood acceptance poses another serious challenge. Just as individuals with mental illness experience stigma, their programs also experience stigma and rejection from local communities. Most programs have faced opposition but have struggled to build good relations with surrounding communities; but discrimination based on fear continues to be a serious problem confronting consumer-run programs.

Social services and mental health agencies control many of the resources that clients need. This means that self-help programs must establish relationships with traditional service agencies so that they can obtain resources. Some of these agencies are resistant to the client population. In addition to their resistance, consumer-run services operate on principles that are counter to the professional credentials and values of many of the traditional agencies. Instead of collaborating, consumer-run programs and traditional agencies are competing for scarce resources in the mental health systems that never have the financial capacity to meet total need.

Self-help groups may begin with leadership and staffing of-fered by people with minimal skills. As they grow, however, these programs require more skilled workers and they must find effec-tive and egalitarian ways to train new workers. As consumer-run organizations expand, they may need to add temporary support staff from trained professionals such as lawyers, community or-ganizers, social workers, nurses and specialists on certain issues.

The Value of Consumer-Run Self-Help Programs

Existing service organizations for mentally ill people who are homeless, or at risk of homelessness, have been less than effective in assisting this population. Self-help programs run by mental health consumers offer a new resource and have demonstrated an ability to communicate with and provide services for and with people who are mentally ill and homeless. These programs paral-lel changes within the mental health system that give more responsibility to patients.

Self-help organizations, located across the United States, are diverse in philosophy and approach. They are also similar in es-sential ways, most importantly in consumer control of services. The programs differ in certain ways from more traditional self-help groups; these differences may increase as they operate over a longer period of time.

They all face challenges, but a consumer-directed effort should be assisted so that these new programs can have more time to develop their unique expertise. Such assistance should come in the form of operating funds and research to track their develop-ment and effectiveness. In their present stage, the self-help programs have added a distinctive approach and voice, including advocacy, to serving severely mentally ill people. They have helped many move out of the cycle of homelessness, and have prevented others from leaving the circle of housing.

Chapter 15

Involuntary Commitment

The Koch Edict

Mayor Edward Koch of New York City sharpened an emerging national debate in September 1987 when he issued an edict instructing city officials to take severely mentally ill homeless people from New York City streets and parks where they live and try to forcibly provide them with medical and psychiatric services. This program expanded earlier efforts to find ways to provide care for mentally ill homeless people who appear unwilling or unable to take care of themselves, particularly in winter. In a real sense, the new program reflected an exaggerated and inappropriate outreach strategy. Forcible outreach implies a substantially different approach to service provision than the more acceptable persuasive strategies generally associated with outreach programs.

There are many obvious flaws in this approach to the mentally ill homeless population. The most glaring is that it represents a misguided effort to institutionalize homeless people as a way of solving the embarrassing problem of homelessness. It returns social policy back to the mid-nineteenth century when institutions were viewed as the panacea to the wide range of social problems because they could contain problems in one place. More important, the earlier institutions set the pattern for all future institutional care. They provide services to people with serious and complex problems in an orderly and efficient manner, frequently at less cost than more individualized care, and they achieve the socially acceptable solution of removing people with problems from public sight. The Koch edict, if fully implemented, could achieve the same goal — to get mentally ill homeless people out of sight and out of mind. Finally, the Koch plan merely offers a simple solution to a complex problem.

Before analyzing the New York policy and its implications, a description of how the plan was designed to work is important as a basis for understanding its intentions and potential.

Mobile vans, staffed with a social worker and a nurse, are sent out with lists of homeless people deemed to be in need of immediate hospitalization and in danger to themselves and others. They are taken to a new 28-bed ward at Bellevue Hospital Center where they are examined, bathed, deloused, given clean clothes, advised of their legal rights and interviewed by a psychiatrist and a social worker. Emergency-room doctors can order a patient to be held involuntarily for 48 hours, when a second psychiatrist must confirm the decision.

On the special ward, patients receive medication and are encouraged to participate in activities with other residents. Once admitted, they are entitled to a hearing before a state judge within five days of requesting one.

Special teams of social workers meet with the patients to arrange placements in community residences, group homes or, if necessary, state psychiatric hospitals. Under initial plans, Bellevue Hospital officials envisioned treating as many as 500 patients a year in the special ward by treating each new patient over a three-week period.

Koch administration officials and other supporters of this plan argue that "the pendulum has swung too far" when concern for the rights of the mentally ill have led to a reduction in care. Acknowledging that the program could lead to the re-introduction of long-term care for mentally ill homeless people, advocates of the policy agree that it is the beginning of the recognition of the need for asylums, asserting that the patients' right to treatment can free them from mental illness, in contrast to the patients' right to refuse treatment, which imprisons them in mental illness and grants them the freedom to die in the streets.

At the same time, civil liberties groups have raised questions about the rights of homeless people. Other critics have called for a delay in the program until the city and the state can deal with overcrowding of emergency rooms and shortages of community residences, hospital beds and drop-in centers for the mentally ill who voluntarily seek help.

This program received worldwide attention when Joyce Brown (alias Billie Boggs in her street life) challenged her involuntary hospitalization and psychiatric treatment in the court and won unconditional release. Clearly, the victory of Joyce Brown relates back to the media saga of Rebecca Smith who refused care in the winter of 1981 and died in the cardboard box that she had fashioned as her home. These two cases exemplify the policy dilemma of liberty versus care, identified by Martin Rein as a critical element in the formulation of any policy.[1] The extent to which the state can intervene in an individual's life for his or her good remains a matter where resolution must carefully balance individual rights and collective responsibilities. It is not a dilemma that lends itself to uniform rules and regulations in democratic societies that respect and value individualism and freedom.

The Koch Edict in the National Context

Mayor Koch's edict crystallized a growing national debate about revision of institutionalization and involuntary commitment policies for chronic mental patients. A number of service providers, political leaders, and family members of mentally ill people across the nation have expressed their conviction that the broadening of patients' rights and the restructuring of community-based services have translated into poor quality care, or no care at all. Their concern is that statutory regulations often constrain practitioners in providing necessary care. Others argue, in contrast, that patients' rights and community care systems have not produced a sufficiently different reorientation of services, and that these policies should be pursued more actively. All agree that increased liberty and deinstitutionalization have not been translated into a positive service approach for the most troubled chronic mentally ill patients.

Prominent among the advocates of revised institutionalization and involuntary commitment procedures are such credible organizations as the State Psychiatric Associations, State Medical Associations, the American Medical Association, Advocates for the Mentally Ill (AMI) and the American Psychological Association.

Opponents include patients' rights organizations, local affiliates of the American Civil Liberties Union, the National Coalition for the Homeless, and Mental Health Associations.

This section summarizes the general positions for and against altered interpretation of involuntary commitment and presents potential areas for compromise. The importance of this issue is self-evident in light of the fact that over half of the states are now considering some version of revisions in involuntary commitment laws.

In essence, those seeking revised commitment laws are attempting to broaden the meaning of the term "danger to self," explicit as a condition of involuntary commitment under present laws, to allow public authorities to force mentally ill people to enter hospitals or community care facilities. The basic thrust of this proposal allows civil authorities to place an individual on a treatment regimen in the community, against his/her wishes, specifying criteria of dangerousness, inability to care for oneself, or need for treatment. The consequences for violation of the treatment regimen may be involuntary admission to an institutional setting with or without further procedural due process. This proposed revision is referred to as involuntary outpatient commitment (IOC).

Those arguing against any changes in the interpretation of involuntary commitment pose the following arguments:

Benevolent coercion rarely provides effective therapy and too quickly begins to serve social control and monitoring functions instead. Therefore, any treatment of people who would prefer to be left alone is of dubious value.

The possibility exists that involuntary outpatient commitment could expand the state's power beyond acceptable limits. Those considered most identifiable for treatment would be chronic patients with disorders that are amenable to psychopharmacology. The most efficient way to do this is through the use of blood tests. If injections and blood tests can be justified for the chronic mentally ill, they could be extended to other situations including substance and sexual abuse.

Dangerousness criteria proposed for IOC are lower and less explicit than inpatient care. This could lead to idiosyncratic, biased and poorly regulated commitment decisions.

IOC could be less expensive to use and more difficult to monitor than inpatient care. This could mean that incentives for detection and repudiation of abuses of the system would be lower as a result. As a cheaper cost alternative to inpatient care, IOC would be too costly to monitor.

A patient's right to refuse treatment would be undermined. Currently, patients can refuse certain treatment in inpatient settings. By definition, a person cannot refuse treatment while being involuntarily committed on an outpatient basis, or on a temporary hold. Over one-half of the states now have laws permitting psychoparmacological treatment following judicial review based upon two medical opinions, regardless of a patient's wishes.

The final argument used against revised involuntary commitment procedures is that IOC would undermine the therapeutic relationship so severely that positive approaches to treating chronic mentally ill people would be more difficult in a system of negative sanctions.

Those who argue in favor of altered interpretations of involuntary commitment present three core positions:

The first, and most pervasive, position asserts that liberty must be considered more broadly in order to formulate reasonable policy for the most severely impaired mentally ill people. This broader conception of liberty emphasizes the freedom *from* quality and liberty. Expanded civil commitment law would replace the present liberty, granting chronic mentally ill people the right to be ignored until they are a public nuisance. If community monitoring can be made a reliable and benign intrusion, there is benefit for a large number of patients for whom continued periodic deprivation of liberty through involuntary hospitalization (the revolving door syndrome) could be avoided.

The second argument in favor of IOC is that it has the potential for improved treatment effectiveness. Treating people in the community could allow for a psychosocial approach that is impossible in the present revolving door syndrome of care in which little more can be done than drug stabilization, time-limited therapy, and placement. Treatment effectiveness could be enhanced by removing the issue of resistance from the realm of the therapist-patient relationship. A court order would rule that both parties are responsible for successful completion of the term of treatment.

Finally, advocates of IOC claim that it could begin a cycle of rehabilitation by introducing patients to the experience of community living in a non-psychotic state under supervision.

Practically no research base exists on this issue. Three major research arenas relate to the subject: 1) administrative law relative to public mental health, 2) law review materials on civil commitment, and 3) two quasi-experimental studies reported at national meetings in 1982 and 1984. Existing literature offers only limited information on the way IOC is presently used. Considerable disagreement exists regarding the definition of this treatment status, and empirical investigations shed little light on factors that promote its efficacy or use. Although promoted as a good or bad idea, there is neither sufficient empirical guidance for its implementation nor a great amount of evidence that it can be effective on a broad scale. Finally, the obvious concern is the question of involuntary commitment to...where? The simple fact is that there are too few beds to even keep people on basic 24-hour holds, let alone long-term stays. One year after the Koch edict, fewer than

200 mentally ill people have been treated under the law. Given the lack of data about IOC, policymakers can either abandon any proposals for changes in involuntary commitment laws until sufficient evidence is produced and accepted as valid, or they can proceed on the basis of compromise between the different positions on the issue.

In light of the strength of interest in revised patients' rights, it would seem more advisable to proceed along lines that would make adjustments between the supporters and critics of revised IOC. Numerous potential areas for compromise have been suggested. Two of the most prominent arenas for adjustment between the two forces relate to eligibility restrictions on IOC patients and limitations on therapeutic treatment.

Eligibility restrictions could clearly identify the types of patients most likely to benefit from IOC status. Two patient types are potentially eligible: patients with demonstrated histories of inpatient hospitalization and those with forced community placements. Patients with these case histories will require care for all of their lives and are at the highest risk of becoming homeless when and if any mishap occurs in their lives. IOC, for these people, could translate to homeless-prevention.

Limitations on therapeutic intervention could be established by law to prevent violations of patients' rights and inappropriate treatment. Such limitations would include the following protections: Only those treatments with demonstrated effects for particular diagnostic groups would be permitted. Some treatments could be required, e.g., psychopharmacology. Other treatments would be offered to patients. A patient would be protected through due process measures when a decision about his or her competency to refuse treatment at the time of the outpatient commitment hearing occurs. Outpatient commitment would have to be under lower criteria than those for inpatient commitment, but must become synonymous with conditional discharge from inpatient care. To prevent patients from deterioration, individuals monitoring outpatient commitment should have some authority to authorize short-term institutional care. Treatment plans would have to be specific and time-limited. Organizational procedures would have to be established to prevent overuse of IOC. Foremost among these would be a requirement that all hearings be held at a court rather than the evaluation site. This changes the atmosphere of the hearing for clients from treatment to due process in a neutral setting. Finally, funding arrangements for all prescribed community care must be made explicit at the time of the hearing and recorded in the court decision.[2]

Justification for IOC as a strategy for protecting chronic mentally ill patients and preventing homelessness would rely upon application of the policy to people who live with their families, in board and care facilities, group homes, or alone. If IOC becomes an excuse for removing the homeless from the streets, it will become another instrument of social control, monitoring, and inappropriate institutionalization. If IOC has any merit as a protection for the rights of mental patients, its use must not be restricted to those who finally sink into the despair of the streets.

Any reconsideration of involuntary commitment laws must place the exercise of such power in the context of the U.S. Supreme Court's warning that commitment is a massive deprivation of liberty. Whether IOC can be rationalized has yet to be tested either in the courts or in practice. The general thrust of recent court decisions on the matter has repeatedly asserted that government does not have the power to hospitalize or otherwise commit harmless people who are capable of meeting their basic survival needs, even if they appear disheveled or their standard of living is below appropriate subsistence.

The Koch edict and Joyce Brown's case dramatize the failure of deinstitutionalization from state mental hospitals. They further dramatize the most fundamental problems in the mental health service delivery sector: scarce community mental health resources and the severe shortage of inpatient beds. Most state mental health systems suffer from this lack of facilities, and are thus subject to the prominent criticism that no mental health system exists for the seriously mentally ill. They have merely been shifted from warehouses in state hospitals to warehouses in the community or the streets.

This lack of care and service availability is not confined to the poor, either. Families that can afford to pay report that there is little service to buy. Private psychiatrists and hospitals frequently refuse to treat schizophrenics for many personal and professional reasons. Current medical thinking attributes schizophrenia to a chemical imbalance. This is of no interest to psychoanalysts, who probe the unconscious. Nor is it of interest to practitioners who prefer to treat patients who can be cured. The result is that treatment, even for those who have financial resources, translates to medication with too little attention to the monitoring of the prescription, which must be carefully adjusted over time.

Despite this abysmal national pattern of inadequate and inappropriate care and substandard housing for the seriously mentally ill, some states have achieved a level of decent care that can serve as a standard for all states. The Public Citizen Health Research Group, sponsored by Ralph Nader and directed by Dr. E. Fuller Torrey, surveyed care of the seriously mentally ill in the United States and ranked states on a series of criteria.

The Health Research Group's report singled out Wisconsin as having above-average state hospitals and the best services in the country for the seriously mentally ill. It particularly cited Dane County in Wisconsin where a full range of services is available in the community. Case managers follow individual clients, and even go out onto the streets to find patients who have not kept their appointments. Locked facilities are available for the most disturbed, and small housing units (for no more than 12 people) and job-training are provided by Goodwill Industries and various local non-profit organizations under contract to the county. The report credits much of this to the fact that Wisconsin requires the counties to pay for hospitalization costs for their own patients, giving them an incentive to develop cheaper community services instead.

Among the programs in other states that the report praises is the clubhouse system in Florida, where the mentally ill are given a place to go during the day to socialize with friends, take classes, find out the available housing and get job-training. The clubhouses are usually associated with a housing project and a jobs program, and are supported by the state of Florida.

The Public Health Citizens Health Research Group ranked Rhode Island and Colorado as the next highest in programs for the seriously mentally ill. Curiously enough, money proved to be a minor factor in the ranking. The highest-rated states achieved better services without spending more money. They spend respectively $20.32, $31.54 and $24.88 per capita per year on their mental health programs. The average for all states is $52.00. California spends $28.88 and New York $74.06, yet their programs are rated far down on the list even though they have the largest homeless populations in the nation.

The states that have achieved excellence without spending more money have done this through careful coordination of care, tracking patients, and setting the seriously mentally ill as a special priority population.

Colorado designates the seriously mentally ill as its first priority for the use of state mental health dollars; if state funds are used to pay psychotherapists to treat the "worried well," there are few funds left over for the seriously mentally ill. Rhode Island provides decent community housing for the mentally ill disabled, a measure approved by voters through 11 bond issues in the last 20 years. Wisconsin fixes fiscal responsibility at the county level and authorizes "the dollar to follow the patient" into the hospital and out to the community. These, and other highly rated states, also depend on effective leadership in their state mental health agencies, supportive governors and legislatures, strong cooperation with Alliance for the Mentally Ill consumer groups, and reliance on outpatient commitment (if the patient stops taking medicine, he or she can be returned to the hospital).[3]

These examples demonstrate that there is little mystery about what needs to be done to provide high-quality yet economical mental health services. The solution lies in public willingness to serve this challenging population and to link expenditures for mental health care to patients rather than institutions.

Without such public will, proposals to extend involuntary commitment laws by reinterpreting the term "danger to self" or expanding the length of involuntary hold time to treat people against their will are suspect of being blatant attempts to justify clearing the streets of people whose behavior is embarrassing, threatening, and attracts attention. Any changes in these laws must be accompanied by sufficient community programs that, when sensitively handled, increase the odds that the mentally ill will seek help, take medication and feel some stake in their own survival. Directives or revised laws that purport to offer treatment to the mentally ill, yet do not provide the necessary resources, are another failed promise, and as serious a breach in trust as the failed promise of deinstitutionalization.

Reinstitutionalization carries the potential to protect and care for mentally ill people who cannot live in unrestricted environments. New-type institutions that provide asylums in smaller human-scale settings hold promise for many of these people who would otherwise be homeless. Excellent models abound of community living facilities for people who cannot live independently. These sincere attempts to provide shelter and care are useful preventive and protective measures. They must be carefully designed and monitored, however, to ascertain that they are not viewed as the paradigm for all mentally ill people, thereby exacerbating the troublesome trend to fill up the old state mental hospitals in an attempt to eradicate homelessness.

Chapter 16

Coordinated Care Among Human Service Systems

Program development through systematic service coordination has been a model of social work organization and practice since the middle of the nineteenth century when the first State Boards of Charity were founded to administer the philanthropic institutions and expenditures of the states and philanthropic agencies. This concept was soon expanded by the Charity Organization Movement that designated coordination of services as one of its primary functions. Subsequently, the community planning councils, now replaced by the United Ways, evolved as organizations that would coordinate service delivery through planning mechanisms that identify community needs and priorities.[1]

Explicit in this valued social work administration practice theory is the idea that organizations and interest groups behave rationally, rendering orderly program development and coordination highly probable. However, this unitary and rational approach to planning ignores the view of people and organizations as irrational and politically and economically self-serving. Neil Gilbert and Harry Specht have criticized the concept of rational central planning and coordination as being as unrealistic as town meetings. Today, newer and more relevant models for coordination through non-unitary planning that seeks to accommodate differences within an integrated service model are more acceptable.[2]

In the context of a non-homeless future, human service systems and laws must be scrutinized to ascertain conflicts between and among laws and systems that contribute to homelessness. A non-homeless world cannot become a reality until all of the social service systems and the courts coordinate programs and laws to prevent homelessness. If one views homelessness as the failure of every human service system — child welfare, mental health, health, welfare, housing and employment — the logical question is, what points in these systems contribute to homelessness? One obvious response is inadequate resources and threatening bureaucratic practices that prevent everybody who needs services from either requesting them or receiving them.

A second and equally compelling analysis lies in organizational policies and practices that either conflict or are inadequately integrated, resulting in homelessness for some, and threats for many who are homeless-vulnerable. For many others, these conflicting policies and uncoordinated service systems mean a persistent gap between needs and services that is particularly acute among some vulnerable groups.

Undoubtedly, closing the gaps between needs and services will require more money, but there are measures that states, counties and the courts can take to eliminate legal conflicts between different human service policies and practices with relatively modest addition or re-allocation of funds and, in some instances, no additional expenditures.

This chapter identifies those points of conflict and weakness among human service systems that contribute to homelessness and recommends immediate measures that could eliminate such problems with a view toward making existing services more effective as homeless-prevention strategies. It also reviews current approaches to service integration.

Child Welfare and Homelessness

Child protective service agencies, operating under their mandate to protect abused and neglected children as well as help families in trouble, all too often worsen their plight.

Social agency staff, hospital personnel and shelter operators frequently complain of the dilemmas they experience if they report homeless families. The law requires that these families be reported to children's service agency officials who are, in turn, authorized to take the children into foster care without a court order. Under the law, homeless children are considered neglected even if they live in a car with their parents who are trying to care for them while seeking employment and housing. This conflict between protecting families and protecting children can lead to further family deterioration, permanent separation and permanent homelessness.

Recognizing this inherent systems conflict, a Superior Court decision in Los Angeles County in June 1986 ordered that children and homeless parents should be kept together to avoid further damage to the family and that efforts should be made to restore the family to stable living conditions. This legal precedent could be adopted throughout the country at no additional cost. As a court decision, it sought to preserve the integrity of protective services by protecting the interests of the family and the children.

A similar case was heard in New York City, where the police responded to reports of a quarrel in Brooklyn between a woman and her husband, a suspected drug trafficker who repeatedly physically abused his wife. The woman and two of her children, three and four years old, were taken to a privately operated shelter for battered women and children. They were rescued from physical jeopardy, but then the children were placed in foster care because their mother, who is deaf, had difficulty coping with the Department of Special Services for Children.

The American Civil Liberties Union took this case to court, representing the children. The basis of the argument in court was that the city should have provided the mother and children with legally required homemaker services, an interpreter, and other help that would enable the children to stay with their mother. A State Supreme Court justice agreed and ordered the family reunited at the shelter, with the necessary services.

The mother and children remained at the shelter for 90 days, the legal limit. Forced to leave, they moved in with her mother, a 14-year-old sister, and her eight-year-old son (from another father), all in a one-bedroom apartment. At the shelter, Special Services staff had told the woman that her mother's apartment was unacceptable because it was too small and her husband knew where it was.

Special Services for Children is charged with helping to find housing for such families. Its sole contribution was to take the mother to a rental broker who said that he could not find an apartment at the rent that welfare paid. On her own, she located affordable housing, but the agency never advanced the security deposit and the first month's rent as it is obliged to do. She lost the apartment.

Because the overcrowded conditions in her mother's apartment were unbearable, the woman and her two younger children returned home — and to the risks of living with an abusive husband. The American Civil Liberties Union requested Special Services to intercede immediately to protect them from danger. It took the agency five days to act. When it did, they took the children away again. They were shuttled first to a group home in the Bronx, then to a foster care family; the agency refused to let their able, loving grandmother visit until the American Civil Liberties Union obtained a court order.

The matter was returned to court. The judge excoriated Special Services for failing to meet its statutorial duty to provide services. The children are now in their grandmother's care, but the agency is still not doing anything.

The number of children who need help soars every year. Many require foster care for good reasons: they are victims of abuse, drug addiction and inattention. But why must Special Services in

New York, and its counterparts in cities and counties across the United States, needlessly break up families by taking children who want and need to be with their parents?

What these families need is to stay together, and what federal and state laws say they are entitled to: modest cash aid to get them over a crisis, help in relocating, homemaker services, day care and counseling.

The money from federal and state funds is there for such services. Yet, court demands and efforts by child welfare advocates to improve care have not been heeded by officials responsible for children's welfare, and horror stories like the anecdote reported here appear on a daily basis in national media.

Special Services claims that it is doing a good job. However, some city officials report that the caseworkers' overload limits their ability to conduct child-abuse investigations and makes it impossible to provide proper care.

Moreover, cities are increasingly relying upon private agency contracts for services. Critics say those agencies refuse to help families with hard problems. The agencies claim that Special Services either does not get around to referring families to them or takes too long. When Special Services does refer a family to a private agency, the division of responsibility between it and the agency is unclear, often leaving the family with no help.

The result of this bureaucratic morass is that Special Services in New York and elsewhere often winds up psychologically damaging the children it claims to be saving. Many of these children and families sink into the life of welfare hotels and homelessness.

Within child welfare systems, the foster care divisions contribute to homelessness through poor discharge planning. As young people reach emancipation, they frequently age out of the system with no job and no place to live on a permanent or long-term basis. Discharge planning of emancipated youth generally amounts to little more than one set of clothing, a temporary place to stay, and a list of possible jobs.

Faced with such difficult obstacles, youth who have grown up in foster homes often end up in the streets, unless they commit a crime and then find a home in jail or prison. The National Coalition for the Homeless has a case pending in the court charging the New York foster care system with neglect of its responsibility to properly plan for discharge upon emancipation, thus causing young people to become homeless.

Integrating Mental Health Services with Related Systems

Since 1980, when President Reagan ordered the Mental Health Systems Act rescinded, the mentally ill have, as a group, suffered from federal cutbacks. Hundreds of thousands have lost their Supplemental Security Insurance benefits; Medicaid and Medicare payments to states have been reduced, resulting in lower reimbursement and shorter hospital stays; vocational and social rehabilitation programs have been reduced; the Comprehensive Employment and Training Act was rescinded; housing for the disabled under Section 8 has become almost non-existent. The list is lengthy but by no means inclusive of the budget-cutting measures that have negatively affected this vulnerable group.

The results of legislative and administrative action have been striking. The mentally ill have been deinstitutionalized and "de-entitlemented." Entitlements that provided for food, shelter and health care have been stripped away. Money has been saved at the expense of the mentally ill. If one accepts a figure of $50,000 as the current cost of mental hospital care, and community care as less than $25,000, then it can be seen that combined federal, state and local expenditures for the homeless mentally ill are much lower. Surplus food and shelter care using volunteers do not cost much.

An estimate of savings of $25,000 a year on each and every mentally ill homeless person might not be unrealistic. Multiplied by a mentally ill homeless population that is perhaps as many as one million, the saving may be on the order of billions.

In a rational and humane society, one must repeatedly ask at what cost such massive savings are achieved. How many families are devastated by the absence of community supports, the inability to locate services, eyeglasses, dental care, housing or health care, before moving to comprehensive solutions? In 1980 the National Leadership Conference for the Homeless Mentally Ill organized as a coalition representing diverse professional and citizen groups. It produced a national plan for the chronic mentally ill that would provide and restore this continuum of care across service systems. The next step is action to put a national plan for the mentally ill into effect to prevent this vulnerable population from the plight of homelessness.

As cited earlier, one of the most damaging weaknesses of current programs for mentally ill people is that "dual-diagnosed" people, those who are both mentally ill and drug and alcohol abusers, fall through the crack between the mental health system and the substance-abuse treatment system. Most mental health agencies will not accept someone for treatment who is currently drunk or high, and most drug and alcohol programs refuse those with mental disorders. This Catch-22 arrangement means that many people who desperately need assistance but are poorly equipped to seek it are excluded from programs and told to go find help elsewhere.[3]

The logical solution to this dilemma is to provide help for dual-diagnosed mental patients. Attempts are being made to find workable solutions for those with dual diagnoses. In spite of these efforts, the barriers remain fundamental ones. Approaches to treatment differ; professionals in one area are not familiar with problems in the other; organizations have specific domains and vested interests in remaining separate. This political difference, at the expense of documented client need, provides a clear example of the irrationality of rational and coordinated service organization.

The Welfare System

It is frequently said that there are more welfare disincentives than incentives built into the entitlement programs that provide Aid to Families with Dependent Children, General Assistance, or Supplemental Security Income. Entitlement benefits provide a source of income and some financial stability. But many people who are at risk of homelessness are so disabled, confused, desperate or alienated that they cannot get and retain eligibility for these programs without someone to help them negotiate a process that is both complex and time-consuming. In one county in California, the welfare form is 32 pages long, and this is true across the country. Even professional agency staff require education about how to complete these forms in order to help clients obtain entitlement benefits. Most people need such help, and when it is given, the results are positive.

The most glaring need for coordination between human service systems is manifested in the housing and welfare systems. The average American spends about 40 to 45 percent of his or her paycheck on housing, as compared with the average European, who spends between 20 and 25 percent. In contrast, people who receive general relief checks from Los Angeles County get $280 monthly and spend more than 80 percent of their income on housing. Toward the end of each month, the number of homeless on the streets increases daily. The number shrinks after the first of the month, when families and individuals receive their welfare checks and are again able to afford rock-bottom housing.

Shelter poverty is a stark reality for many middle-income American families. For those receiving public entitlement benefits, it is more stark and dispiritedly unavoidable. Faced with 20 percent of their total income to meet all after shelter costs, more people are choosing to live in the streets than in the derelict housing that is available to them.

A solid homeless-prevention program tied to the welfare system would peg benefit levels closer to the cost of the least expensive housing. Homeless-prevention programs located in welfare offices that are designed to help families at risk of homelessness are important and effective. But they must be accompanied by realistic benefit levels, or those families who receive help in finding and securing housing will not be able to maintain it for more than six months. Project Alert in New York and the Homeless Prevention Program, begun in Los Angeles, are positive attempts to prevent homelessness by coordinating housing programs with public welfare departments, but even these well-conceived programs keep beneficiaries at risk of homelessness because they do not address the high cost of low-income housing and the inadequacy of welfare benefit levels.[4]

One of the most common contradictions in the welfare system is its requirement that beneficiaries show proof of residence to be eligible for benefits. Presumably, this requirement prohibits people from claiming benefits in more than one place. It also discourages people from moving to states and counties that provide the most generous benefits. This concern for maintaining and protecting the welfare system from those who would take advantage of it dates back to fourteenth-century England when the Statute of Laborers was passed requiring proof of residency for poor law relief and protecting local authorities against sturdy vagabonds and beggars.[5] Little evidence has ever been produced to prove the notion that people move to obtain benefits.

What has become clear through mounting evidence is that residency requirements contribute to individual homelessness. Typically, when a person loses a job, and eventually loses his or her home because of an inability to pay rent or meet mortgage payments, he or she loses credit and does not have money to pay move-in costs for a new and cheaper dwelling. The only recourse is public welfare. But without an address, even public welfare is unavailable, thus perpetuating the cycle of homelessness. Proof-of-residency requirements make sense to those who are concerned about the proverbial "welfare cheat." It makes no sense to those who are concerned about preventing people from becoming homeless.

Fortunately, public welfare agencies and personnel have acknowledged this flaw in the system and have made many different kinds of flexible arrangements with community social agencies, designating them as legal payees for recipients who do not have a permanent address. This has helped numerous people regain housing and employment while using welfare as their aid in transition.

Another area of public welfare that poses difficulties regarding early detection of welfare recipients who are homeless-vulnerable is the separation of income and social service functions. This policy was mandated by the Department of Health, Education and Welfare in 1972. The manifest reasons for separating the two functions were twofold: first, to eliminate use of coercion of recipients to use social services, and second, to clarify the distinction between determining eligibility for public welfare funds and the need for social services. The separation of social services from income maintenance in public welfare law directly responded to the arguments of sympathetic reformers who claimed that if people were poor, they needed money. Some may need services as well, but this should be an individualized matter.

These intentions were fair, but they have not been realized. Many people who have serious problems and need social services receive income only, and frequently fall through the crack between income and social services. Some of these become homeless. One empirical study, the single study assessing the separation of services and income, suggests greater utilization of services and greater satisfaction by service recipients and providers in the pre-separation organization.[6]

Most of the states have retained this separation plan, but many are now reconsidering a return to the earlier merged plan. In the context of homelessness, merging services and income would coordinate services and enable early identification of people with problems that are likely to lead to homelessness.

While it may be premature, in the absence of sufficient empirical studies, to advocate the merged model, common sense suggests that it removes a major obstacle in the way of coordinating service systems at those key points that involve clients, and could help people in need of counseling and other personal social services to obtain them in the current arrangement of public assistance programs.

Public Housing

The early public housing projects did not start out to be the crime-infested tenements that many have become. At their best, they provided a full range of social services in recognition of the many problems experienced by public housing tenants. Youth and recreation workers, social workers assigned to individuals and families with special needs, and community-relations workers were regular features of public housing. This resulted in a positive environment that offered housing plus services.

Few public housing projects today hire anybody but custodial workers. If the earlier plan of locating human services workers in public housing projects were revived, people who live at risk of homelessness for any number of reasons could be identified early with a view toward keeping them in the circle of housing and stability.

The most needed resource, for those with mental illness in particular, is housing. This is also the most difficult to provide. Without housing that is appropriate for people with a mental illness, the provision of other services is bound to be less than effective. Even when a client has an income, there is little or no housing that can be afforded at the income levels provided by either entitlements or low-paying jobs.

Andranovich and Rosenblum, cited by the Rand Corporation, report in their study of case management: "Above all other concerns, the availability of low-cost housing coupled with supportive services for individuals who are seriously mentally disabled affects the potential success of any case management effort. Without stable, permanent housing, a client is less likely to be able to adjust to the community and to participate fully in other available services."[7] This compelling need for housing emphasizes the lack of public housing on any scale, as well as the importance of coordinating housing and services.

Coordination Among Levels of Government

The National Governor's Association has described serious obstacles placed in their way by the federal government in their attempts to increase state responsibilities in housing, welfare and child care. This demonstrates that disaccord between agencies is aggravated by conflicts among government levels that retard attempts to provide services that would prevent homelessness.

The governors and mayors alike call for a coordinated effort and genuine partnership among all levels of government and the private sector. They argue that the federal government's role in providing affordable housing is crucial and that the Congress and the Administration must assume leadership roles. But since there are significant differences in the nature and extent of housing problems, efforts to provide housing should be tailored to local needs and geographic differences. The National Governors Association is seeking more leeway in designing housing programs for state and local governments. As things now stand, the continuing reduction in federal funds threatens to make the shortage of low-income housing worse. At the same time, federal laws and regulations inhibit the ability of state and local governments to devise solutions of their own.

The general focus of excessive or unacceptable federal laws and regulations is on the multiple federal agencies that state and local governments, as well as private developers, are required to deal with on a single project. Governors and mayors almost universally complain about burdensome requirements from Washington that are not accompanied by federal funds and, they say, prevent states and localities from meeting their own critical needs.

Ultimately, a national homeless-prevention policy should be based upon partnership with the states, local governments and the private sector. The foundation of such a policy should be based upon an exploration of the costs and benefits of integrating housing subsidies, public assistance, job training and tax benefits to develop more effective programs for poor families.

Federalism, the complex and constantly shifting set of power relationships between the states and the central government in Washington, is at the center of intense debate about how the nation is to be governed and its citizens served. The drama of states, local governments and the federal government each attacking the other for not meeting its responsibilities to provide services and funds, has resulted in making people — especially those who rely on public services — pawns in the power struggle.

The federal-state relationship changed substantially during the Reagan presidency, both strengthening and weakening the states. Most observers believe that the relationship will change again by the 1990s when the federal government will be forced by circumstances to play a more activist role, particularly in human services. Few, however, envision a return to the 1960s when nearly every program was initiated, controlled, and mostly financed by Washington. The federal budget deficit is likely to continue to limit federal spending.

What the governors would like to see happen is for the federal government to earmark its spending more precisely to populations and areas of greatest need rather than apply money uniformly to the entire country. Generally, the states would carry a larger share of the financial responsibility than in the past, and they would be the major social and economic innovators.

Revision in the welfare system is frequently cited as a step in this direction. The Family Security Act allows for a wide range of approaches to the task of converting welfare recipients into jobholders. The law requires that most federal welfare funds be spent on those who need it most. And they are based on a variety of innovative welfare-to-jobs programs established by the states in recent years.

The governors are calling for similar coordinated arrangements in the areas of housing, child care and transportation. They generally assume that in the absence of a federal compelling role like civil rights enforcement, social and economic programs are best attended to at the state and local level. Officials at these levels are presumed to be more accountable and responsive to local conditions.

The mammoth Stewart B. McKinney Homeless Assistance Act, passed by Congress in July 1987, represents the type of federal-local arrangement sought by the National Governors Association. The Act gave grants for emergency shelters to cities and counties that qualify for Community Development Block Grants, and established numerous competitive programs for rehabilitating old SROs, housing for the handicapped homeless, transitional housing and some innovative prevention programs.

The McKinney Act, like many well-intended laws, posed serious implementation problems, particularly related to coordination. It overwhelmed local governments with a maze of funding programs under several federal agencies and departments, and it had one of the shortest scheduling periods in history, from the time of publication of the Act to deadlines for applications. Most programs under the McKinney Act are uncoordinated. Six agencies are authorized to administer 15 programs. This has placed heavy responsibility on local governments and the voluntary sector agencies to make sure that all of the resources are used.

State governments have also cut funds for homeless programs in anticipation of receiving McKinney funds. This hardly supports the governors' position that the states should retain major responsibility for services. It merely exacerbates the federalism debate.

One overriding concern about the McKinney Act is what will happen to it under the Gramm-Rudman-Hollings budget-balancing process. In 1987 Congress authorized $442 million in McKinney money for fiscal 1987, but appropriated only $355 million. A total of $617 million was authorized for fiscal 1987-88, but this appropriation will also be cut.[8]

Given the precedent of the McKinney Act, constructive federalism directed at homelessness and homeless-prevention remains problematic and complex.

Inappropriate Use of Jails

Debilitated persons who live at the margins of society without assistance are increasingly becoming the subjects of criminal proceedings. As a result, the criminal-justice system is inappropriately saddled with the responsibility of acting as a social agency of last resort, a role that it performs inefficiently and at great expense.

The criminal-justice system has been forced to assume this role as a result of recent cuts in public funds for treatment programs to assist drug abusers. Without their criminal activity, including drug possession and drug intoxification, thefts, traffic offenses and aberrant or violent drug-induced acts, the criminal-justice system's workload could easily be reduced.

The largest group of offenders needing treatment are drug abusers. Many chronic drug abusers can be effectively treated in drug programs. Defendants committed to drug programs by court order have a cure rate higher than volunteer patients, and considerably higher than defendants sentenced to jail.

Another staple of the courts is mental illness. The bizarre behavior and delusions of the poor and unattended mentally ill generally bring them into contact with law enforcement. Cuts in mental health services have resulted in extreme increases in the number of mentally ill persons enmeshed in the criminal-justice system.

Criminal-justice professionals are constantly looking for programs in which to place such persons, but few exist. Because prisoners receive priority for scarce space in county psychiatric facilities, police officers are encouraged to make mercy bookings — arrests of the mentally ill to enhance their chances of receiving at least some minimal psychiatric attention and to get them away from the dangers of the streets. As a result, jails have become large psychiatric hospitals.

A third category of needy persons, often inappropriately under the auspices of the criminal-justice system, is the homeless, who overlap with, but are not confined to, the mentally ill. Homeless people usually commit public-nuisance crimes such as sleeping in parks, drinking in public or loitering, and sometimes minor property crimes. Often the solution to their problems is simply a safe place to live, where they could get food, clothing and counseling. Unfortunately, these programs remain scarce, and all too frequently the vagrant released from a few days in jail returns to the park to sleep for lack of any place else to go.

Ironically, the process of criminalizing the debilitated has achieved only false economies, because the savings derived from cuts in human services are more than offset by increased expenditures on the criminal-justice system. It is as least three times as expensive to commit a mental patient through the criminal-justice system as to commit directly.

There is a direct correlation between homelessness and the lack of short-term inpatient psychiatric treatment, which stabilizes the condition of such persons, making them better able to function. Yet since 1979, due to budget cuts, the number of spaces in acute-care psychiatric facilities has been reduced dramatically.

Such cuts in human services do not save money. They simply shift the burden of care to a criminal-justice system that is not equipped to deal with it. In this respect, conservative critics of social programs are correct. The public's money is being thrown at social problems through expansion of the criminal-justice system at a time when more economic, practical and thoughtful — not to mention humane — solutions are being ignored.

Jail is no place for social work. Drug abusers, the mentally ill and the homeless do not belong there.

A Conceptual Framework for Coordinated Services to Prevent Homelessness

Chapter 12 describes an ideal service typology for a comprehensive and coordinated mental health system that is client-centered and organized through case management. This typology, if extended to all human service systems, could become the framework for coordinating programs, practices and policies to prevent conflicts that force people through the cracks in the system. Exhibit 2 (p. 226) depicts a range of human service systems and strategies required for treating mentally disabled people. This model could be extended to become a client-centered comprehensive human service system. As such, it would weave a web of entitlements around all people, especially those who are the most vulnerable, and would move the agenda of homeless-prevention forward by leaps.

In a volume describing various attempts to unify services, John Talbott defined ten elements of an ideally integrated service system: a common theoretical basis for the system, a single point of entry, a single point of funding allocation, a single person in control, a no-refusal-of-treatment policy, a division of labor among members of the treatment/service team, a tracking mechanism for patients, separation of service-delivery and service-monitoring, a single service plan and flexibility of staff assignments in the system.[9] Similarly, Bachrach has identified the key characteristics of successful model service systems for the chronic mentally ill.[10]

Such programs specifically target chronic patients, link resources, have an overall functional integrity, provide individually tailored treatment, are relevant and sensitive to their cultural context, have specially trained staff, develop close liaisons between community and hospital services, and conduct ongoing internal evaluations of the quality and costs of services.

The prototype for such programs was developed in Dane County, Wisconsin over a decade ago, and its characteristics and success have been extensively described elsewhere.[11] Summarized briefly, the responsibility for public mental health services in Wisconsin was decentralized from the state to the county level. In Dane County, far-sighted administrators and clinicians organized a system of services to encourage cost-effective community-based care for the chronically mentally ill by ensuring that funding followed patients from the hospital to the community. They integrated services into their Training in Community Living (TCL) program which includes a crisis intervention service, a mobile community treatment team, a daytime supportive activity program, and specialized living arrangements. A core service team forms the heart of this system. This team assumes responsibility for a defined group of patients, provides primary somatic and psychosocial treatments, and sees to it that a patient's needs are met in all areas of life by coordinating services, collaborating with other providers and advocating for resources. In a randomized experiment, patients in the TCL program utilized considerably fewer hospital days and were less symptomatic, more functional and more satisfied with their lives compared to patients treated in a more traditional, hospital-oriented manner. The costs of the TCL program did not differ significantly from the control treatment.[12] This model program has been replicated elsewhere with similar success.[13]

In theory, an integrated service system holds many advantages over the more typical, loosely associated system of agencies for improving both the quality and efficiency of services. First, integrated systems may improve quality of care by means of greater continuity, comprehensiveness and flexibility of services. When a provider accepts responsibility for all of the client's needs, service gaps and service duplications are more readily identified and addressed. This reduces unnecessary burdens on patients and their families (e.g., having to invent their own ways to fill service gaps or acting as the informal case managers between providers who do not communicate directly with each other), reduces the risk of untoward clinical decisions due to lack of adequate communication (e.g., unnecessary hospitalizations due to inadequate information by admitting officers), reduces negative interactions between providers (e.g., turf battles over who is responsible for a patient in crisis), and increases coordination of interventions (e.g., not changing medications just as the patient enters a new residence, or successfully linking a reduction in medication with the patient's progress in a vocational training program).

Second, integration also should improve the efficiency of services by eliminating duplication, substituting new programs which reduce the need for more expensive ones (e.g., day treatment programs or family respite services which reduce the use of emergency and inpatient care), improving communications to reduce costly omissions or duplications (e.g., eliminating delays in hospital discharge summaries which lead to inadequate outpatient follow-up care and rapid rehospitalizations; repetition of psychological and medical tests due to failure to communicate results as the patient moves from one provider to another), and creating provider incentives to enhance efficiency (e.g., better staffing of outpatient services made possible by elimination of unnecessary inpatient utilization).

Integration also permits better coordination of workforce resources to improve the rational distribution and availability of qualified personnel. In summary, an ideally integrated system develops and distributes services to meet patients' needs in the most cost-effective manner.

If effective models for service integration already exist, then what stands in the way of general implementation? Bachrach has argued that this failure to generalize lies in the differences between model programs and service systems. Because model programs have more control over their resources and whom they serve, they succeed much more often than do service systems in creating rational service arrays to address patients' needs.[14] In contrast, mental health systems must provide a wider variety of services to a wider variety of patients, thus reducing their capacity to plan and to match patients with services. Mental health systems lack the clear boundaries of model programs and are more susceptible to the influences of governing bodies, advocacy groups and the like. Model programs can focus their funding, personnel, and material resources on their target population, but mental health systems encompass competing priorities among multiple patient groups and providers. In essence, systems cannot control and regulate themselves in the way that models can. Other barriers to integrated service systems exist. Agencies and providers naturally seek to maintain their own integrity, fearing the loss of control and resources that may accompany integration, and setting up the "turf battles" with which we are all too familiar. Concerns about confidentiality in such a system are also common. Integration requires that information flow readily among providers. Currently, confidentiality exists between a given provider and a patient, and providers understandably worry about the transfer of information in such a system. We do need an effective and safe mechanism by which a patient establishes a confidential relationship with an integrated system of providers rather than with individual providers. Finally, the development of integrated services relies upon a shared concept and knowledge base of care for the chronically mentally ill. Existing systems often encompass disparate or simply unarticulated views, and there exists a severe shortage of personnel who are specifically trained to work with this population.

The desire to stimulate and encourage human service providers to adopt the practices of integrated service models has prompted four new policy initiatives. These policies assume the superiority of integrated models over existing systems and seek both the elimination of barriers to their application and the creation of positive incentives and pressures for providers to adopt them.

The goal is to achieve service integration at the service-patient interface. To accomplish this, each of the four policies directly attempts to unify one or more of three system functions: clinical responsibility, funding and regulation. These four policy initiatives are 1) continuous treatment terms, 2) establishment of local mental health authorities, 3) integrated entitlement, and 4) capitation payment systems.

Continuous-Treatment Teams: This policy option directly unifies clinical responsibilities by requiring that the same mental health team accept responsibility indefinitely for a given chronically mentally ill patient, no matter where the patient is — hospital, foster home, shelter, family, own apartment — and no matter what the patient's needs. Team functions include outreach, patient assessment, treatment-planning, provision of services, referral for other services, advocacy and crisis intervention. At times, development of natural support systems, advocacy for community resource development, monitoring of service quality and public education are also required.

The advantages to this approach have already been discussed with regard to the Dane County, Wisconsin experiment. However, the problems with the model are formidable if the development of these teams is not linked with other system changes. Torrey encountered considerable resistance in his attempt to create continuous-care teams at St. Elizabeth's Hospital.[15] Obstacles included rigid job descriptions and union rules, staff resistance to changes in work hours and inflexibility in hours of services, interprofessional turf struggles regarding role definition, supervision and uncertainty about who should be responsible for patients who migrate or who refuse to participate in treatment. The Dane County experiment succeeded in overcoming these obstacles because the development of continuous-care teams occurred within the context of considerable systemic control by the principal developers. Attempts to create continuous-care teams without such systemic control seem doomed in most settings.

There are some new initiatives to stimulate the development of continuous-care teams. In Arizona continuous or "clinical/case management" teams are being developed under new regional mental health authorities and a capitation payment system. These teams directly provide patients' assessment, treatment and service plans, long-term case management, supportive services, crisis intervention, outreach, transportation, medications and access to medical care; purchase arrangements from the continuum of other care providers; establish working relationships with legal guardians; and conduct service evaluations. Some cities included in the Robert Wood Johnson Program for Chronic Mental Patients may develop continuous-care teams under local mental health authorities.[16] Both the Arizona and Johnson Foundation projects will be evaluated over the next several years. It is important to note that these programs do not specify the details of clinical services to the degree encompassed in the Dane County experiment, but like Dane County, they do link continuous-care team development with other system changes.

In summary, the crux of continuous care teams is the integration of services at the service team level. This policy option, though the most direct means for ensuring that service providers work together, is unlikely to succeed unless implemented within the context of other system changes which reduce administrative barriers and create incentives for personnel and agencies to cooperate. The other three policy options do not directly dictate the creation of continuous-care teams, but often attempt to foster their development through less direct, though forceful systemic changes.

Local Mental Health Authorities: A local health authority may be either a government agency, such as a city health authority, or a private, non-profit corporation. The authority oversees all local services for the chronically mentally ill through a variety of mechanisms currently utilized by state mental health authorities: establishment and enforcement of local regulations and requirements for operation, determination of reimbursement eligibility, purchase of services by contract, and direct operation of programs. In theory, such authorities possess the clout to ensure that providers comply with a community-wide plan of integrated services and, compared to statewide authorities, have greater sensitivity to local issues and greater flexibility to respond quickly to local needs. Although the authority integrates programs at a local administrative level, it does not necessarily dictate how services are to be provided or who should provide them, unlike the Dane

County model. The authority may opt to contract for services from both the public and private sectors on a competitive bidding basis. Such authorities can allow considerable opportunity for creative and culturally specific service development. Their major risks are that they may lack the resources or energy to change services, thus becoming a passive conduit of funds, or worse, yet another layer of bureaucracy with which providers must deal.

In the Arizona model, nine regional authorities will be established as public corporations with boards of directors, including family members. The regional authority will exercise a broad range of functions including development of requests for proposals, bidding mechanisms and awarding of bids; establishment of patient eligibility criteria, assignment of eligible patients to treatment teams, enforcement of licensing, certification and standards of care as established by the state, maintenance of a patient-tracking system; technical assistance to treatment teams; advocacy; and regional planning, among others.[17]

In New York State, Monroe and Livingston counties have established a non-profit private corporation, Integrated Mental Health, Inc.(IMH), to integrate all public mental health services in the two-county area. This corporation centralizes the flow of money for services through contracts with funding sources and then distributes these funds by contracts to local "lead agencies" (community mental health centers). These lead agencies, in turn, may subcontract for certain services, such as supervised housing, with other providers. IMH has the authority to establish a Contract Revenue System (CRS), a network of payor contracts between and among New York State, the two counties, the United Way of Greater Rochester, and IMF, which centralizes on a local level service funding streams; a Capitation Payment System (CPS) for the chronically mentally ill and a Management Information System (MIS) for all participating agencies to monitor patient outcomes, support financial and management reporting, and to permit provider agencies to monitor and plan services. Although IMH contracts with lead agencies require that each chronically mentally ill person under CPS have an approved treatment plan, monitored on a performance basis by IMH, IMH itself does not dictate required services to the extent apparently planned in the Arizona model.

A third example of the local mental health authority option is the Robert Wood Johnson Program for the Chronically Mentally Ill, which funds the development of local mental health authorities in Philadelphia, Baltimore, Charlotte, Columbus, Cincinnati, Toledo, Austin, Denver and Honolulu. Each of these cities has proposed a somewhat different model for the authority, but each authority will exercise considerable control over the distribution of funding and the regulation and/or direct provision of services.

In summary, the concept of local mental health authorities seems to have captured the interest of several locales. The authorities thus far conceived share the features of centralized control of funding streams and regulation of local services, but vary according to the degree to which they dictate specific service plans for individual patients and the degree to which they are involved in the direct provision of services. For each of these initiatives to create local authorities, evaluations are planned. Therefore they will become valuable sources of data to guide policy over the next several years.

Integrated Entitlements: Although the models of local mental health authorities include integration of funding streams on a local level, such integration may be accomplished at higher governmental levels. Clinicians, patients and their families are all amply aware of the problems that arise when funds for mental health, general health, substance abuse, social, vocational and housing services flow from different sources, producing uncoordinated and frequently irrational service arrays for the chronically mentally ill.

Recently, Talbott and Sharfstein proposed the creation of a single Social Security entitlement for the chronically mentally ill, pooling all existing funding streams for this population. The principal goal of such a funding change would be to strongly encourage states and locales through capitation grants to develop comprehensive, efficient and effective systems of services for the chronically mentally ill. They emphasize that the responsibility for implementing such systems must ultimately rest with states and locales, but integrating funding at the federal level will greatly facilitate this. They specifically cite the development of state and local mental health authorities focusing on the integrated care of the chronically mentally ill as a desired goal of such an entitlement program. In effect, this option, by using the leverage of federal dollars, would encourage all states to implement the changes in local mental health service authorities currently under development in the Arizona, Monroe and Livingston Counties, Johnson Foundation and Dane County projects.[18]

The problems and risks in such an option include the difficulties of estimating the costs according to level of disability rather than diagnosis, the risk of loss or reduction in funds when hospital beds are no longer directly linked to funding sources, and the risk that the cost of patients' basic supportive needs will displace the provision of treatment and rehabilitation. With regard to stimulating continuous-care teams, there is also the problem that restructuring of federal entitlements is very distal from the service-patient interface. Clearly the incentives at that level must somehow trickle down to the local level, and would have to precipitate a cascade of changes; e.g., federal entitlement integration would lead to state funding integration, leading to local funding integration, which would ultimately result in the development of continuous-care teams. Nonetheless, Talbott and Sharfstein have made an urgent call for movement in this direction to ameliorate the ills of the currently disjointed array of entitlements.

Capitation Payment Systems: As usually defined, capitation is a method of payment for services in which a provider is paid a prospectively determined sum for each person served during a given time period. Typically, the mix of services covered is also predetermined and limited, particularly in the area of mental health. The advantages of capitation payment systems for the chronically mentally ill include the identification of a single provider who assumes responsibility for providing designated services for the patient, provider incentives to intervene early in crises and to offer adequate maintenance and rehabilitation services to reduce unnecessary and costly hospitalizations, and opportunities to create innovative, cost-effective service programs. The risks include inadequate resources in the capitation amount to cover needed services, incomplete coverage for services needed by more disabled patients in plans to protect providers against financial losses, and the lack of patients' and families' choice in selecting providers if they are dissatisfied with the services rendered. Chronic illnesses in general pose special problems for capitation payment systems because they are so costly to providers.[19]

As already noted, both the local mental health authority models and the integrated entitlement model rely heavily upon capitation, although in theory they need not. While capitation funds for the chronically mentally ill will most certainly derive from public sources, there is no theoretical reason why private-sector providers cannot agree to contract for them. Whether or not the private sector enters this market will depend upon the financial viability of capitation plans for the chronically mentally ill.

The most explicitly specified capitation plan for this population is that developed in Rochester, New York. This plan establishes categories of chronically mentally ill patients, based upon prior use of state hospital services, and sets different capitation rates and different required services for these categories. More generally, planners of this scheme have proposed a method of capitation for chronic mental patients which includes integrated public entitlements, payment to public sector providers or designated private sector providers, coverage for all psychiatric, medical, social and rehabilitation services, and multiple-risk-adjusted capitation rates. Other capitation experiments for the CMI are currently planned or in progress in Arizona, Philadelphia, South Carolina and Wisconsin. Capitation seems to be at the core of several initiatives. By integrating payments to providers, capitation may stimulate providers to create integrated, effective and cost-efficient services. Whether such incentives truly are experienced by providers serving the chronically mentally ill under capitation funding mechanisms remains a very open question.

To summarize, the predominantly shared goal for changing how we serve the chronically mentally ill and others who need social services and income is the integration of responsibility and authority for delivery of services and income at the front-line provider level, creating the circumstances for motivated, creative and well-trained service teams to develop and deliver individualized, comprehensive, cost-effective and continuous services for people and their families. The policy options reviewed either explicitly or implicitly seek to create such continuous-care teams, and differ mainly in their level of intervention, i.e., service team vs. funding vs. regulation; local vs. state vs. federal. In fact, most of the existing or planned initiatives combine more than one level of intervention to increase their likelihood of success.

Conclusion

A Non-Homeless Future

Beyond Shelter

Across the United States, people who work directly with homeless persons in shelters, soup kitchens, outreach programs and transitional living facilities bemoan the nagging moral dilemma that they constantly face. Their empathy for the plight of homeless people compels them to serve in any kind of setting that is permitted to provide homeless services in their communities. They sincerely wish to make life better for people who live in such insufferable conditions. On the other hand, those who are deeply enough concerned about homelessness amidst plenty raise questions about why homelessness exists, why it has proliferated despite their best efforts, how homelessness can be ended, and how it can be prevented. The growing number of people asking these questions complain that they are too caught up in meeting the immediate, and frequently desperate, needs of the homeless people they encounter every day to address these fundamental questions in more concrete ways.

Not all people who work with homeless populations experience this moral dilemma. For many, work with homeless men, women, children and families satisfies a personal need to do good. Others see the more traditional opportunity to do God's work among the homeless by trying to save the souls of those who have been predestined to misfortune in the moral ethics of stewardship and evangelism.

Viewed from the perspective of homeless people or service providers, shelters, soup kitchens and all other emergency responses to homelessness have emerged as one of the cruelest forms of bureaucratic dehumanization in spite of the fact that homeless advocates, religious activists, and public and private leaders praise them. Indeed, the more entrenched the shelter system becomes, including a growing number of shelter-based services like health care, job banks and welfare entitlement offices, the more institutionalized the system grows. Even the best and most humane shelters, that manage to help some homeless people regain stable lives, are part of a new arrangement for providing relief to those in desperate straits that resembles the workhouses and poorhouses of earlier times. The ultimate question that the shelter response raises is, have we returned to the early Elizabethan poor law tradition of indoor relief? Unless we move beyond shelters and turkeys at Thanksgiving and Christmas to emphases on preventing homelessness in the first place, this reinstitutionalization of indoor relief will become a permanent fixture of social services in the 1990s. We will have to sadly affirm the reappearance of the poorhouse.

By opting for a strategy of "the right to shelter," homeless advocates, led by the National Coalition for the Homeless, expressed decent intentions. Nine years after the Callahan v. Carey consent decree in New York asserting the right to shelter, it has become all too clear that well-intentioned homeless advocates, along with many sincere public officials, allowed themselves to be diverted from the need for permanent and preventive solutions in the press for emergency responses to a growing and desperate problem.

One justification for developing so many emergency services is that, in truth, few people perceived the problem of homelessness as more than temporary.

There is no satisfaction from hindsight, but if homeless advocates had pressed for the "right to housing," rather than shelter, they would have focused more directly on the nature of homelessness and its prevention. It is still not too late!

The most effective way to deal with a person who is homeless is to address that person's need for housing in a straightforward and expedient manner. If one must subject a homeless person to a secondary experience like living in a shelter or transitional housing, going to jail, or to a mental hospital, then that person must adjust to the intermediate situation. Adjusting to living in their unique "housing situations" is often the bitter lesson of a lifetime. This adjustment may involve a considerable detour for the person, and distract him or her from what needs to be done to return to an ordinary life in regular housing. There seems to be a correlation between having lived in what Erving Goffman referred to as a "total institution" and being homeless later on.[1]

As they exist today, even the best shelters merely alleviate the individual and collective guilt of society by appearing to help homeless people. Dennis Culhane and Marc Fried convey the force of this assertion by claiming that the shelter system

> ...only serves to keep people alive and communicates its message to the homeless, that keeping alive is all that can be done for them. As institutions of social control, the shelters tend to confirm people's self-blame, to increase their feeling of helplessness, and to perpetuate their powerlessness by denying virtually all opportunities to allow people to control their own lives. In the rituals of obtaining food and shelter, the homeless are forced to be utterly dependent and without a voice, often denied even the minimal chances to improve their situation.[2]

This dehumanization process is further developed by the use of the popular and acceptable term, "the homeless." By dropping the words *people, persons, man, woman, child* or *family*, advocates, scholars, journalists, clergy and direct care givers have stripped the humanness and individual faces and personalities from homeless people. A faceless problem becomes more tolerable than one which is attached to a person with a name, face and unique situation.

Those who continue to view shelters as part of a solution to the problem of homelessness also need reminding that shelters are unsatisfactory because there are never enough of them. Faced with inadequate, temporary and emergency services, homeless people have been converted to permanent victims who all too frequently are blamed for their plight. Discredited ideas of the past have accompanied the new wave of homelessness as organizations and governments have attempted to cope with the growing need. Among these ideas are:

> "Some people are going to soup kitchens voluntarily because the food is free and that's easier than paying for it."
>
> — Edwin Meese

> "The Sunday newspapers list thousands of jobs for which there is no taker, and some homeless people are sleeping on grates by choice."
>
> — Ronald Reagan

> "If we don't make homelessness as unpleasant as possible, everyone will want to be homeless."
>
> — Edward Koch

To be sure, there are homeless people who are incompetent and irresponsible. Many are seriously disabled drug addicts. Others are aggressive panhandlers. But the pervasive tendency to blame homelessness on people's flaws serves more to assuage public and private guilt, divert attention and problem-solving from systemic failures, and rationalize reinstitutionalization in state hospitals. Focusing on the worst examples of the homeless population also allows the general public to ignore the far greater number of innocent and unfortunate who experience this tragedy.

The purpose of this book has been to challenge emergency responses to homelessness, as well as views of homeless people as unfortunate failures, and shift to a paradigm of prevention. This shift involves raising questions about the ways in which our society facilitates the process of falling through the cracks economically, socially and psychologically. A more precise understanding of the human process of skidding to the most marginal places in society moves beyond temporary solutions to an agenda of prevention.

Nothing in this position suggests that shelters should be closed down. They should, however, be acknowledged for what they are — temporary havens for people with serious problems. This message cautions against converting such a temporary situation to permanence.

Beyond the Reluctant Welfare State

No set of problems challenges the commitments of caring Americans to meet the demands of equity and common decency more than mass homelessness. The agenda of the Social Security Act remains unfinished while homelessness continues. An affirmative government, with the consent and participation of its governed, can only fulfill the promise of economic security for all Americans by investing in programs that assure income, housing and health care.

A non-homeless future does not imply a socialist state; nor would it necessarily foster dependency and irresponsibility, as many challengers of welfare statism contend. When people are threatened by the prospect of homelessness they are more likely to become dependent, compliant, irresponsible and incapable of saving themselves. People who are free from dependency are capable and free to assert their individual responsibility and independence.

This book has drawn upon theory from such diverse bodies of knowledge as economics, family policy, housing and urban planning, social welfare policy, and mental health practice in an effort to demonstrate that large-scale interventions in the economy, the housing sector and the mental health system could reverse the massive growth of homelessness in the United States. It has proposed a series of recommendations designed to keep people who are increasingly at risk of homelessness within their circle of housing.

In the economic sector, this agenda features national industrial policies of full employment with adequate wages. Families, increasingly reliant on two worker parents, need policies that allow them to compete successfully and remain in the workplace while meeting their responsibilities to their children, and more frequently, their aging parents. Taxation trends have become too regressive to protect low-wage earners from inflation. These low earners comprise the highest proportion of homeless-vulnerable people. Unemployment compensation is now collected by only one-third of people who are out of work. This benefit should be extended to respond to the realities and exigencies of today's unemployed who do not meet the criteria established in the 1935 Social Security Act. Proposals for an increase in the minimum wage are welcome homeless-prevention measures that would make a paycheck worth more than a welfare check. Finally, welfare reform focused on adequate and decent benefits rather than workfare programs that prepare people for the lowest-paying jobs and permanent poverty, hold great promise for preventing homelessness that is caused by economic conditions. Given the fact that no state has yet to set benefit levels at the official poverty level, this welfare standard should be acceptable even in conditions of scarcity and large deficits. Welfare reform has such great potential for homeless-prevention because the massive cuts in welfare benefits that began in 1980-81 forced many people into homelessness. The time is right for a reversal of these cuts.

Because homelessness has so many direct ties to a lack of low-cost affordable housing, by definition, multiple strategies to provide such housing are essential components for preventing homelessness. Homeless-prevention programs, targeted to people who face eviction or temporary reductions in income, assist people to remain in their homes through grants or loans for rent and mortgage payments, or security deposits on replacement housing. These programs, few but growing, offer families assistance to prevent eviction or foreclosure through tangible help with short-term needs such as utility payments, landlord-tenant problems, and rent or mortgage help in times of crisis.

State and local government-sponsored home ownership and

rental assistance programs have stimulated construction of new low- and moderate-priced houses by offering reduced interest and first mortgage loans, as well as lower rates favoring builders. These programs, augmented by federal resources, could multiply and meet the need for affordable housing.

Housing rehabilitation programs, financed through mortgages and deferred payback plans, shared-equity loans, forgiven loans and resale controls, can maintain the existing stock of low-cost shelter.

Non-profit housing, mutual cooperative housing and employer-assisted housing have emerged as other partial solutions to the problem of affordable housing.

Hartman's model of social housing offers a sound basis for homeless-prevention because it acknowledges the existence of a segment of the population who cannot participate in the private housing sector, no matter how fully it may be subsidized by the government. Social housing would establish a third stream of housing which is neither private nor public in the traditional sense.

Inclusionary zoning, shared housing and rent control can produce new stock and protect the scarce supply of affordable housing.

Finally, there must be a return to the construction and subsidization of public housing. The absence of an adequate public housing sector has resulted in five-year waiting lists exceeding 200,000 people across the United States. Despite their many flaws, public projects have maintained a circle of housing around many of the nation's poorest people who are the most homeless-vulnerable.[3] Criticisms of large public tracts as drug-infested targets of gang violence and abuse may be correct, but they do not justify the elimination of public housing. They do warrant greater vigilance of public housing sites, as well as the re-introduction of social services at the sites. It is also important to acknowledge that much public housing is scattered, garden-type, and indistinguishable from private housing.

None of these housing strategies depends upon government spending alone. They rely upon a more realistic combination of groups capable of financing social resources at the end of the twentieth century — creative financing arrangements that feature cooperative ventures between the government, the corporate sector, the non-profit sector, and community-based organizations. These arrangements are currently in place as demonstrations on small scales at the local level. It is time that they move beyond this and become national plans with the federal government acting as financier or catalyst. Newer cooperative arrangements for financing low-cost housing would include the construction industry as a partner in the financing pool. They would also contribute to the nation's much-needed productivity through the multiplier effect that new construction has on a community by creating new jobs, businesses, tax sources and general revenues.

In the mental health arena, the singular homeless-prevention measure of importance remains the institutionalization of deinstitutionalization. Instead, we are moving in the opposite direction, towards reinstitutionalization. To achieve this goal we must return to the implementation of the Community Mental Health Centers Act plan to establish 2,000 community mental health facilities and standardized programs of continuous care including case management, outreach, medication, care and advocacy in inpatient and outpatient settings, crisis response services, rehabilitation schemes, supports for the families of mentally ill people, income support and entitlements, housing and health care. These services should be organized so that they are coordinated, accessible, available and acceptable to people who are mentally ill and to their families.

Where possible, programs that are run by mental-health consumers should be encouraged as a means of empowering mentally disabled people and adding to the pool of personnel available as caregivers.

Relaxed involuntary commitment laws are the wave of the future. Over one-half of the states have begun to ease restrictions on commitment. As civil libertarians and mental health professionals are pitted against each other in their mutually sincere efforts to serve the mentally ill population and protect them from homelessness, all who are involved in the mental health system must note the futility of easier commitment laws in the absence of enough available services to treat people once they are committed.

For mentally ill people, homelessness translates to the availability of acceptable treatment. Arguments that street people refuse to accept treatment and care are diversionary because the few who do refuse are atypical of the many who want it and would accept it but are refused care because of laws constraining the duration of treatment and the glaring lack of resources to treat all who need and want help.

Homelessness Outside of the United States

International comparisons are by their very nature imperfect. Social and political contexts, including cultural norms and different situational conditions dissuage policymakers from transporting strategies and ideologies from one country to another. Nevertheless, we are living in a global economy where nations' strengths and weaknesses have become more similar than different. The problems associated with homelessness in the United States exist in almost every advanced industrial country in Western Europe. In the capitalist countries, these problems have been identified with the systemic factors of a diminished supply of affordable housing and a changed economic structure that has rendered between 10 and 15 percent of most advanced nations' employable population superfluous.

In the socialist countries, homelessness exists on a different dimension. The basic problem in socialist Eastern Europe is to provide housing for all social groups. This is a different problem because it does not involve unequal deprivation in a land of plenty.

Only the United States includes mental illness as an antecedent of homelessness, so that one preventive measure, mental health services, must be in place in other countries. As British homelessness has grown, analysts have acknowledged a new dimension to the problem, domestic violence and abuse among immigrants and against women. By adding this explanation, the British have begun to blame the victims of homelessness as Americans do.

All international comparisons of social and economic policies ultimately turn to Sweden. Despite its inefficacy as a rational model for all nations because of its small and homogeneous population, it retains examples of equity and efficiency for all societies that value individuality and accept responsibility for collective well-being.

In the context of homelessness, Sweden retains its integrity as an exemplar for other nations. A survey of homelessness conducted there in November 1987 found fewer than 100 homeless people in Stockholm, the largest city in Sweden, and only one person in Gothenburg, the second largest city.

These startlingly low figures, in contrast to other nations, merits some explanation as a basis for understanding preventive action elsewhere. Sweden clearly has a different history from other European nations. Nearly 180 years of peace, rapid urbanization, high economic growth, powerful unions, a powerful construction industry, and a strong set of egalitarian social goals have all made their mark on the nation's development. Nevertheless, all problems facing housing policymakers can be found in Sweden. Their severity, however, is less prevalent because of the conditions described above.[4]

The Swedish model of housing policy is mainly influenced by the fact that it ignores the imperatives of the private housing market sector. Out of Sweden's immense volume of housing subsidies, the bulk serve to raise the housing standards of people. This is both a strength and a weakness. It allows the government to set policies such as issuing acquisition loans to low-income families with children to buy used single-family dwellings. Sellers, of course, know this and frequently raise prices. However, the government generally ignores such divisive market behavior, thereby sanctioning the private housing market without directly subsidizing it. Housing policy in the public sector, which accounts for a major proportion of Sweden's housing supply, co-exists with the commercial housing sector but each operates separately. In this way, the Swedes are protected from homelessness by social policy, rather than private housing market policy.

Several key strategies for the preservation of housing in Sweden have contributed to the relative stability of housing in that country. These practices perform a redistributional task and keep people in housing and maintaining a housing stock.

Rent levels are set in negotiations between tenant organizations and their landlord counterparts. Rent leaders are semi-public bodies. A basic formula for setting rents is to keep the difference between negotiated rents and market rents as low as possible. People are not allowed to sell their tenancy agreements, but they may switch them for another, or hand them over to the seller of a single-family dwelling that they buy.

Practically all single-family dwellings recently constructed have received heavily subsidized government loans. This has resulted in housing for many, but it has not confined subsidies to those who really need them. In practice, one questions a social policy that subsidizes houses for rich people as well as poor. Nevertheless, the presence of subsidies has prevented homelessness by maintaining an affordable housing supply.

From 1949 to the present day, some 2.6 million dwellings have been completed. The whole population could be very well housed without utilizing any part of the housing heritage from centuries past.[5]

Most Western European countries played active roles in providing good-quality government-owned or built housing until the second half of the 1970s. Between 1951 and 1979 there was a high degree of consensus on national housing objectives. This steady postwar improvement in housing conditions has been reversed by new policies that attempt to reduce the size of the state sector, expand home ownership and revive the private rental sector. Australia and New Zealand, once strong proponents of public support for a large housing sector, have also moved to privatize large parts of the public housing supply. Homelessness that resembles conditions in the United States has emerged with these shifts from public responsibility for housing to private enterprise.

France reports the number of its homeless people to be between 200,000 and 400,000.[6] In 1986, England identified 102,980 homeless people.[7] All European countries report similar data and disclaim the accuracy of such data (suggesting that the numbers are higher) because of the inherent obstacles to obtaining a precise count of those without housing.

The growing problems of affordable housing, unemployment and homelessness coincided with the general international retreat from welfare state policies and programs. The new conservative governments in the mid-1980s came to power at a time when market liberalism and encouragement of laissez-faire were reappearing as a dominant economic theory. As nations returned to arguments that the revitalization of domestic economics required renewed support for entrepreneurialism by creating a climate of greater competition and new patterns of investment, the shift in housing policy became quite radical.

Housing policy was a central feature of the postwar development of social-democratic Labor Party administrations throughout Western Europe, Australia and New Zealand. These economies were largely shaped by Keynesian economic theories emphasizing the control of demand for commodities rather than upon the supply of money. The first two decades after World War II were marked by economic growth and only minimal periods of downward fluctuation. In these years, inflation was modest, unemployment rates were low and economic growth was obtained and sustained. As the 1960s approached, the Western industrialist nations began to falter. Inflation and unemployment became acute problems and presented a new "crisis" for capitalist nations.[8]

State intervention into this problem was reorganized during the 1960s with an emphasis on using new technological skills and relying upon improved economic management. The 1970s became the decade when the break with postwar social democratic welfare state policy occurred. Nearly all Western nations during this period adopted policies of fiscal austerity, shifting from supports for the demand side of the economy to the supply side, especially of money.

This emphasis on monetarism was accompanied by a revival of market individualism and deregulation, creating a new entrepreneurial culture in place of the former welfare culture. In the human service sector, market forces translated to the "privatization" of services. The result has been the growth of private medical insurance, proprietary health-delivery organizations and, in housing, the expansion of owner-occupied housing and private market control over housing construction and rehabilitation.

These changes were less marked in the United States than in other countries because it always relied on housing policy that encouraged free market control over the housing supply, even in the construction of public housing. The United Kingdom, under the Thatcher government, most radically shifted housing policy by redefining the role of the state in housing. Today England has become a residual housing provider, only entering the housing arena when the private market cannot meet the demands. Policy has therefore moved from support for public housing to one encouraging the further expansion of home ownership and the revival of the private rental sector. There is little difference between the housing policies of Britain and the United States today, in marked contrast to the pre-Thatcher government.

Britain has achieved its conservative policies largely through the taxation system by offering assistance to owner-occupiers through tax relief on mortgage interest payments, exemption from capital gains and inheritance tax, and discounts on the sale of council housing. These forms of assistance collectively provide over nine billion pounds annually. The second area where this conservative direction is clear is in provisions for homeless people. British local authorities are required to house the homeless by statutory obligation. In order to carry out this requirement, local authorities have adopted temporary solutions much the same as those in the United States. They are spending increasingly large amounts of money on temporary accommodations in both hotels and bed-and-breakfast boarding houses. The costs of these provisions are well in excess of the costs of providing more permanent solutions in the form of new housing stock, particularly in London. This solution is consistently blocked by the Conservative Central Government's opposition to the expansion or maintenance of the public stock and its control over local authorities' capital expenditures.

France is experiencing homelessness that resembles America's experience. The problem is large, visible, and a regular media feature. Housing policy analysts in France view the problem of homelessness as stemming from the fact that housing is more for profit than for social purposes.

The mutual problems of poverty and homelessness in France are being addressed partly by public policies and partly by private ones through collaboration. The voluntary associations organize flexible and innovative programs that are targeted to special homeless populations throughout the country. The state provides affordable housing for handicapped and elderly people, while voluntary organizations address the more urgent problems and especially provide emergency shelters.

The French response to homelessness has been as short-sighted as those of the United States and Britain. However, more associated programs provide various forms of affordable housing and attempt to provide help before eviction. Special collective social funds have been set up. The voluntary organizations are doing more than their counterparts in other countries to prevent homelessness by helping people with rent payments and housing expenses. Earlier public laws guaranteeing tenants rights under the socialist government served as a strong protection against homelessness. Many of these laws have been rescinded. In general, the categorical programs adopted to meet the urgency of poverty and homelessness in France have unfortunately relied upon emergency responses, ranging from shelters to extensive use of the underground railroad stations as protection during the coldest winter months.

The retreat from the welfare state in Australia and New Zealand has been similar to the general withdrawal of other nations. This has resulted, as expected, in accelerated housing costs and a deterioration in the supply of affordable dwellings. Neither country has challenged the cultural norm of owner-occupation. They have merely developed policies designed to facilitate ownership in spite of the diminished capacity of moderate- and low-income earners to afford home ownership.

In both nations, state governments have initiated programs to reduce the costs of house purchase. These schemes have two major features: they offer a cash grant to help with the deposit for home purchase and a repayment plan designed around a constant real rate of interest and fixed percentage of household income. The levels of interest rates in both countries are three percent, and a repayment level of 25 percent of total household income. The repayments and the amount loaned are also indexed to inflation to ensure a smoother repayment pattern and a more equitable return to the lender than a conventional mortgage.

Evaluation data of this policy suggest that these schemes have helped two groups of people, those with substantial deposits but with low income, (e.g., those who have money as a result of divorce and unemployment) and moderate-income earners. The appeal of these plans to low-income earners who lack savings is minimal. Nor do they appeal to moderate- and upper-income earners because they do not offer capital gains.[9]

Despite the targeted effort to prevent the erosion of affordable housing through reduced deposit and repayment plans, the general economic restructuring in Australia and New Zealand around market individualism and monetarism has resulted in fiscal restraint, and dire housing consequences for low- and moderate-income earners have grown substantially. Waiting lists for public housing have grown and overcrowding has increased. This has put pressure upon the cheaper end of the private rental market, pushing up rents, and homelessness is now appearing.

Another approach to homeless-prevention through the housing supply has grown in many European countries, that of self-help housing. This is both a new and old strategy. Self-help is a tradition that dates to the feudal era. It is logical that governments would encourage self-help in times of crisis and retreat from welfare expenditures and responsibilities. In England, the government and the National Housing Corporation stimulate self-help housing in several ways: tax and mortgage facilities and housing cooperatives. The German government did this in the 1920s and 1930s. They also organized a Standing Committee of Self-Help after World War II. Swedish people have built over 20,000 houses by themselves. Self-help building is a central feature of Belgian culture. In Latin American, Asian and African countries, self-help housing and squatting is frequently the only chance for most people to obtain housing. The phenomenon of self-help has occurred on a large scale in the Netherlands. Today more than half of the Dutch population can be regarded as self-builders. It is alleged that more than 600,000 people who are capable of doing any kind of construction work can be qualified as experts in the field.[10]

Self-help dwellers function as exemplars of individualism and the positive values ascribed to personal autonomy over one's life. One the other hand, reliance upon self-help to guarantee housing reflects a dangerous decline of planning as governments have abandoned the welfare state. Even in areas where monetarism and individual markets hold the power, there does need to be a substantial level of cooperation between local governments and communities and those citizens who engage in self-help housing. In any political and economic arrangement, there remains a need for a healthy balance between the interests of private citizens and the collective needs of communities and the polity. This means that governments cannot abandon their regulatory responsibilities even if they dismantle their welfare functions.

It is by now clear that homelessness is not exclusively an American problem. The fact that the United Nations sponsored an International Year of Shelter for the Homeless in 1987 is sufficient testimony to this. The major flaw in the United Nations program was that it ignored the existence of homelessness in any industrialized state. No mention was ever made of homelessness in the advanced industrialist countries. The purposes of the International Year of Shelter was to address the need for renewed commitment to house people in the developing countries. This obvious omission reflects the politics of the United Nations which emphasize development of Third World countries and preclude raising issues that embarrass the advanced nations.

Nevertheless, numerous conferences and scholarly papers did address the need to attack the root causes of homelessness and poverty. Major institutions, including Harvard University, the Executive Office of Human Services of the Commonwealth of Massachusetts, and the University of British Columbia Center for Human Settlements, committed themselves to continuous work on homelessness. The result is that within the reports and proceedings of the International Year of Shelter, lie concepts about homelessness, its causes and its prevention that elucidate the nature of problems and solutions in the advanced countries.[11]

What has become apparent in comparing and contrasting housing policies and homelessness outside of the United States, is that just as housing policy was a key ingredient of the postwar development of social-democratic countries, the abandonment of housing policy since the 1970s has been a major factor in the decline of these nations. The broad retreat from the welfare state model, with whatever mix of capitalism it included, has left the advanced industrial nations with staggering growth in homelessness and poverty. In most of these lands, a substratum of people has begun to live in conditions that resemble those in the developing countries. This is the reverse direction for advanced societies. If nations have entered a global economy, the more advanced countries should lead the developing lands. Instead, they are following the Third World. Does this imply that a fourth world combining the negative features of the developed and developing nations will emerge?

As the streets of New York City, London, Paris and Sydney have begun to resemble those of Mexico City, Lagos and Calcutta with armies of beggars, the differences between developed and developing nations have become muddled, and the similarities clear.

The Politics of a Non-Homeless Future

For the past decade, advocates for homeless people have promoted the evolution of a three-tiered housing system. Such a continuum of housing would move from shelter to transitional housing and onto permanent living facilities. This is a useful metaphor but it never facilitated the establishment of the third tier, and the middle tier still plays a relatively minor role in service provision for homeless people and those at risk of homelessness.

Planners of a non-homeless future must change the metaphor of a line to a circle. This metaphor would focus on keeping people in their circle of housing with all necessary social and economic supports. The image of the circle emphasizes the fact that it is easier to keep people out of the circle once they have left than it is to get them out in the first place. A circle of housing combines the dual concepts of stabilization and prevention.

The circle of social supports also strongly suggests the need for a more robust system of universal human welfare entitlements to income through family allowances, housing allowances, unemployment compensation, health insurance, child and family supports such as day care and elder care, and a more prominent commitment to equality and equity.

Welfare provisions in the United States never approached such a system of universal entitlements. The Northern European nations did adopt universal entitlements as the basis for social policy, and the outcome was a more solid safety net for their citizens. The ideas of universal entitlements never precluded capitalism, individual reward or private earnings. Nor did universalism in welfare ever seek to equalize income and redistribute wealth. The major objectives of universal welfare entitlements was to insure individuals against the vagaries of the free market by guaranteeing a fundamental set of economic and social rights as a benefit of citizenry, regardless of private means.[12]

Even though the European nations have withdrawn from the welfare models adopted after World War II, they have not dismantled those systems that have become permanent fixtures of their society. Nor did the universal entitlement model ever attain standards of adequacy sufficient to eliminate poverty and its effects. Nevertheless, even today when Europe and the other industrial nations have adopted the reluctant welfare state model of the United States, clear differences remain. The United States will spends less on social aid than Northern Europe — 12 percent of the gross national product compared with 20 percent in Northern Europe. Spending levels are but one indicator of the intent and effectiveness of welfare in a nation or state. A more important indicator is how welfare programs are organized and how they are distributed to people. American social benefits that do reach those who need them remain fragmented and heavily means-tested, thus demeaning and stigmatizing recipients. The more coordinated and universal forms of social aid in other countries protect people against misfortune without humiliating them. They also prevent the poor from social isolation by lifting the sense of shame associated with the dole in the United States.

Faced with austerity and a federal budget deficit of $500 billion, it is doubtful that the expansion of public spending for welfare can occur in the present focal climate of personal and public commitments to individualism, personal wealth, and a fail-proof defense preparedness. The fundamental question then is how to limit public and private spending in austerity, and the answer to this lies in political will and choices.

In developing his argument that equality and efficiency coexist, Kuttner reminds us that there can be major differences in how spending is limited:

...In Sweden, wage levels generally have been cut by about six percent, but the lowest paid workers have received the most favorable treatment. In France, the Mitterand government has reduced total social spending but raised the minimum wage, minimum pensions and family allowances for the poorest families. In Holland, where pension benefits are indexed to wage levels, the entire society has taken a three percent cut. Only in Britain and the United States has austerity fallen disproportionately on the poor.[13]

Questions of who bears the brunt of austerity in economic stagnation are not economic matters subject to the vagaries of the free market and personal fortune or misfortune. These are questions of political will and choice. Economic laws do not require poverty, homelessness and other forms of inequality. Political choices dictate who wins and who loses in any economic system.

The spectre of thousands of homeless people can be the singular compelling force to reverse the rollback of the welfare state. The United States Census Bureau data released in September 1988 document the steady trend to a wider gap between the rich and the poor. It further documents the sobering fact that poverty among children, black and Latino people is more than twice as high as among whites, and increasing at a steady rate. The persistent growth of poverty and its disproportionate distribution confronts the travesty whereby the poorest 40 percent of the

American population continue to receive only 15.4 percent of the country's national income, the lowest percentage ever recorded, and the wealthiest 40 percent received a record 67.18 percent of national income.[14]

Such a discrepancy cannot be attributed solely to chance or the rules of the market. It requires choices about who benefits. Serious social costs and negative consequences can be visited upon the United States and its economy. These pretenses will not be confined to the least fortunate individuals and families if we do not shift political will toward reversing the gap between the rich and the poor. The failure to prevent the growth of homelessness represents the most careless inattention to the consequences of a smaller middle class, a larger poverty class, and a pervasive diminution of equality.

The fact that large pockets of poverty continue, and are more visible because of the growth of homelessness at a time of decreasing unemployment, suggests that job growth alone is an incomplete solution. The federal government must re-enter the arena of social aid and play an active role once again in helping the poor. In the housing sector, continued cuts in new construction and rental assistance for low-income housing, along with no emergency homeless prevention programs and gentrification, will lead to a homeless and hidden homeless population of 18 million people by the year 2000.[15]

This is not an assessment that supports minimal public welfare targeted only to the frailest members of society. These data unequivocally assert that the safety net has disintegrated beyond repair.

Remedies are clear. Many of them are unoriginal. Expanding the earned-income tax credit and the minimum wage would help working poor families. Welfare reform legislation to move people into secure jobs paying adequate wages would build a new and stronger safety net, as would increased welfare benefits to help poor single mothers. Expanded health and education services would give poor children a second chance. Adequate and appropriate health and mental health services would keep individuals and families more stable and secure from childhood to old age. New housing policies that recognize the diversity of America's changing families and their needs must acknowledge the discrepancy between the rich and the poor. As families have grown smaller and poorer, the houses that are being built are larger and costlier. This is an unacceptable irony!

Numerous contemporary historians, exemplified by Arthur Schlesinger have observed that the 1990s are ripe for a cyclical shift to the left that would involve a return to an activist government and a commitment to social aid and entitlements. Schlesinger's hypothesis is based upon a cyclical analysis of history rather than his personal preference for a more liberal policy.[16] Robert Reich argues more pragmatically that the pervasive sense of decline in American society has stimulated consensus between conservative and radical left economists. The narrowness of the contemporary debate retains the American emphasis on rugged individualism, a distaste for authority and centers of power, and the need for heavier investment and sacrifice. Dissensus remains about whether to leave these matters to the private sector or whether the government has a significant role to play.[17]

Reich and Schlesinger both note that whenever there has been a crisis, such as the First World War, the Depression, and Second World War, extraordinary social harmony has prevailed. It is this sense of crisis, shared by most Americans and universally symbolized by mass homelessness, that can forge ultimate consensus between left, right and center to deal with our present crisis. Historically and chronologically, the approach of another century naturally raises fundamental questions about the direction of a nation and its people. At the end of the twentieth century these questions must be addressed on worldwide dimensions because of our global independence.

There is clearly a broad consensus that something must be done about solving our homeless.

The 1988 presidential elections called attention to the sense of crisis in the American economy by acknowledging issues of employment, housing and compassion in human services. The Congress has begun to demonstrate interest in the problems of homelessness and has set a benchmark date for the production of a major housing bill in 1989. Numerous Senate and House committees have held public hearings on homelessness and its correlates. Interest groups, coalitions, think tanks, scholars, advocacy organizations and individuals, and the media are all attempting to address the problem of homelessness and poverty amidst plenty. Charitable agencies that service homeless people are strained beyond their capacity to serve. Surging data analyzing homelessness and calling for action confront us.

This kind of public activity provides the impetus for political action and social change. It is what legislators at every level respond to. Growing Congressional interest has been accompanied by expanded proposals for legislation to provide for homeless people and is beginning to address homeless-prevention by including provisions for low-cost housing. Some legislation is more complete than others. At the federal level, the proposed bill before the U.S. Congress sponsored by Representative Ronald Dellums incorporates systemic views of homelessness and its prevention and calls for 45.5 billion in grants for shared housing.[18] Proposition 84 in California, the Housing and Homeless Bond Act, will raise as much as $300 million annually for housing, food, job-training programs and construction of low-income housing.[19]

The more modest proposal, The Affordable Housing Act, sponsored by Representative Barney Frank, calls for $15 billion in expenditures for housing every year for the next five years.[20]

Other examples of laws and programs operating at state and local government levels under a variety of auspices featuring public sector, private sector and non-profit organizations acting alone or cooperatively abound in this book. All of these programs demonstrate a readiness and a will to attack the roots of homelessness. Not one of them is sufficient on its own, given the limited resources of private organizations and the reduced amount of government activity to meet the ultimate challenge of eliminating homelessness without large-scale funding that can only come from the federal level of government.

Austerity and the deficit can either mock this goal of homeless-prevention or serve it as a way of preserving the American political economy in crisis by raising new questions that seek respectable living arrangements for all citizens.

Housing is so basic a human need that governments around the world have historically adopted an affirmative role in helping people meet their housing needs. The budget deficit does not justify the present retreat from this public responsibility. Austerity dictates that clear choices must be made about who suffers in hard times. Contemporary choices have allowed suffering to fall cruelly and disproportionately on the poorest and frailest members of society. New choices would spread the suffering so that all would share responsibility for reducing the deficit and accepting the sacrifices required in an austere economy.

Epilogue

This book has been concerned with primary prevention of homelessness. Primary prevention is a concept derived from the field of public health. As originally developed, public health prevention emphasized the control of communicable disease, epidemics, clean and healthy water, effective sanitation and sewage systems, epidemiology and, in some communities, treating medically indigent people. As the field of public health expanded, it included chronic disease control, the organization of medical care, and the health needs of specific high-risk populations such as mothers, children and industrial workers. When the field of mental health began to focus on community-based services, in contrast to institutional care, primary-prevention concepts were borrowed from public health and evolved into a three-part conceptual framework for prevention, which included the following elements:

- Primary prevention to promote health in individuals, families and their communities; and specific interventions referred to people and groups who are designated as at risk of experiencing difficulties, to intercept the causes of problems before they involve such people;

- Secondary prevention relies on early diagnosis and prompt treatment in order to halt the spread and further decline of a problem or condition;

- Tertiary prevention directed at maximizing the competence of people with irreversible conditions to limit the extent of their disability.[1]

This three-fold framework, in effect, means prevention, treatment and rehabilitation. Unfortunately, all three approaches entered the professional lexicon as prevention, and the term has become confused and elusive. As the term "prevention" became prominent in all social services, it became almost useless because it meant all things to all people, hence it meant little or nothing specific. To invoke the term prevention came to be as formidable as invoking the deity, and equally frustrating. This has resulted in the labeling of many endeavors as preventive that are not at all preventive.

For clarification purposes, the National Mental Health Association's Commission on the Prevention of Mental-Emotional Disabilities defined prevention in a special report in 1986 as follows:

Prevention means literally to keep something from happening. Within the field of mental health, it means intervening in a deliberate and positive way to counteract harmful circumstances before they cause disorder or disability.

Early identification and treatment are essential mental health services, but if treatment is needed, the disability has not been prevented.[2]

Within the framework of this book, primary prevention is concerned with reducing the incidence of homelessness or the number of new people losing their housing. This requires utilizing the wealth of data about what groups of people, experiencing which kinds of problems, are at risk of becoming homeless, and working with those people to keep them within the circle of their housing.

For some people, employment and income guarantees can prevent homelessness. For others, family support to alleviate the stresses of overwork and underpay, the hazards of aging, and domestic violence and abuse comprise homeless-prevention. Diminished wage scales, coupled with the demise of low-cost housing, call for homeless-prevention through the provision of affordable housing accommodation and decent wages. Mentally ill people need appropriate and acceptable treatment and care, as do their families, to keep them stable enough to avoid homelessness.

The general confusion over the many meanings of prevention has also led to a series of arguments claiming that prevention does not work. Critics of preventive theory assert that there is no research base applicable to primary prevention and there is no conceptual basis to support it. Critics also claim that there are no practice models of preventive activities. Perhaps the sharpest challenge to primary prevention is that it cannot be achieved short of a social revolution and that the public is unwilling to use tax money for such purposes because it does not lend itself to quick and easy solutions.

To counteract these criticisms, proponents of prevention, e.g., Bernard Bloom, George Albee and Stephen Goldston, have asserted that the following basic ideas form the foundation of primary prevention:

- Communities produce counterproductive stressful situations that make the political and social environment a key factor affecting general well-being. These factors can be identified and either reduced or eliminated.

- The well-being of a community is reflected in its institutions, e.g., schools, hospitals, recreation programs and housing. The corollary of this is that key community leaders such as teachers, doctors, police, clergy and business people have major impacts on the status of a community.

• The growing body of knowledge about stressful life events has led to a shift from predisposing or developmental factors in individual and group psychopathology to an emphasis on precipitating factors, those here-and-now life-stress situations faced by people.

• Crisis theory and crisis intervention approaches provide clear opportunities to understand and anticipate stress points, and thereby develop preventive interventions.

These fundamental ideas indicate a series of preventive functions that all human service workers and political leaders can perform. Foremost among these functions are consultation, education, community organization, training of key caregivers and community agents in the principles and techniques of prevention, and facilitating effective policy development.

Goldston identifies a commonly shared ideology about prevention which underlies the paradigm for homeless-prevention in this book. This ideology affirms:

• A commitment to raising the quality of life of the entire community, not just the casualties who appear for direct help and treatment services;

• Involvement in community institutions and systems to promote health and security;

• The relevance of public health concepts and practices, particularly notions about populations at risk, incidence rates, epidemiological techniques and analyses. Finally, two related public health questions are part of this common ideology. No condition has ever been controlled by treating the victims; therefore the key question is, "How well is the community?" rather than "How sick?"[3]

The soundness of this logic and the imperative nature of the growing incidence of homelessness demand a return to primary preventive responses to homeless people. Shelters, no matter how well-intended and decent, do not prevent homelessness.

Notes

Prologue

1. Ralf Dahrendorf "The Erosion of Citizenship and Its Consequences for Us All" *New Statesman*, June 12, 1987.

2. Fred Muir, "Nattily Dressed Homeless Man Has a Mission," *Los Angeles Times* (March 26, 1988).

Introduction

1. Susan J. Smith, "New Thinking About the Homeless: Prevention, Not Cure," *Governing* (I:5, February 1988), pp. 24-30.

2. Kim Hopper and Ellen Cox Baxter, *Private Lives/Public Spaces: Homeless Adults on the Streets of New York City*, mimeographed (New York: Community Services Society of New York, February 1981).

3. Jonathan Kozol, *Rachel and Her Children: Homeless Families in America* (New York: Crown, 1988).

4. Randy Young, "The Homeless: The Shame of the City," *New York Magazine* (December 21, 1981), pp. 26-32.

5. John R. Coleman, "Diary of a Homeless Man," *New York Magazine* (February 21, 1983), p. 30.

6. Patricia Sexton, "The Life of the Homeless," *Dissent* (30;1, 1983), pp 79-84.

7. Mark J. Stern, "The Emergence of the Homeless as a Public Problem," *Social Service Review* (58:2, 1984), pp. 291-301.

8. William W. Vosburgh, "Voluntary Associations, The Homeless and Hard-To-Serve Populations: Perspectives from Organizational Theory" (17:1, 1988), pp. 10-23.

9. Kim Hopper and Jill Hamburg, *The Making of America's Homeless: From Skid Row to the New Poor, 1945-1984* (New York: Community Service Society of New York, 1985).

10. Philip Kasinitz, "Gentrification and Homelessness: The Single Room Occupancy and Inner City Revival," *Urban and Social Change Review* (17:1, 1984), pp. 9-14.

11. Michael Sloss, "The Crisis of Homelessness: Its Dimensions and Solutions," *Urban and Social Change Review* (17:2, 1984), pp. 18-20.

12. Roger K. Farr, M.D., *A Mental Health Treatment Program for the Homeless Mentally Ill in the Skid Row Area*, mimeographed (Los Angeles County Department of Mental Health, December 1, 1985).

13. H. Richard Lamb, "Deinstitutionalization and the Homeless Mentally Ill," in H. Richard Lamb, Ed., *The Homeless Mentally Ill, A Task Force Report of the American Psychiatric Association on the Homeless Mentally Ill* (Washington, D.C.: American Psychiatric Association, 1984), pp. 55-74.

14. Hopper and Hamburg, *The Making of America's Homeless*.

15. Ellen Bassuk, "The Homelessness Problem," *Scientific American* (251:1, 1984), pp. 40-45.

16. Thomas Main, "The Homeless of New York," *The Public Interest* (72:Summer, 1983), p. 3028.

17. Donald Bauman and Charles Grigsby, *Understanding the Homeless: From Research to Action* (Hogg Foundation for Mental Health; The University of Texas; Austin, Texas 1988).

18. "The City's Homeless Pose $100 Million Quandary," *New York Times* (October 10, 1984).

19. Callahan et al v. Carey et al., Index No. 42582/79, Supreme Court of the State of New York.

20. Josh Barbanel, "Alternatives to Despair: Private Shelters Hearten New York's Homeless," *New York Times* (March 13, 1988); Madeleine R. Stoner, Ph.D., "An Analysis of Public and Private Sector Provisions for Homeless People," *Urban and Social Change Review* (17:1, 1984), pp. 3-81.

21. Partnership, Inc., *The Short-Term Housing System of Los Angeles County: Serving the Needs of the Homeless: An Analysis of Operating Characteristics and Funding Activity* (Los Angeles: The Partnership, August 1987).

22. Smith, "New Thinking About the Homeless," Shelter Partnership, Ibid. *The Short-Term Housing System.*
23. Shelter Partnership, *The Short-Term Housing System.*
24. Smith, ibid. "New Thinking About The Homeless."
25. U.S. Congress. Stewart B. McKinney, *Homeless Assistance Act,* H.R. 4352 99th. Cong., 1st sess.; U.S. Congress, *Urgent Relief for Homeless Act,* Public Law 100-77, 100th Cong., 1st sess.
26. Shelter Partnership, "The Short-Term Housing System."
27. Madeleine R. Stoner, Ph.D., "An Analysis of Public and Private Sector Provisions for Homeless People," *Urban and Social Change Review* (17:1, 1984), pp. 3-8.
28. These data are estimates presented by the National Coalition for the Homeless.

Chapter 1

1. *The Growth of Hunger and Homelessness in America's Cities in 1985: A 25 City Survey,* United States Conference of Mayors (Washington, D.C., The Conference, January 1986)
2. Michael Sosin, Paul Colson, Susan Grossman. *Homelessness in Chicago: Poverty and Pathology, Social Institutions and Social Change* (University of Chicago, School of Social Service Administration, 1988), p. 281.
3. Louis Uchitelle, "Reliance on Temporary Jobs Hint at Economic Frugality," *New York Times* (March 16, 1988).
4. Ibid.
5. Barbara Ehrenreich, Ph.D., *Social Welfare: The Attack from the Right,* The Robert J. O'Leary Memorial Lecture Series (Columbus: The Ohio State University College of Social Work, October 22, 1986).
6. Sosin, et al., *Homelessness in Chicago,* p. 280.
7. Mary Jo Bane, "Household Composition and Poverty," in Sheldon H. Danziger and Daniel H. Weinberg, eds., *Fighting Poverty: What Works and What Doesn't* (Cambridge, Mass.: Harvard University Press, 1986), pp. 209-31.
8. Center on Budget and Policies Priorities, *Smaller Slices of the Pie: The Growing Economic Vulnerability of Poor and Moderate Income Americans* (Washington, D.C.: Center on Budget and Policy Priorities, November 1985).
9. Bennett Harrison, Chris Tilly and Barry Bluestone, "Wage Inequality Takes a Great U-Turn," *Challenge* (March-April 1986), pp. 26-32.
10. Ehrenreich, *Social Welfare.*
11. William Ryan, *Equality* (New York: Vintage Books, 1981), pp. 3-36.
12. Joel Blau, *The Homeless of New York: A Case Study in Social Welfare Policy,* mimeographed doctoral dissertation (New York: Columbia University, 1987), p. 156.
13. Ibid.
14. Ibid., p. 158.

15. Ibid., p. 159.

16. Ibid.

17. Laurie J. Bassi and Orley Ashenfelter, "The Effect of Direct Job Creation and Training Programs on Low-Skilled Workers," in Danziger and Weinberg, *Fighting Poverty*, pp. 133-51.

18. Ibid.

19. Ibid.

20. John Kenneth Galbraith, *Economics in Perspective: A Critical History* (Boston: Houghton Mifflin, 1987), Chap. XXI.

21. Robert Kuttner, *The Economic Illusion: False Choices Between Prosperity and Social Justice* (Boston: Houghton Mifflin, 1984); Michael Harrington, *The Next Left: The History of a Future* (New York: Henry Holt, 1986); Robert McElvaine, *The End of the Conservative Era: Liberalism After Reagan* (New York: Arbor House, 1987); Arthur Schlesinger, Jr., *The Cycles of American History* (Boston: Houghton Mifflin, 1986).

22. U.S. Bureau of the Census, *Characteristics of the Population Below the Poverty Level*. Current Population Reports, ser. p. 60, no. 130. (Washington, D.C.: GPO, 1981).

23. Kuttner, *The Economic Illusion*.

Chapter 2

1. Rebecca M. Blank and Alan S. Blinder, "Macroeconomics, Income Distribution and Poverty," in Sheldon H. Danziger and Daniel H. Weinberg, eds., *Fighting Poverty: What Works and What Doesn't* (Cambridge, Mass.: Harvard University Press, 1986).

2. Ibid.

3. Ibid.

4. U.S. Congress, *Employment Act of 1946*, Public Law 304, 79th Cong., 2d sess.

5. Robert S. McElvaine, *The End of the Conservative Era* (New York: Arbor House, 1987), pp. 228-63.

6. Robert Kuttner, *The Economic Illusion: False Choices Between Prosperity and Social Justice* (Boston: Houghton Mifflin, 1984) Chap. 4.

7. U.S. House of Representatives, *Minimum Wage Bill*, H.R. 1834, 100th. Cong., 1st sess.; U.S. Senate, *Minimum Wage Bill*, S. 837, 100 Cong., 1st sess.

8. The Deficit Reduction Act of 1984 expanded the Earned Income Tax Credit slightly.

9. "Go Take a Hike," *The New Republic*, No. 3,826 (May 16, 1988), pp. 7-8.

10. Michael Harrington, *The Next Left: The History of the Future* (New York: Henry Holt, 1986), p. 172.

11. William K. Stevens, "Economic Swat Team Saves Jobs in Pennsylvania," *New York Times* (March 28, 1988)

12. James Flanigan, "Debate Over Plant Closings Misses Point," *Los Angeles Times* (April 27, 1988).

13. Harrington, pp. 164-70.
14. Ibid., pp. 170-73.
15. Ibid.
16. Robert Lekachman, *Visions and Nightmares* (New York: MacMillan, 1987) Chap. 6. Also in Harrington, *The Next Left.*
17. Kuttner, *The Economic Illusion*, p. 264.

Chapter 3

1. U.S. Bureau of the Census, *Current Population Reports Consumer Income Series P-60* (Washington, D.C.: Government Printing Office) August 1985.
2. Family Policy Panel, *Work and Family in the United States: A Policy Initiative* (New York: United Nations Association of the United States of America, 1985), pp. 10-11.
3. U.S. Senate, *Family and Medical Leave Act*, S. 249, 100th Cong., 1st sess., 1987. Sponsored by Senators Christopher Dodd and Arlen Specter; U.S. House of Representatives, *Family and Medical Leave Act*, H.R. 925, 100th Cong., 1st sess., 1987.
4. Sheila Kammerman, "Child Care Services: A National Picture," *Monthly Labor Review* (December 1983), p. 37.
5. Martin O'Connell and David E. Bloom, *Juggling Jobs and Babies: America's Child Care Challenge* (Population Reference Bureau, Inc. No. 12, February 1987), p. 12.
6. Kammerman, "Child Care Services."
7. O'Connell and Bloom, *Juggling Jobs and Babies*, p. 15.
8. U.S. Bureau of the Census, *Current Population Reports.*
9. U.S. Bureau of the Census, *Money, Income and Poverty Statistics of Families and Persons in the United States 1984*, Current Population Survey (August 1985), pp. 60-149.
10. The National Citizens' Board of Inquiry into Health in America, *Health Care USA: 1984, Volume 1, The National Report* (Washington, D.C.: October 1984), pp. 16-20.
11. U.S. Senate, *Minimum Health Care for All Workers Act*, S12625, 100th Cong., 1st sess., 1987, Sponsored by Senator Ted Kennedy.
12. Family Policy Panel, pp. 38-39.
13. Leonore Weitzman, *The Divorce Revolution* (New York: Free Press, 1985).
14. Ibid.
15. Institute for Policy Studies Working Seminar on Employment, Welfare and Poverty, *Women, Families and Poverty: An Alternative Policy Agenda for the Nineties* (March 1987), p. 7.
16. Family Policy Panel, *Work and Family*, pp. 60-63.
17. Michael R. Sosin, Paul Colson and Susan Grossman, *Homelessness in Chicago: Poverty and Pathology, Social Institutions and Social Change* (School of Social Service Administration: The University of Chicago, 1988), pp. 52-55.

Chapter 4

1. Rebecca M. Blank and Alan S. Blinder, "Macroeconomics, Income Distribution and Poverty," in Sheldon H. Danziger and Daniel H. Weinberg, *Fighting Poverty: What Works and What Doesn't* (Cambridge: Harvard University Press, 1986), p. 192.

2. U.S. Department of Labor, Bureau of Labor Statistics, *Employment and Earnings, Various Issues*; Department of Labor (1979, tables 32C and 33C).

3. Blank and Blinder, *Macroeconomics*, p. 191.

4. Ibid., p. 192.

5. U.S. House of Representatives, Committee on Ways and Means, *Unemployment Compensation, Background Material on Poverty* (Washington, D.C.: GPO, 1984).

6. U.S. Department of Labor, Bureau of Labor Statistics, *Handbook of Labor Statistics* (Washington, D.C.: GPO, 1984).

7. Blank and Blinder, *Macroeconomics*, pp. 200-03.

8. Ibid.

9. Robert S. McIntyre, *Sharing the Sales Tax Burden* (Washington, D.C.: Citizens for Tax Justice, 1988).

10. Ibid.

11. Deborah C. Eisenstedt and Peter Ciroux, "Benefits of Low-Income Housing," *Taxation For Accountants* (January 30, 1987).

Chapter 5

1. U.S. Congress, *The Family Welfare Reform Act*, Public Law 100-485, Amendment to H.R. 1720, 100th Cong., 2d sess.

2. These data on general relief and AFDC were obtained from the Los Angeles County Department of Social Services.

3. Charles Murray, *Losing Ground* (New York: Basic Books, 1984).

4. Barbara Ehrenreich, Ph.D. *Social Welfare: The Attack from the Right*, The Robert J. O'Leary Memorial Lecture Series (Columbus: The Ohio State University College of Social Work, October 22, 1986).

5. William Julius Wilson, *The Truly Disadvantaged: The Inner City, the Underclass and Public Policy* (Chicago: The University of Chicago Press, 1987).

6. Robert S. McElvaine, *The End of the Conservative Era: Liberalism After Reagan* (New York: Arbor House, 1987), pp. 84-94.

7. Melinda Bird, Bob Newman and Josh Bernstein, *Monitoring the New Homeless Assistance Program*, mimeographed memorandum, Los Angeles Western Center on Law and Poverty (February 9, 1988).

8. Lawrence Mead, *Beyond Entitlement* (New York: Free Press, 1986).

9. David T. Ellwood, *Poor Support: Poverty in the American Family* (New York: Basic Books, 1988).

10. Wilson, *The Truly Disadvantaged*, pp. 160-63.

Chapter 6

1. David C. Schwartz, Richard C. Ferlauto and Daniel Hoffman, *A New Housing Policy for America: Recapturing the American Dream* (Philadelphia: Temple University Press, 1988), Chap. 1.

2. Robert Kuttner, "Bad Housekeeping," *The New Republic* (3,823: April 25, 1988), p. 22.

3. James Brown and John Yinger, *Home Ownership and Housing Affordability in the United States, 1963-1985* (Cambridge, Mass.: Joint Center for Housing Studies of MIT and Harvard, 1986), p. 6.

4. Schwartz et al., *A New Housing Policy,* p. 23.

5. Margery Austin Turner, *Housing Needs to the Year 2000* (Washington, D.C.: National Association of Housing and Redevelopment Officials, 1986), p. 14 and bibliography.

6. Louis Uchitelle, "Labor's Lost Strength," *New York Times* (August 23, 1988), p. 1.

7. Michael Stone, "Housing and the Economic Crisis" in Chester Hartman, ed., *America's Housing Crisis* (Washington, D.C.: Institute for Policy Studies, 1983), pp. 99-150.

8. Kuttner, *Bad Housekeeping.*

9. U.S. Department of Housing and Urban Development, *Programs of HUD, 1985/1986* (Washington, D.C.: The Department, April 1986).

10. Kuttner, *Bad Housekeeping,* pp. 23-24.

11. National Coalition for the Homeless, *Homelessness in America* (Washington, D.C.: The Coalition, 1986), p. 7 ff; U.S. Conference of Mayors, *Status Report: Emergency Food, Shelter and Energy Programs in Twenty Cities* (Washington, D.C.: The Conference, 1987); Partnership for the Homeless, *National Growth in Homelessness* (New York: The Partnership, Winter, 1987), pp. 6-7.

12. Schwartz et al., *A New Housing Policy,* p. 123.

13. Partnership for the Homeless, *National Growth in Homelessness,* p. 9.

14. William Tucker, "Where Do the Homeless Come From?" *National Review* (39: September 25, 1987), p. 32; "Then There's Rent Control," *New Republic* (198:15, April 11, 1988), p. 22.

15. Karl Mannheim, "Housing is Necessary, So Rent Control is Justified," *Los Angeles Times,* March 6, 1988.

16. William Trombley, "Economy to Muffle Slow-Growth Moves," *Los Angeles Times,* June 17, 1988.

17. U.S. Department of Housing and Urban Development, *The President's National Urban Policy Report* (Washington, D.C.: The Department, 1986), pp. 25-27; E. Jay Howenstine, *Housing Vouchers: A Comparative International Analysis* (New Brunswick, N.J.: Center for Urban Policy Research of Rugters, 1986).

18. Turner, *Housing Needs*, p. 12; Marjorie Tiven and Barbara Ryther, *State Initiatives in Elderly Housing: What's New, What's Tried and True* (Washington, D.C.: Council of State Agencies and National Association of State Units on Aging, 1986), p. ix.

19. Sandra Newman and Raymond Struyk, *Housing and Supportive Services: Federal Policy for the Frail Elderly and Chronically Mentally Ill* (Cambridge, Mass.: MIT Press, 1987), pp. 2-6 and bibliography.

20. William C. Agpar, Jr., *The Housing Haves and Housing Have-Nots: The Growing Disparity* (Washington, D.C.: RAM Digest, 1985), p. 10.

21. Turner, *Housing Needs*, p. 12.

22. R. First, D. Roth and B. Arewa, *Homelessness: Understanding the Dimension of the Problem for Minorities* (Columbus, Ohio: Ohio State University, School of Social Work, June 1987) Conference presentation.

Chapter 7

1. Chester Hartman and Michael E. Stone, "A Socialist Housing Alternative for the United States," in Rachel G. Bratt, Chester Hartman and Ann Meyerson, eds., *Critical Perspectives on Housing* (Philadelphia: Temple University Press, 1986), pp. 484-513; and John I. Gilderbloom and Richard P. Applebaum, *Rethinking Rental Housing* (Philadelphia: Temple University Press, 1988).

2. Robert Ball, "Employment Created by Construction Expenditures," *Monthly Labor Review* (December, 1981), pp. 38-44.

3. Data presented to the author by the National Association of Homebuilders, May 1988.

4. David C. Schwartz, Richard C. Ferlauto and Daniel N. Hoffman, eds., *A New Housing Policy for America: Recapturing the American Dream* (Philadelphia: Temple University Press, 1988), Chap. 2.

5. New Jersey Department of Community Affairs, *Homelessness Prevention Program, Preventing Homelessness in New Jersey: Fact Sheet, Fiscal Year 1987* (Trenton: New Jersey Department of Community Affairs, 1987), and interviews with program staff in June 1988.

6. William Ryan, *Equality* (New York: Vintage Books, 1981).

7. Pennsylvania Housing Finance Agency, data presented to the author in interviews, May 1988; Homelessness Prevention Project of the Community Exchange, Washington, D.C., mimeographed reports, July 1987.

8. Ibid., Homelessness Prevention Project.

9. ACTION-Housing, *Addressing the Problems of the Homeless in Pittsburgh and Allegheny County: A Comprehensive Plan* (Pittsburgh: Action Housing, June 1985), pp. 20-22.

10. Homelessness Prevention Project.

11. State of Connecticut, Department of Housing, *Housing Programs* (Hartford: State of Connecticut, 1986), p. 14.

12. Schwartz et al, *A New Housing Policy*, pp. 91-103.

13. New Jersey Housing and Mortgage Finance Agency (NJHMFA), *Annual Report* (Trenton: The Agency, 1986).

14. Council of State Housing Agencies (CHSA), *Housing Initiatives of State Housing Finance Agencies* (Washington, D.C.: The Council, 1987), p. 12.

15. Ibid., p. 16.

16. Council of State Community Affairs Agencies (COSCAA), *State Housing Initiatives: A Compendium* (Washington, D.C.: The Council, 1987).

17. Schwartz et al., *A New Housing Policy*, p. 74; Deborah C. Eisenstadt and Peter Ciroux, "Benefits of Low Income Housing," *Taxation for Accountants* (30: January 1987), p. 22.

18. Schwartz et al., *A New Housing Policy*, pp. 81-82.

19. Robert Kuttner, "Bad Housekeeping," *The New Republic* (3,823: April 25, 1988), p. 24.

20. Joseph B. Frazier, "Christian Finds a Fuller Life by Building Homes for the World's Poor," *Los Angeles Times* (August 6, 1988).

21. Schwartz et al., *A New Housing Policy*, pp. 155-158.

22. Ibid., pp. 158-61.

23. Burlington County NAACP v. Township of Mount Laurel (Mount Laurel, IL), 92NJ456, A2d. 390 (1983).

24. New Jersey, Revised Statutes, *Fair Housing Act of 1985*, Public Law 1975, L. 291; L. 1985, L. 222.

25. Dolores Hayden, *Redesigning the American Dream: The Future of Housing, Work and Family Life* (New York, London: W.W. Norton, 1984), pp. 13, 57, 184; Marjorie Tiven and Barbara Ryther, *State Initiatives in Elderly Housing: What's New, What's Tried and True* (Washington, D.C.: Council of State Housing Agencies and National Association of State Units on Aging, 1986), pp. 7-8; Data presented to the author by American Association of Retired Persons, August 1988.

26. Schwartz et al., *A New Housing Policy*, pp. 104-12. 27. Michael Dear and S. Martin Taylor, *Not on Our Streets: Community Attitudes to Mental Health Care* (London: Pion, Ltd., 1982).

Chapter 8

1. James Brown and John Yinger, *Home Ownership and Housing Affordability in the United States, 1963-1985* (Cambridge, Mass.: Joint Center for Housing Studies of MIT and Harvard, 1986), pp. 7-9, 10-30; John L. Gilderbloom and Richard P. Applebaum, *Rethinking Rental Housing* (Philadelphia: Temple University Press, 1988).

2. Grace Milgram and Robert Bury, *Existing Housing Resources vs. Need.* Congressional Research Service Report No. 87-81 E (Washington, D.C.: CRS, Library of Congress, 1987), p. 4 ff.

3. Ibid.

4. Robert Kuttner, "Bad Housekeeping," *The New Republic* (3,823: April 25, 1988), p. 22.

5. Margery Austin Taylor, *Housing Needs to the Year 2000* (Washington, D.C.: National Association of Housing and Redevelopment Officials, 1986), p. 14 ff.

6. Phillip L. Clay, *At Risk of Loss: The Endangered Future of Low-Income Rental Housing Resources* (Washington, D.C.: Neighborhood Reinvestment Corporation, 1987).

7. David C. Schwartz, Richard C. Ferlauto and Daniel N. Hoffman, eds., *A New Housing Policy for America: Recapturing the American Dream* (Philadelphia: Temple University Press, 1988), pp. 73-75.

8. State of Massachusetts, *EOCD Resource Guide* (Boston: Executive Office of Community Development, 1987).

9. Schwartz et al., *A New Housing Policy*, pp. 125-26.

10. Data reported to the author in an interview with the Los Angeles Community Redevelopment Agency, July 1988.

11. Iver Peterson, "Battery Park City: A New Phase Begins," *New York Times* (June 19, 1988).

12. John I. Gilderbloom and Richard P. Applebaum, *Rethinking Rental Housing* (Philadelphia: Temple University Press, 1988); Anthony De Palma, "Pace of Building Abandonment Tumbles," *New York Times* (July 10, 1988).

13. Schwartz et al., *A New Housing Policy*, pp. 240-44; Anthony De Palma, "The Rocky Road to Tenant Management," *New York Times* (June 26, 1988).

14. John Atlas and Peter Dreir, "The Tenant's Movement and American Politics," in Rachel G. Bratt, Chester Hartman and Ann Meyerson, eds., *Critical Perspectives on Housing* (Philadelphia: Temple University Press, 1986).

15. ACORN Legislative Report, March 11, 1987, ACORN National Legislative Office (Washington, D.C.: ACORN Newsletter, Summer 1986), p. 1.

16. Schwartz et al., *A New Housing Policy*, p. 237.

17. Gilderbloom and Applebaum, *Rethinking Rental Housing*.

18. Allen David Heskin, "Rather than Help the Landlords, Make Rent Laws Help the Renters," *Los Angeles Times* (August 29, 1988); Karl M. Mannheim, "Housing is Necessary, So Rent Control is Justified," *Los Angeles Times* (June 17, 1988).

19. New York Senate, *Illegal Eviction Law, 1982,* Introduction 3538-B, Amendment to the Multiple Dwelling Law of New York, Amendment Section 302-D.

20. Jonathan Kozol, *Rachel and Her Children: Homeless Families in America* (New York: Crown, 1988); Josh Barbanel, "Koch Plans to Move Homeless Families from Hotels by 1990," *New York Times* (August 2, 1988).

Chapter 9

1. Robert Morris, *Social Policy of the American Welfare State: An Introduction to Policy Analysis* (New York: Harper & Row, 1979), p. 100.

2. Ibid., p. 103.

3. Ibid., pp. 103-05.

4. Ibid., pp. 124-28.

5. Bruce S. Jansson, *Theory and Practice of Social Welfare Policy: Analysis, Processes and Current Issues* (Belmont, CA: Wadsworth Press, 1984), p. 380.
6. David C. Schwartz, Richard C. Ferlauto and Daniel N. Hoffman, *A New Housing Policy for America: Recapturing the American Dream* (Philapdelphia: Temple University Press, 1988), pp. 56-60.
7. Stephen Crystal, *Chronic and Situational Dependency: Long-Term Residents in a Shelter for Men* (New York: Human Resources Administration, May 1982), p. iv.
8. Schwartz et al., *A New Housing Policy*, pp. 221-22.
9. Dolores Hayden, *Redesigning the American Dream: The Future of Housing, Work and Family Life* (New York, London: W.W. Norton, 1984), pp. 195-96.

Chapter 10

1. Robert Morris, *Social Policy of the American Welfare State: An Introduction to Policy Analysis* (New York: Harper & Row, 1979), p. 106.
2. David C. Schwartz, Richard Ferlauto and Daniel N. Hoffman, eds., *A New Housing Policy for America: Recapturing the American Dream* (Philadelphia: Temple University Press, 1988), pp. 60-64.
3. U.S. Congress, H.R. 3891, *Community Housing Partnership Act*, 100th Cong., 1st sess.
4. Council of State Community Affairs Agencies (COSCAA), *State Housing Initiatives: A Compendium* (Washington, D.C.: The Council, 1986); U.S. Congress, H.R. 4727; H.R. 4990, *The Affordable Housing Act*, 100th Cong., 2d sess.
5. Schwartz et al., *A New Housing Policy*, pp. 170-171; Center for Community Change, "National Citizen's Project Monitoring Community Development," (Washington, D.C.: The Center, 1980-1985).
6. Robert Kuttner, "Bad Housekeeping," *The New Republic* (3,823: April 25, 1988), p. 25.
7. N.R. Kleinfeld, "The Ripple Effects of Housing," *Mortgage Banking* (43:13 September 1983), pp. 10-21.
8. Joseph Guggenheim, *Tax Credits for Low Income Housing* (Washington, D.C.: Simon Publications, 1986).
9. Schwartz et al., *A New Housing Policy*, p. 132.
10. Chester Hartman and Michael Stone, "A Socialist Housing Alternative for the United States," in Rachel G. Bratt, Chester Hartman and Ann Meyerson, eds., *Critical Perspectives on Housing* (Philadelphia: Temple University Press, 1986), pp. 484-513; John L. Gilderbloom and Richard P. Applebaum, *Rethinking Rental Housing* (Philadelphia: Temple University Press, 1988).
11. Kuttner, "Bad Housekeeping," p. 25.
12. Pamela Edwards Kammer, "Demountable Space," *L.A. Architect*, November 1987.

13. Alan Murie and Ray Forrest, "The New Homeless in Britain," in Jurgen Freidrichs, *Affordable Housing and the Homeless* (Berlin, New York: Walter de Gruyter, 1988), pp. 129-46; Steve Schiffres, "The Dilemmas of British Housing Policy," in Bratt et al., *Critical Perspectives*, pp. 514-34.

14. Arne Karyd, "Affordable Housing and the Market—Generalized Swedish Experiences," in Friedrichs, *Affordable Housing*, pp. 59-74; Richard P. Applebaum, "Swedish Housing in the Postwar Period: Some Lessons for American Housing Policy," in Bratt et al., *Critical Perspectives*, pp. 535-57.

15. Jill Hamburg, "The Dynamics of Cuban Housing Policy," in Bratt et al., *Critical Perspectives*, pp. 558-85.

16. Kim Hopper and Jill Hamburg, *The Making of America's Homeless* (New York: Community Service Society, 1984) Working Papers on Social Policy Series.

Chapter 11

1. Rodger K. Farr, M.D., *A Mental Health Treatment Program for the Homeless Mentally Ill in the Los Angeles Skid Row Area*, mimeograph, December 1, 1985 (published by American Psychiatric Association in subsequent book); Richard Lamb, "Deinstitutionalization and the Mentally Ill," in Jon Erickson and Charles Wilhelm, eds., *Housing the Homeless* (Rutgers: The State University Press, 1986), pp. 262-78; George Vernez, et al., *Review of California's Program for the Homeless Mentally Disabled*, Working Draft (Rand Corporation, prepared for the State Department of Mental Health-R-3631-SDMH, L988, June 1988), p. vi.; Michael J. Dear and Jennifer R. Wolch, *Landscapes of Despair: From Deinstitutionalization to Homelessness* (Princeton: Princeton University Press, 1987), Chap. 8.; F. Stevens Redburn and Terry F. Buss, *Beyond Shelter: The Homeless and Public Policy* (New York: Praeger, 1986), Chap. 5.

2. James Baumohl and Steven Segal, "The New Chronic Patient," in Lonnie Snowden, ed., *Reaching the Underserved: Mental Health Needs of Neglected Populations* (Beverly Hills, CA: Sage Publications, 1982).

3. Joel Blau, *The Homeless of New York: A Case Study in Social Welfare Policy*, mimeographed doctoral dissertation (New York: Columbia University, 1987), pp. 177-79.

4. Ibid.

5. Bernard L. Bloom, *Community Mental Health: A General Introduction* (Monterey, CA: Brooks/Cole, 1976).

6. Ellen L. Bassuk, "The Homelessness Problem," in Erickson and Wilhelm, eds., *Housing the Homeless*, pp. 258-60.

7. Leona L. Bachrach, Ph.D., "Research on Services for the Homeless Mentally Ill," *Hospital and Community Psychiatry* (35:9, September 1984), pp. 910-13.

8. Rand Corporation, *Review of California's Homeless*, pp. vi-vii.

9. Leona L. Bachrach, Ph.D., "Interpreting Research on the Homeless Mentally Ill," *Hospital and Community Psychiatry* (35:9, September 1984), pp. 914-16; *Diagnostic and Statistical Manual*, Third Edition (DSM III), p. 1980.

10. Dean R. Owen, California Department of Mental Health, reported to Los Angeles Advocates for Mental Health, April 10, 1986, based upon data presented in E. Fuller Torrey and Sidney M. Wolfe, *Care of the Seriously Mental Ill: a Rating of State Programs* (Washington, D.C.: Public Citizen Health Research Group, 1987).

11. Stephen E. Goldston, Ed.D., M.S.P.H., ed., *Concepts of Primary Prevention: A Framework for Program Development* (California: Department of Mental Health, Office of Prevention, 1987).

12. F.L. Jessica Ball and Barbara Havassy, "A Survey of the Problems and Needs of Homeless Consumers of Acute Psychiatric Services," *Hospital and Community Psychiatry* (35:9, September 1984), pp. 917-21.

13. Frank R. Lipton, M.D., Suzanne Nutt, M.P.H. and Albert Sabatini, M.D., "Housing the Homeless Mentally Ill: A Longitudinal Study of a Treatment Approach," *Hospital and Community Psychiatry* (39:1, January 1988), pp. 40-45.

14. Rand Corporation, *Review of California's Homeless*, pp. 85-86.

15. James Intagliata, "Improving the Quality of Community Care for the Chronically Mentally Disabled: The Role of Case Management," *Schizophrenia Bulletin* (8:4, 1982), pp. 655-74.

16. Marie Weil and James M. Karls, *Case Management in Human Service Practice: A Systematic Approach to Mobilizing Resources for Clients* (San Francisco: Jossey-Bass, 1985).

17. The Chicago Coalition for the Homeless, *When You Don't Have Anything: A Street Survey of Homeless People in Chicago* (Chicago, Illinois, The Coalition, 1983).

18. Carlyn Lampert and Tina Shaps, *Homeless Youth Project: Initial Data Summary*, (Los Angeles Free Clinic, 1985), mimeographed unpublished report to the National Institute of Mental Health.

19. George Wolkon, "Patient Compliance in the Mental Health Continuum of Care," *Journal of Compliance in Health Care* (1:1, 1986).

20. Marsha A. Martin and Jane W. Hausner, "Mobilizing Services for Homeless People," *The Social Welfare Forum* (Washington, D.C.: National Conference on Social Welfare, 1985), pp. 238-39.

21. Daniel Goleman, "Experts Say Poor Supervision Plagues New York Mentally Ill," *New York Times*, (September 11, 1987).

22. Robert W. Surber, et al, "Medical and Psychiatric Needs of the Homeless— A Preliminary Response," *Social Work* (33:2 March-April, 1988), pp. 116-19.

23. Bachrach, *Research on Services*, p. 913.

Chapter 12

1. U.S. Congress, Senate, *State Comprehensive Mental Health Plan Act*, Public Law 99-960, 98th Cong., 2d sess.

2. Jacqueline Parrish, R.N., M.S., *Ideal Community-Based Mental Health Service System for Adults with Long-Term, Disabling Mental Illnesses*, mimeographed excerpt from *Toward a Model Plan for a Community-Based Mental Health Service System*, (Rockville, MD: National Institute of Mental Health, Division of Education and Service Systems Liaison, October, 1987), pp. 5-6.

3. U.S. Congress, Senate, *The Protection and Advocacy for Mentally Ill Individuals Act of 1986*, Public Law 99-319, 98th Cong., 1st sess.

4. Parrish, *Ideal Community-Based Mental Health Service System for Adults with Long-Term, Disabling Mental Illnesses*

5. Elaine Lomas, L.C.S.W. and Dale Weaver, M.S.W., *Skid Row Mental Health Services, Department of Mental Health* (County of Los Angeles, January 1985), unpublished report; Gold Award, "A Network of Services for the Chronic Mentally Ill," *Hospital and Community Psychiatry* (37:11, 1986), p. 4.

6. U.S. Department of Health and Human Services, *Helping the Homeless: A Resource Guide* (Washington, D.C.: the Department, Summer 1984), pp. 81-84.

7. Ibid.

8. Harris Chaikin, Ph.D., *Report on the Homeless* (University of Maryland, School of Social Work and Community Planning, January 1985), Unpublished manuscript.

9. Marie Nordberg, "Hope for the Homeless," *Emergency Medical Services* (14:5, 1985), pp. 25-33.

10. National Council of Community Mental Health Centers, *Trends in Community Mental Health* (Washington, D.C.: The Council, 1987).

11. George W. Albee, "The Rationale and Need for Primary Prevention," in Stephen E. Goldston, ed., *The Concepts of Primary Prevention: A Framework for Program Development, California Department of Mental Health Office of Prevention*, 1987; Paul V. Lemkau, "A Conceptual Model of Prevention," in Morton O. Wagenfeld, Paul V. Lemkau and Blair Justice, eds., *Public Mental Health: Perspectives and Prospects* (Beverly Hills, London, New Delhi: Sage Publications, 1982).

Chapter 13

1. David C. Anderson, "Streetwise Streetworker," *New York Times* (April 8, 1985).

2. Marsha A. Martin and Jane W. Hausner, "Mobilizing Services for Homeless People," in National Conference of Social Welfare, *The Social Welfare Forum* (Washington, D.C.: National Conference of Social Welfare, 1985), pp. 235-41.

3. Robert W. Surber, et al., "Medical and Psychiatric Needs of the Homeless: A Preliminary Response," *Social Work* (33:2, March-April 1988), pp. 116-19.

4. Nina Berman, M.S.W., *Outreach Programs for the Chronically Mentally Ill*, mimeographed report (Los Angeles: University of Southern California School of Social Work, May 1988).

5. June Axinn and Herman Levin, *Social Welfare: A History of the American Response to Need* (New York: Dodd, Mead & Co., 1975), Chap. 4.

6. Samuel H. Taylor, "Community Liaison," in Samuel H. Taylor and Robert W. Roberts, eds., *Theory and Practice of Community Social Work* (New York: Columbia University Press, 1985), pp. 197-98.

7. Madeleine R. Stoner, "Mental Health Settings," in Taylor and Roberts, eds., *Theory and Practice*, pp. 296-302.

8. Ibid., pp. 309-10.

9. Josh Barbanel, "New Psychiatric Ward to Aid Homeless Plan," *New York Times* (September 14, 1987).

10. Ibid.

Chapter 14

1. Lawrence A. Long, *Consumer-Run Self-Help Programs Serving Homeless People With A Mental Illness, Vol. III.*, mimeographed report (Rockville, MD: National Institute of Mental Health, Division of Education and Service Systems Liaison, Contract #304666, June 1988).

2. Clifford Beers, *A Mind That Found Itself* (Pittsburgh: University of Pittsburgh Press, 1908).

3. Anton Boison, *Exploration of the Inner World* (New York: Harper & Row, 1936).

4. Abraham Low, *Mental Health Through Will Training* (Boston: Christopher, 1950).

5. Lewis Yablonsky, *Synanon: The Tunnel Back* (Baltimore: Penguin Books, 1967).

6. Maxwell Jones, *The Therapeutic Community* (New York: Basic Books, 1953).

7. National Mental Health Consumer's Association, *Preliminary Highlights of the National Organizing Survey* (Philadelphia: National Mental Health Consumer's Association, 1987).

8. Frank Reissman, "The Helper Therapy Principle," *Social Work* (10:4, 1965), pp. 27-32.

9. U.S. Congress, Senate, *The Protection and Advocacy for Mentally Ill Individuals Act of 1986*, Public Law 99-319, 98th Cong., 1st sess.

10. Long, *Consumer-Run Self-Help Programs*, pp. 28-47.

11. Alan Gartner and Frank Riessman, *Self-Help in the Human Services* (San Francisco: Jossey-Bass, 1977).

Chapter 15

1. Martin Rein, *Social Policy* (New York: Random House 1970), Chap. 12.

2. Edward P. Mulvey, Jeffrey L. Geller and Loren H. Roth, "The Promise of Involuntary Outpatient Commitment," *American Psychologist* (42:6, June 1987).

3. E. Fuller Torey and Sidney M. Wolfe, *Care of the Seriously Mentally Ill: a Rating of State Programs* (Washington, D.C.: Public Citizen Health Research Group, 1987).

Chapter 16

1. Paul A. Kurzman, "Program Development and Service Coordination as Components of Community Practice" in Samuel H. Taylor and Robert W. Roberts, eds., *Theory and Practice of Community Social Work* (New York: Columbia University Press, 1985), pp. 96-101.

2. Neil Gilbert and Harry Specht, *Dimensions of Social Welfare Policy* (Englewood Cliffs, N.J.: Prentice-Hall, 1974), pp. 178-99.

3. George Vernez, et al., *Review of California's Program for the Homeless Mentally Disabled*, working draft (Rand Corporation, prepared for the State Department of Mental Health, R-3631-SDMH, 1988), pp. 85-100.

4. Susan J. Smith, "New Thinking About the Homeless: Prevention, Not Cure," *Governing* (1:5, February 1988), pp. 24-30; Melinda Bird, Bob Newman and Josh Bernstein, *Monitoring the New Homeless Assistance Program*, mimeographed memorandum, Los Angeles Western Center on Law and Poverty, February 9, 1988.

5. June Axinn and Herman Levin, *Social Welfare: A History of the American Response to Need* (New York: Dodd Mead & Co., 1975), Chap. 2.

6. Bruce S. Jansson, *Theory and Practice of Social Welfare Policy: Analysis, Processes and Current Issues* (Belmont, CA: Wadsworth, 1984), p. 300.

7. George Vernez, et al., *Review of California's Program for the Homeless Mentally Disabled*.

8. Smith, "New Thinking," p. 30.

9. J.A. Talbott, "Unified Mental Health Systems: Utopia Revisited," *New Direction for Mental Health Services* (San Francisco: Jossey-Bass Social and Behavioral Sciences Series, No. 26, 1983).

10. Leona Bachrach, "Model Programs for Chronic Mental Patients," *American Journal of Psychiatry* (137: 1031, 1980).

11. L.I. Stein, "Test MA: The Training in Community Living Model," *New Directions for Mental Health Services* (San Francisco: Jossey Bass Social and Behavioral Sciences Series, No. 26, 1983).

12. B.A. Weisbrod, "A Guide to Cost-Benefit Analysis, as Seen Through a Controlled Experiment in Treating the Mentally Ill," in A. Razin, E. Helpman and E. Sadka, eds., *Social Policy Evaluation* (New York: Academic Press, 1983).

13. L. Hoult, et al., "Psychiatric Hospital versus Community Treatment: The Results of Randomized Trial," *Australian and New Zealand Journal of Psychiatry* (17: 1983), pp. 160-67.

14. Bachrach, "Overview."

15. E. Fuller Torrey, "Continuous Treatment Teams in the Care of the Chronic Mentally Ill," *Hospital and Community Psychiatry* (37: 1986), pp. 1245-47.

16. Robert Wood Johnson Foundation, *Program for the Chronically Mentally Ill* (1986).

17. John K. Iglehard, "The Future of HMOs," *New England Journal of Medicine* (303: 1982), pp. 451-56.

18. J.A. Talbott and S.S. Sharfstein, "A Proposal for Future Funding of Chronic and Episodic Mental Illness," *Hospital and Community Psychiatry* (37: 1986), pp. 1126-30.

19. M. Schlesinger, "On the Limits of Expanding Health Care Reform: Chronic Care in Prepaid Groups," *Millbank Quarterly* (64: 1986), pp. 189-215; J.K. Iglehart "Medicine Turns to HMOs," (312: 1985), pp. 132-36.

Conclusion

1. Erving Goffman, *Asylums* (Chicago: Aldine Publishing Co., 1961).

2. Dennis Culhane and Marc Fried, "Paths in Homelessness: A View From the Street," in Jurgen Friedrichs, ed., *Affordable Housing and the Homeless* (Berlin, New York: Walter de Gruyter, 1988), pp. 182-83.

3. Council of Large Public Housing Authorities, *Public Housing Today* (Boston: The Council, 1986).

4. Anne Karyd, "Affordable Housing and the Market-Generalized Swedish Experiences," in Friedrichs, ed., *Affordable Housing,* p. 60.

5. Ibid., p. 61.

6. Dan Ferrand-Bechmann, "Homelessness in France, Public and Private Policies," in Friedrichs, ed., *Affordable Housing,* p. 147.

7. Alan Marie and Ray Forrest, "The New Homeless in Britain," in Friedrichs, ed., *Affordable Housing,* p. 133.

8. David C. Thorns, "Who Gets Housed: The Changing Nature of Housing Affordability and Access in Advanced Capitalist Countries," in Friedrichs, ed., *Affordable Housing,* pp. 28-56.

9. Ibid., p. 38.

10. Wouter Turpijn, "Shadow-Housing: Self-Help of Dwellers in the Netherlands," in Friedrichs, ed., *Affordable Housing,* pp. 103-14.

11. Rudolph H. Knight, "Homelessness: An American Problem?" in Richard D. Bingham, Roy E. Green and Sammis B. White, eds., *The Homeless in Contemporary Society* (Newbury Park, CA: Sage Publications, 1987), pp. 249-71.

12. Robert Kuttner, *The Economic Illusion: False Choices Between Prosperity and Social Justice* (Boston: Houghton Mifflin, 1984), p. 238.

13. Ibid., p. 264.

14. U.S. Bureau of the Census, *Number and Median Income of Families and Persons,* September 1988.

15. James Brown and John Yinger, *Home Ownership and Housing Affordability in the United States, 1963-1985* (Cambridge, Mass.: Joint Center for Housing Studies of MIT and Harvard, 1986), p. 6 ff.

16. Arthur M. Schlesinger, Jr., *The Cycles of American History* (Boston: Houghton Mifflin Co., 1986).

17. Robert B. Reich, *Tales of a New America: The Anxious Liberal's Guide to the Future* (New York: Times Books, 1987).

18. U.S. Congress, H.R. 4727, *Affordable Housing Act*, 100th Cong., 2d sess.

19. SB 1692 and 1693, *Housing and Homeless Initiatives*, State of California General Obligation Bond.

20. U.S. Congress, H.R. 4990, *Affordable Housing Act*, 100th Cong., 2d sess.

Epilogue

1. Stephen E. Goldston, Ed.D, M.S.P.H., *Concepts of Primary Prevention: A Framework for Program Development* (California, Department of Mental Health Office of Prevention, 1987), p. 2.

2. Ibid., p. 3.

3. Ibid., p. 6.

Bibliography

ACORN. Legislative Report, Washington, D.C., ACORN National Legislative Office, 11 March 1987.

——— Newsletter, Washington, D.C., ACORN National Legislative Office, Summer 1986.

ACTION - Housing, *Addressing the Problems of the Homeless in Pittsburgh and Allegheny County: A Comprehensive Plan*. Pittsburgh: Action Housing, June 1985.

Agpar, William C., Jr. *The Housing Haves and Have-Nots: The Growing Disparity*. Washington, D.C.: RAM Digest, 1985.

American Psychiatric Association. *Diagnostic and Statistical Manual of Mental Disorders*, 3rd Ed. Washington, D.C.: American Psychiatric Association, 1980.

Axinn, June, and Levin, Herman. *Social Welfare: A History of American Response to Need*. New York: Dodd, Mead & Co., 1975.

Bachrach, Leona L., Ph.D. "Interpreting Research on the Homeless Mentally Ill." *Hospital and Community Psychiatry* 35:9, September 1984.

——— "Model Programs for Chronic Mental Patients." *American Journal of Psychiatry* 137:1031, 1980.

——— "Research on Services for the Homeless Mentally Ill." *Hospital and Community Psychiatry* 35:9, September 1984.

Ball, Jessica F.L., and Havassy, Barbara. "A Survey of the Problems and Needs of Homeless Consumers of Acute Psychiatric Services." *Hospital and Community Psychiatry* 35:9. September 1984.

Ball, Robert. "Employment Created by Construction Expenditures." *Monthly Labor Review,* December 1981.

Barbanel, Josh. "Koch Plans to Move Homeless Families from Hotels by 1990." *New York Times,* 2 August 1988.

—— "New Psychiatric Ward to Aid Homeless Plan." *New York Times,* 14 September 1988.

—— "Alternatives to Despair: Private Shelters Hearten New York's Homeless." *New York Times,* 13 March 1988.

Bassuk, Ellen. "The Homelessness Problem." *Scientific American* 251:1, 1984.

Bauman, Donald, and Grigsby, Charles. *Understanding the Homeless: From Research to Action.* Austin, Texas: Hogg Foundation for Mental Health, The University of Texas, 1988.

Beers, Clifford. *A Mind that Found Itself.* Pittsburgh: University of Pittsburgh Press, 1908.

Berman, Nina, M.S.W. *Outreach Programs for the Chronically Mentally Ill.* Mimeographed report. Los Angeles: University of Southern California School of Social Work, May 1988.

Bingham, Richard D.; Green, Roy E.; and White, Sammis B., eds. *The Homeless in Contemporary Society.* Newbury Park, CA; Sage Publications, 1987.

Bird, Melinda; Newman, Bob; and Bernstein, Josh. *Monitoring the New Homeless Assistance Program.* Mimeographed memorandum. Los Angeles: Western Center on Law and Poverty, 9 February 1988.

Blau, Joel. *The Homeless of New York: A Case Study in Social Welfare Policy.* Mimeographed doctoral dissertation. New York: Columbia University, 1987.

Bloom, Bernard L. *Community Mental Health: A General Introduction.* Monterey, CA: Brooks/Cole, 1971.

Boison, Anton. *Exploration of the Inner World.* New York: Harper & Row, 1936.

Brown, James, and Yinger, John. *Home Ownership and Housing Affordability in the United States, 1963-1985.* Cambridge, Mass.: Joint Center for Housing Studies of MIT and Harvard, 1986.

Callahan et al. v. Carey et al. Index No. 42582/79. Supreme Court of the State of New York.

Center on Budget and Policies Priorities. *Smaller Slices of the Pie: The Growing Economic Vulnerability of Poor and Moderate Americans.* Washington, D.C.: Center on Budget and Policies Priorities, November 1985.

Chaiken, Harris, Ph.D. *Report on the Homeless.* Unpublished manuscript. University of Maryland: School of Social Work and Community Planning, January 1985.

The Chicago Coalition for the Homeless. *When You Don't Have Anything: A Street Survey of Homeless People in Chicago.* Chicago: The Coalition, 1983.

Clay, Phillip L. *At Risk of Loss: the Endangered Future of Low-Income Rental Housing Resources.* Washington, D.C.: Neighborhood Reinvestment Corporation, 1981.

Coleman, John R. "Diary of a Homeless Man." *New York Magazine*, February 21, 1983.

Conference of Mayors. *The Growth of Hunger and Homelessness and Poverty in 1985: a 25-City Survey.* Washington, D.C.: the Conference, January, 1986.

Council of Large Public Housing Authorities, *Public Housing Today.* Boston: The Council, 1986.

Council of State Community Affairs Agencies (COSCAA). *State Housing Initiatives: A Compendium.* Washington, D.C.: The Council, 1987.

Council of State Housing Agencies (CSHA), *Housing Initiatives of State Housing Finance Agencies,* Washington, D.C.: The Council, 1987.

Crystal, Stephen. *Chronic and Situational Dependency: Long-Term Residents in a Shelter for Men.* New York: Human Resources Administration, May 1987.

Dahrendorf, Ralf. "The Erosion of Citizenship and Its Consequences." *New Statesman,* 12 June 1987.

Danziger, Sheldon H., and Weinberg, Daniel. *Fighting Poverty: What Works and What Doesn't.* Cambridge, Mass: Harvard University Press, 1986.

Dear, Michael J., and Taylor, Martin S. *Not on our Streets: Community Attitudes to Mental Health Care.* London: Pion, Ltd., 1982.

Dear, Michael J., and Wolch, Jennifer R. *Landscapes of Despair: From Deinstitutionalization to Homelessness.* Princeton: Princeton University Press, 1987.

De Mott, Benjamin. "Rediscovering Complexity." *Atlantic* 26:3, September 1988.

Ehrenreich, Barbara, Ph.D. *Social Welfare: The Attack from the Right.* The Robert J. O'Leary Memorial Lecture Series. Columbus: The Ohio State University College of Social Work, 22 October, 1986.

Eisenstadt, Deborah C. and Ciroux, Peter, "Benfits of Low Income Housing." *Taxation for Accountants,* 30 January 1982.

Ellwood, David T. *Poor Support: Poverty in the American Family.* New York: Basic Books, 1988

Erickson, Jon and Wilhelm, Charles, eds. *Housing the Homeless.* Rutgers: The State University Press, 1986.

Family Policy Panel. *Work and Family in the United States: A Policy Initiative.* New York: United Nations Association of the United States of America, 1985.

Farr, Rodger K., M.D. *A Mental Health Treatment Program for the Homeless Mentally Ill in the Los Angeles Skid Row Area.* Mimeographed. Los Angeles: Los Angeles County Department of Mental Health, 1 December 1985.

Flanigan, James. "Debate Over Plant Closings Misses Point." *Los Angeles Times,* 27 April 1988.

Frazier Joseph B. "Christian Finds a Fuller Life by Building Homes for the World's Poor." *Los Angeles Times,* 6 August 1988.

Friedrichs, Jurgen, ed. *Affordable Housing and the Homeless.* Berlin, New York: Walter de Gruyter, 1988.

Galbraith, John Kenneth. *Economics in Perspective: A Critical History*. Boston: Houghton Mifflin, 1987.

Gartner, Alan and Riessman, Frank. *Self-Help in the Human Services*. San Francisco: Jossey-Bass, 1977.

Gilbert, Neil and Specht, Harry. *Dimensions of Social Welfare Policy*. Englewood Cliffs, NJ: Prentice-Hall, 1974.

Gilderbloom, John I. and Applebaum, Richard P. *Rethinking Rental Housing*. Philadelphia: Temple University Press, 1988.

Goffman, Erving. *Asylums*. Chicago: Aldine Publishing Co., 1961.

Gold, Award. "A Network of Services for the Chronic Mentally Ill." *Hospital and Community Psychiatry* 37:11, 1986.

Goldston, Stephen E., Ed.D., M.S.P.H., ed. *Concepts of Primary Prevention: a Framework for Program Development*. California Department of Mental Health, Office of Prevention, 1987.

Goleman, Daniel. "Experts Say Poor Suspension Plagues New York Mentally Ill." *New York Times*, 11 September 1987.

Guggenheim, Joseph. *Tax Credits for Low Income Housing*. Washington, D.C.: Simon Publications, 1986.

Harrington, Michael. *The Next Left: The History of the Future*. New York: Henry Holt, 1986.

Harrison, Bennet; Tilly, Chris; and Bluestone, Barry. "Wage Inequality Takes a Great U-Turn." *Challenge*, March-April 1986.

Hartman, Chester and Meyerson, Ann, eds. *Critical Perspectives on Housing*. Philadelphia: Temple University Press, 1986.

Haskin, Allen David. "Rather Than Help the Landlords, Make Rent Laws Help the Renters." *Los Angeles Times*, 19 August 1988.

Hayden, Dolores. *Redesigning the American Dream: The Future of Housing, Work and Family Life*. New York-London: W.W. Norton, 1984.

Homelessness Prevention Project of the Community Exchange. Mimeographed reports. Washington, D.C.: Community Exchange, July 1987.

Hopper, Kim, and Baxter, Ellen. *Private Lives/Public Spaces: Homeless Adults on the Streets of New York City*. New York: Community Services Society of New York, 1981.

Hopper, Kim, and Hamburg, Jill. *The Making of America's Homeless: From Skid Row to the New Poor, 1945-1984*. New York: Community Service Society of New York, 1985.

Hoult, L., Reynolds, I., Charbonneau, Pouris, Weeks, P. and Briggs, J. "Psychiatric Hospital versus Community Treatment: The Roots of Randomized Trial." *Australian and New Zealand Journal of Psychiatry* 17, 1983) pp. 160-167.

Howenstine, E. Jay. *Housing Vouchers: A Comparative International Analysis*. New Brunswick, N.J.: Center For Urban Policy Research of Rutgers, 1986.

Iglehart, John K. "The Future of HMO's," *New England Journal of Medicine* 303, 1982.

———— "Medicare Turns to HMO's," *New England Journal of Medicine* 312:1985

Institute For Policy Studies Working Seminar on Employment, Welfare and Poverty. *Women, Families and Poverty: An Alternative Policy Agenda For the Nineties*. March 1987.

Intagliata, James. "Improving the Quality of Community Care for the Chronically Mentally Disabled: The Role of Case Management." *Schizophrenia Bulletin* 8:4, 1982.

Jansson, Bruce S. *Theory and Practice of Social Welfare Policy Analysis: Processes and Current Issues*. Belmont, CA: Wadsworth Press, 1984.

Johnson Foundation, Robert Wood. *Program for the Chronically Mentally Ill*, 1986.

Jones, Maxwell. *The Therapeutic Community*. New York: Basic Books, 1953.

Kammer, Pamela Edwards. "Demountable Space." *LA Architect*, November 1987.

Kammerman, Sheila. "Child Care Services: A National Picture." *Monthly Labor Review*. December 1983.

Kasinitz, Philip. "Gentrification and Homelessness: The Single Room Occupancy and Inner City Revival." *Urban and Social Change Review* 17:1, 1984.

Kleinfeld, N.R. "The Ripple Effects of Housing." *Mortgage Banking*. 13 September 1983.

Kottner, Robert. *The Economic Illusion: False Choices Between Prosperity and Social Justice*. Boston: Houghton Mifflin, 1984.

——— "Bad Housekeeping." *The New Republic* 3, 823. 25 April 1988.

Kozol, Jonathan. *Rachel and Her Children: Homeless Families in America*. New York: Crown, 1988.

Lamb, H. Richard, ed. The Homeless Mentally Ill. *A Task Force Report of the American Psychiatric Association on the Homeless Mentally Ill*. Washington, D.C.: American Psychiatric Association, 1984.

Lampert, Carlyn and Shaps, Tina. *Homeless Youth Project: Initial Data Summary*. Mimeographed unpublished report. Los Angeles: Los Angeles Free Clinic, 1985.

Lekachman, Robert. *Visions and Nightmares*. New York: MacMillan, 1987.

Lipton, Frank R., M.D.; Nutt, Suzanne, M.P.H.; and Sabatini, M.D. "Housing the Homeless Mentally Ill. A Longitudinal Study of a Treatment Approach." *Hospital and Community Psychiatry* 39:1, January 1988.

Lomas, Elaine, L.C.S., and Weaver, Dale, M.S.W. *Skid Row Mental Health Services*. Unpublished report. Los Angeles: County Department of Mental Health, January 1985.

Long, Lawrence A. *Consumer-Run Self-Help Programs Serving Homeless People with a Mental Illness*, Vol. III. Mimeographed report. Rockville, MD: National Institute of Mental Health, Division of Education and Service Systems Liaison, Contract #304666, June 1988.

Low, Abraham. *Mental Health through Will Training*. Boston: Christopher, 1950.

Main, Thomas. "The Homeless of New York." *The Public Interest* 72: Summer, 1983.

Mannheim, Karl. "Housing is Necessary, So Rent Control Is Justified." *Los Angeles Times*, 17 June 1988.

Mead, Lawrence. *Beyond Entitlement*. New York Free Press, 1986.

Milgram, Grace, and Burg, Robert. *Existing Housing Resources vs. Need*. Congressional Research Service Report Nos. 87-81 E. Washington, D.C.: CRS, Library of Congress, 1987.

Morris, Robert. *Social Policy of the American Welfare State: An Introduction to Policy Analysis*. New York: Harper & Row, 1979.

Mulvey, Edward P.; Geller, Jeffrey L.; and Roth, Loren H. "The Promise of Involuntary Outpatient Commitment." *American Psychologist* 42:6, June 1987.

Murray, Charles. *Losing Ground*. New York: Basic Books, 1984.

McElvaine, Robert. *The End of the Conservative Era: Liberalism After Reagan*. New York: Arbor House, 1987.

McIntyre, Robert S. *Sharing the Sales Tax Burden*. Washington, D.C., Citizens for Tax Justice, 1988.

The National Citizens' Board of Inquiry into Health in America. *Health Care USA: 1984. Vol. 1. The National Report*. Washington, D.C.: The National Citizens' Board, October 1984.

National Coalition for the Homeless. *Homelessness in America*. Washington, D.C.: The Coalition, 1986.

National Conference on Social Welfare. *The Social Welfare Forum*. Washington, D.C.: National Conference on Social Welfare, 1985.

National Council of Community Mental Health Centers. *Trends in Community Mental Health*. Washington, D.C.: The Council, 1987.

National Institute of Mental Health. *Toward a Model Plan for a Community Based Mental Health Service System*. Rockville, MD: National Institute of Mental Health, Division of Education and Service Systems Liaison, October, 1987.

National Mental Health Consumer's Association. *Preliminary Highlights of the National Organizing Survey*. Philadelphia National Mental Health Consumer's Association, 1987.

New Jersey Department of Community Affairs Homeless Prevention Program. *Preventing Homelessness in New Jersey: Fact Sheet, Fiscal Year 1987*. Trenton: New Jersey Department of Community Affairs, 1987.

New Jersey Housing and Mortgage Finance Agency (NJH MFA), *Annual Report*. Trenton: The Agency, 1986.

Newman, Sandra, and Struy K. *Housing and Supportive Services: Federal Policy for the Frail Elderly and Chronically Mentally Ill*. Cambridge, Mass.: MIT Press, 1987.

Nordberg, Marie. "Hope for the Homeless." *Emergency Medical Services* 14:5, 1985.

O'Connell, Martin, and Bloom, David E. *Juggling Jobs and Babies: America's Child Care Challenge*. Population Reference Bureau, Inc. No. 12. February 1987.

Partnership for the Homeless. *National Growth in Homelessness*. New York: The Partnership, 1987.

Peterson, Iver. "Battery Park City: A New Phase Begins." *New York Times*, 19 June 1988.

Redburn, F. Stevens, and Buss, Terry F. *Beyond Shelter: The Homeless and Public Policy*. New York: Praeger, 1986.

Reich, Robert B. *Tales of a New America: The Anxious Liberal's Guide to the Future.* New York: Times Books, 1987.

Rein, Martin. *Social Policy.* New York: Random House, 1970.

Reissman, Frank. "The Helper Therapy Principle." *Social Work* 10:4, 1965.

Ryan, William. *Equality.* New York: Vintage Books, 1981.

Schlesinger, Arthur, Jr. *The Cycles of American History.* Boston: Houghton Mifflin, 1986.

Schlesinger, M. "On the Limits of Expanding Health Care Reform; Chronic Care in Prepaid Groups." *Millbank Quarterly* 64:1986, pp. 189-215.

Schwartz, David C.; Ferlauto, Richard C.; and Hoffman, Daniel. *A New Housing Policy for America: Recapturing the American Dream.* Philadelphia: Temple University Press, 1988.

Sexton, Patricia. "The Life of the Homeless." *Dissent* 30:1, 1983.

Shelter Partnership, Inc. *The Short-Term Housing System of Los Angeles County: Serving the Needs of the Homeless: An Analysis of Operating Characteristics and Funding Activity.* Los Angeles: The Shelter Partnership, 1987.

Sloss, Michael. "The Crisis of Homelessness: Its Dimensions and Solutions." *Urban and Social Change Review* 17:2, 1984.

Schorr, Lisbeth B. *Within Our Reach: Breaking the Cycle of Disadvantage.* New York: Doubleday, 1988.

Smith, Susan J. "New Thinking About the Homeless." *Governing* 1:5, February 1888.

Snowden, Lonnie, ed. *Reaching the Underserved: Mental Health Needs of Neglected Populations.* Beverly Hills, CA: Sage Publications, 1982.

Sosin, Michael; Colson, Paul; and Grossman, Susan. *Homelessness In Chicago: Poverty and Pathology: Social Institutions and Social Change.* Chicago: University of Chicago, School of Social Service Administration, 1988.

State of California General Obligation Bond. *Housing and Homeless Initiative.* SB 1692 and 1693.

State of Connecticut, Department of Housing. *Housing Programs.* Hartford: State of Connecticut, 1986.

State of Massachusetts. *EOCD Resource Guide.* Boston: Executive Office of Community Development, 1987.

Stein, L.I. "Task MA: Training in Community Living Model," *New Directions for Mental Health Services.* San Francisco: Jossey-Bass Social and Behavioral Sciences Series, No. 26, 1983.

Stern, Mark J. "The Emergence of Homelessness as a Public Problem." *Social Service Review* 58:2, 1984.

Stevens, William K. "Economic Swat Team Saves Jobs in Pennsylvania." *New York Times,* 28 March 1988.

Stoner, Madeleine R. "An Analysis of Public and Private Sector Provisions for Homeless People." *Urban and Social Change Review* 17:1, 1984.

Surber, Robert W., Dwyer, Eleanor, Ryan, Katherine J., Goldfinger, Stephen M. and Kelly, John T. "Medical and Psychiatric Needs of the Homeless — A Preliminary Response." *Social Work* 33:2, March-April, 1988.

Talbott, J.A., and Sharfstein, S.S., "A Proposal for Future Funding of Chronic and Episodic Mental Illness." *Hospital and Community Psychiatry* 37, 1986.

—— "Unified Mental Health Systems: Utopia Revisited." *New Directions for Mental Health Services*. San Francisco: Jossey-Bass Social and Behavioral Science Services, no. 26, 1983.

Taylor, Samuel H., and Roberts, Robert W., eds. *Theory and Practice of Community Social Work*. New York: Columbia University Press, 1985.

Tiven, Marjorie, and Ryther, Barbara. *State Initiatives in Edlerly Housing: What's New, What's Tried and True*. Washington, D.C.: Council of State Housing Agencies and National Association of State Units on Aging, 1986.

Torrey, B. Fuller. "Continuous Treatment Terms in the Care of the Chronic Mentally Ill." *Hospital and Community Psychiatry* 37, 1986.

Torry, E. Fuller, and Wolfe, Sidney M. *Care of the Seriously Mentally Ill: A Rating of State Programs*. Washington, D.C.: Public Citizen Health Research Group, 1987.

Trombley, William. "Economy to Muffle Slow-Growth Moves." *Los Angeles Times*, 17 June 1988.

Tucker, William. "Where do the Homeless Come From?" *National Review* 39. 25 September 1987.

—— "Then There's Rent Control." *New Republic* 198:15, 11 April 1988.

Turner, Margery Austin, *Housing Needs to the Year 2000*. Washington, D.C.: National Association of Housing and Redevelopment Officials, 1986.

Uchitelle, Louis. "Reliance on Temporary Jobs Hints at Economic Frugality." *New York Times*, 10 March 1988.

—— "Labor's Lost Strength." *New York Times*, 23 August 1988.

U.S. Bureau of the Census. *Characteristics of the Population Below the Poverty Level*. Current Population Reports, no. 130, p.60. Washington, D.C.: Government Printing Office, 1981.

—— *Current Population Reports: Consumer Income Series*, p. 60. Washington, D.C.: Government Printing Office, August 1985.

—— *Money, Income and Poverty Statistics of Families and Persons in the United States 1984, Current Population Survey*. Washington, D.C.; Government Printing Office, August 1985.

—— *Number and Median Income of Families and Persons*. September 1988.

U.S. Conference of Mayors. *Status Report: Emergency Food, Shelter and Energy Programs in Twenty Cities*. Washington, D.C.: The Conference, 1987.

U.S. Congress. *Employment Act of 1946*. Public Law 304. 70th Cong., 2d sess.

—— *The Protection and Advocacy for Mentally Ill Individuals Act of 1986*. Public Law 99-319, 98th Cong., 1st sess.

—— *State Comprehensive Mental Health Plan Act*. Public Law 99-960. 98th Cong., 2d sess.

—— *Urgent Relief for the Homeless Act*. Public Law 100-77. 100th Cong., 1st sess.

U.S. Congress, House of Representatives. *Affordable Housing Act*. H.R. 4990. 100th Cong., 2d sess.

———*Community Housing Partnership Act.* H.R. 3891. 100th Cong., 1st sess.

———*Family and Medical Leave Act.* H.R. 925, 100th Cong., 1st sess. 1987.

———*Minimum Wage Bill.* H.R. 1834. 100th Cong., 1st sess. 1987.

———*Stewart B. McKinney Homeless Assistance Act.* H.R. 4352, 99th. Cong., 1st sess.

U.S. Congress, House of Representatives, Committee on Ways and Means. *Unemployment Compensation, Background Material on Poverty.* Washington, D.C.: Government Printing Office, 1984.

U.S. Congress, Senate. *Family and Medical Leave Act.* S. 249. 100th Cong., 1st sess. 1987.

———*Minimum Health Care for All Workers Act.* S. 12625, 100th Cong., 1st sess. 1987.

———*Minimum Wage Bill.* S. 837. 100th Cong., 1st sess. 1987.

U.S. Department of Health and Human Services. *Helping the Homeless: A Resource Guide.* Washington, D.C.: the Department, Summer 1984.

U.S. Department of Housing and Urban Development. *The President's National Urban Policy Report.* Washington, D.C.: the Department, 1986.

———*Programs of HUD, 1985/1986.* Washington, D.C.: The Department, April 1986.

U.S. Department of Labor, Bureau of Labor Statistics. *Handbook of Labor Statistics.* Washington, D.C.: Government Printing Office, 1984.

———*Employment, Earnings, Various Issues.* Table 32C and 33C. Washington, D.C.: Government Printing Office, 1979.

Vernez, George, et al. *Review of California's Program for the Homeless Mentally Disabled.* Working Draft. Los Angeles: Rand Corporation, prepared for the State Department of Mental Health. R-3631-SDMH, 1988, June 1988.

Vosburgh, William W. "Voluntary Associations, The Homeless and Hard-To-Serve Populations: Perspectives From Organizational Theory." *Journal of Voluntary Action Research* 17:1, 1988.

Wagenfeld, Morton O.; Lemkau, Paul V.; and Justice, Blair, eds. *Public Mental Health: Perspectives and Prospects.* Beverly Hills, London, New Delhi: Sage Publications, 1982.

Weil, Marie, and Karl, James M. *Case Management in Human Service Practice: A Systematic Approach to Mobilizing Resources for Clients.* San Francisco: Jossey-Bass, 1985.

Weisbrod, B.A. "A Guide to Cost-Benefit Analysis, As Seen Through a Controlled Experiment in Treating the Mentally Ill," in Razin A.; Helpman E.; and Sadka, E., eds. *Social Policy Evaluation.* New York: Academic Press, 1983.

Weitzmann, Leonore. *The Divorce Revolution.* New York: Free Press, 1985.

Wilson, William Julius. *The Truly Disadvantaged: The Inner City, the Underclass and Public Policy.* Chicago: The University of Chicago Press, 1983.

Wolkon, George. "Patient Compliance in the Mental Health Continuum of Care." *Journal of Compliance in Health Care* 1:1, 1986.

Yablonsky, Lewis. *Synanon: The Tunnel Back.* Baltimore: Penguin Books, 1967.

Young, Randy. "The Homeless: The Shame of the City." *New York Magazine,* December 21, 1981.

——— "The City's Homeless Pose $100 Million Quandary." *New York Times,* 10 October 1984.

——— "Go Take a Hike." *The New Republic* 3, 826, 16 May 1988.

Index

Debra A. Dagavarian

SAYING IT AIN'T SO

American Values As Revealed in Children's Baseball Stories 1880–1950

American University Studies: Series II (Anthropology and Sociology). Vol. 16
ISBN 0-8204-0583-3   223 pages   hardback US $ 32.50/sFr. 42.25

Recommended prices – alterations reserved

Saying It Ain't So explores the themes which emerge from popularly-read children's stories about baseball. This book examines the first piece of baseball fiction, which appeared in 1882, and was written for children. Why does baseball – more than other sports – teach values of supportiveness, responsibility, and fairness? How do children's stories bring out these values? This work reveals the unique qualities of baseball which set it apart from other sports and truly make it our national pastime.

Contents: This research analyzes children's baseball stories in terms of thematic content. The values which emerge support the didacticism of the fictional literature throughout the span under study: 1880 to 1950.

PETER LANG PUBLISHING, INC.
62 West 45th Street
USA – New York, NY 10036